STEVE BLANDFORD

Jimmy McGovern

Manchester University Press
MANCHESTER AND NEW YORK

distributed in the United States exclusively by Palgrave Macmillan

Copyright © Steve Blandford 2013

The right of Steve Blandford to be identified as the author of this work has been asserted by him in accordance with the Copyright, Designs and Patents Act 1988.

Published by Manchester University Press
Oxford Road, Manchester M13 9NR, UK
and Room 400, 175 Fifth Avenue, New York, NY 10010, USA
www.manchesteruniversitypress.co.uk

Distributed in the United States exclusively by
Palgrave Macmillan, 175 Fifth Avenue, New York, NY 10010, USA

Distributed in Canada exclusively by
UBC Press, University of British Columbia, 2029 West Mall, Vancouver, BC, Canada V6T 1Z2

British Library Cataloguing-in-Publication Data
A catalogue record for this book is available from the British Library

Library of Congress Cataloging-in-Publication Data applied for

ISBN 978 0 7190 8248 1 *hardback*

First published 2013

The publisher has no responsibility for the persistence or accuracy of URLs for any external or third-party internet websites referred to in this book, and does not guarantee that any content on such websites is, or will remain, accurate or appropriate.

Typeset in Scala with Meta display by
Koinonia, Manchester
Printed in Great Britain by
TJ International Ltd, Padstow

For Mitch, who gets me through it all
and with whom I spend the best of times,
and for Sam and Beth,
setting off on their own journeys now

Contents

GENERAL EDITORS' PREFACE		*page* ix
ACKNOWLEDGEMENTS		xi
	Introduction	1
1	Soaps, series and serials: *Brookside, Cracker, Hearts and Minds, The Lakes*	24
2	'Hybrid' forms: *The Street, Moving On, Accused*	64
3	Documentary and historical drama: *Hillsborough, Sunday, Dockers, Gunpowder, Treason and Plot*	111
4	Single plays and a conclusion	152
	REFERENCES	174
	INDEX	181

General editors' preface

Television is part of our everyday experience, and is one of the most significant aspects of our cultural lives today. Yet its practitioners and its artistic and cultural achievements remain relatively unacknowledged. The books in this series aim to remedy this by addressing the work of major television writers and creators. Each volume provides an authoritative and accessible guide to a particular practitioner's body of work, and assesses his or her contribution to television over the years. Many of the volumes draw on original sources, such as specially conducted interviews and archive material, and all of them list relevant bibliographic sources and further reading and viewing. The author of each book makes a case for the importance of the work considered therein, and the series includes books on neglected or overlooked practitioners alongside well-known ones.

In comparison with some related disciplines, Television Studies scholarship is still relatively young, and the series aims to contribute to establishing the subject as a vigorous and evolving field. This series provides resources for critical thinking about television. While maintaining a clear focus on the writers, on the creators and on the programmes themselves, the books in this series also take account of key critical concepts and theories in Television Studies. Each book is written from a particular critical or theoretical perspective, with reference to pertinent issues, and the approaches included in the series are varied and sometimes dissenting. Each author explicitly outlines the reasons for his or her particular focus, methodology or perspective. Readers are invited to think critically about the subject matter and approach covered in each book.

Although the series is addressed primarily to students and scholars of television, the books will also appeal to the many people who are interested in how television programmes have been commissioned, made and enjoyed. Since television has been so much a part of personal and public life in the twentieth and twenty-first centuries, we hope that the series will engage with, and sometimes challenge, a broad and diverse readership.

Jonathan Bignell
Steven Peacock

Acknowledgements

I would like to thank my many colleagues and friends at the University of Glamorgan for their help and support whilst I was writing this book. In particular I would like to thank those colleagues whose interest in television drama has provided insights and collegial discussions that have contributed a great deal to the ideas that shaped this volume, particularly Huw Jones, Stephen Lacey, Ruth McElroy, Catriona Noonan and Rebecca Williams. A number of other colleagues in Drama, Film and the Centre for the Study of Media and Culture in Small Nations at the University of Glamorgan have also been of enormous help and support in various ways, particularly Jodie Allinson, Michael Carklin, Ross Garner, Steve Fisher, Richard Hand, Lesley Harbidge, Lisa Lewis, Marta Minier, Ieuan Morris and Daryl Perrins. I would also like to thank Matthew Frost at Manchester University Press for his support in developing this volume and Jonathan Bignell at the University of Reading, who encouraged its development.

Finally, of course, I would like to acknowledge the work of a large number of scholars who have developed the growing field of television drama studies and whose work I have relied upon and, to the best of my ability, acknowledged, in developing the framework for this book.

Introduction

In one sense the rationale behind this book is very simple. For a writer who now occupies such a prominent place in the recent history of British television drama, currently there barely exists any extended writing on Jimmy McGovern at all apart from Mark Duguid's very useful *Cracker*, in the BFI's Television Classics series. What does exist is in small fragments dotted around larger studies of genre or accounts of particular periods in television history. In such accounts McGovern's name is frequently little more than a footnote and usually associated with just one particular example of his now extensive and wide-ranging output. He is most frequently mentioned as one of the writers who came to prominence on the team that produced *Brookside* (1982–2003) and which was central to the early history of Channel 4 (see for example Brown, 2007).

Very striking indeed is the total absence of McGovern's name from the index of Robin Nelson's excellent *State of Play*, which sets out to 'broadly review the output of "quality" TV drama between the mid-1990's and 2006' (2007: 1). By contrast, the names of Russell T. Davies, Paul Abbott, Stephen Poliakoff and several others are referenced frequently. Whilst it can be a distortion to focus too heavily on a single volume, the comparative lack of full-length work on British television drama since 2000 has helped make Nelson's work a key definer of the British television drama canon.

Alternatively, as exemplified by Lez Cooke's *British Television Drama, a History* (2003), McGovern is almost solely associated with one or other of the 'controversies' that have been central to his work, in this case the documentary drama based upon the events that took place at Hillsborough Stadium in Sheffield in 1989. It is of course understandable that, in a book with such a broad historical sweep, any one television author should receive only a brief individual mention, and Cooke does acknowledge that not only is his book limited in that respect, but that scholarship in general has been neglectful of television writers, often focusing on just one or two figures whose contributions to the development of British television drama then become distorted. The list of neglect is in itself helpful to the case for this volume:

> there is still much to be done. There is a need for books on television dramatists other than the ubiquitous Dennis Potter – on Alan Bleasdale, John Hopkins, Lynda La Plante, Tony Marchant, Jimmy McGovern, Paula Milne and Alan Plater for example; there is a need for books on producers such as Tony Garnett, Verity Lambert, David Rose and Ken Trodd; on directors such as Alan Clarke, Stephen Frears, Gavin Millar and Philip Saville. (Cooke, 2003: 5)

Since the appearance of Cooke's history a number of the writers, directors and producers that he mentions have received significant coverage, some at book length and some in the series in which this volume appears, but McGovern remains seriously neglected and this book hopes to at least partly redress that balance and, maybe more importantly, stimulate others to explore his work with the depth and seriousness that it deserves.

However, whilst he remains neglected by television and drama academics, it is interesting to note the number of times that McGovern's work has been cited by those working in other disciplines such as sociology and criminology (see for example Walker, 1996 and Woodin, 2005). These two phenomena may not be unrelated, it seems to me. As I will attempt to explore at greater length later in the book, it appears that McGovern's readiness to engage with highly charged contemporary controversy tends to distance him from those whose discipline focuses on the formal, aesthetic or even institutional dimensions of television drama.

Also, this seems to signal a further injustice that I hope to rectify during the course of the book, namely that McGovern is widely regarded solely as a writer who deals with issues and is therefore unconcerned with form. Apart from anything else it is hard to name a television dramatist whose work has encompassed such a broad formal and generic spectrum and moreover, within that framework, who has used popular forms in such innovative ways. In fact it is almost McGovern's defining characteristic that he works so frequently within popular, accessible forms only to continually surprise his audience with the use that he makes of them. This alone makes his work worthy of serious consideration, though, as I will go on to discuss, there is a great deal more.

This volume will therefore argue that, whilst much of McGovern's writing can be associated with a class-based radicalism rooted in a British social-realist tradition, there are also complexities both to McGovern's recurrent social and political concerns and to his stylistic range. McGovern's frequently antagonistic relationship with the organised left is key to the first of these complexities, particularly in relation to what he has often referred to as the appropriation of the left of centre in British politics by middle-class special interest groups, particularly feminists. If there is such a thing as a single mission across McGovern's work it is perhaps an attempt to give voice to those most neglected by organised politics. Clearly the white working-class male is very prominent in this, but it is also possible to identify strong females as being amongst McGovern's most memorable and enduring characters, from *Brookside* right through to some of those caught up in the criminal justice system in *Accused*.

The other inescapably central preoccupation, one that tends to distinguish McGovern from most of his contemporaries, is the use that his work makes of the Catholic Church and its role in working-class life. This book will seek to understand what is, clearly, a very complicated relationship for McGovern both in simple autobiographical terms and in terms of the way that he sees the functioning of the Church alongside other forces that shape individual destiny.

In stylistic terms this book will argue that the placing of McGovern in an unambiguously social-realist tradition ignores a much greater range than has hitherto been recognised. Particularly in his later work, McGovern (and the collaborators working under his guidance) has displayed a tendency to push at the boundaries of the aesthetic traditions with which he is most commonly associated and in the direction that might tentatively be called magic realism. As the chapters make clear, there are limits to this, but there are clear indications both in the works themselves and in interviews that McGovern's approach to narrative has, in recent years, indicated a strong interest in the intrusion of the fantastical into the fabric of everyday life.

The book's format is relatively simple. Rather than a chronological approach I have chosen to focus on television forms. One consequence of this is to emphasise the quality of McGovern's work that is mentioned above, namely the sheer versatility of his output, but also the way that he has, largely, chosen to work in particular genres and innovate from that position.

This approach inevitably leads to a certain amount of compromise and grouping together of work that does not always have an obvious relationship. Thus the first chapter includes not only work separated by long time-lapses such as *Brookside* (1982–2003) and *The Street* (2006–10), but also work belonging to very different genre such as *Cracker* (1993–2007) and *Hearts and Minds* (1995). Nevertheless, when engaging with a writer whose absolute commitment has been to television and its ability to speak to a mass audience, it seemed vital to place emphasis on categories that made sense in terms of the institutional context of television, even if those categories change and mutate so radically over time.

An advantage of such an approach is perhaps obvious, but worth stating clearly here, which is that there is, particularly in Chapter 1, the clear opportunity to examine how McGovern's work in similar formats has changed and developed over quite a lengthy time frame. Whilst *Brookside* and *The Street*, for example, are clearly very different in so many ways, they both have much to tell us about not only the changes in McGovern as a writer, but also about the evolution of television dramatic fiction in a period that has seen such enormous change in the shape of television in general. It is salutary to think that McGovern began his career as a writer in the vanguard of what seemed such a radical change at the time, the introduction of a fourth channel and the creation of institutional space for independent producers, only to still be going strong in the multi-channel, internet era of fragmented audiences and ever-increasing competition.

Whilst it is not the function of this book to tell anything approaching the full story of the radical changes that have shaped television in the period from 1980 to the time of writing, the nature of Jimmy McGovern's career does, nevertheless, offer the opportunity to reflect on institutional change, particularly the ways that such changes have impacted upon drama production. This introduction will then attempt to provide an outline map, not only of the chronology of McGovern's career, but also the ways in which it has become linked to changes in television and, in particular, changes in television drama production.

As has already been indicated, McGovern's career was irrevocably shaped by the arrival of Channel 4 in 1982 and its commitment to providing an alternative voice to the three existing channels, an aspiration summed up by John Ellis in the *Screen* dossier that marked the Channel's twenty-fifth anniversary:

> The various groups involved in formulating the new channel hoped that its programming would address some of the issues of social divergence that were seen to be opening up in British society. Channel 4 was based on the idea that significant minorities existed in society who were not well served by the existing broadcasting set-up. (Ellis, 2008: 333)

However, as Ellis goes on to say, the idea of 'minorities' was, as he puts it, convenient rhetoric that glossed over the deep divisions that existed within the forces in British television (and wider British society) that helped bring Channel 4 into being. In Ellis's formulation there were two 'halves' of the idea of minorities:

One held that immigration and other social developments had produced a society that was far more heterogeneous than that of the 1950s, and that relatively cohesive minority groups had emerged that were in danger of being marginalized. The other belief was more economic. It held that consumer society was developing away from mass-market practices towards ever greater segmentation and diversity of tastes. In addition, the programme-makers were interested in a channel that would be shocking and outrageous, offering opinionated and experimental programming. (Ellis, 2008: 333)

In a sense McGovern's break into television via *Brookside* owed something to both of these underlying forces. On the one hand, especially in the early days, there was a sense that *Brookside* was attempting to reinvent the soap opera both through its mush more issue-based approach and its representation of minorities. On the other, *Brookside* also represented a key aspect of Channel 4's attempt to reach out beyond its core audience and develop a wider following that might be drawn in by the likes of *Brookside* and stay for more challenging programming.

As will be discussed later, *Brookside*'s issue-based radicalism was to be relatively short-lived and McGovern's departure was one measure at least of the beginning of the show's declining inclination towards the difficult and contentious storyline (though not for the sensational). Although McGovern's departure from *Brookside* took place well before the acceleration of the ratings imperatives that were to change Channel 4 so drastically in the 1990s, it can perhaps fairly be seen as an early harbinger of a general trend.

In the period immediately after leaving *Brookside* McGovern worked on a number of single dramas, mainly for the BBC, including *Traitors* (1990) *Needle* (1990) and *Gas and Candles* (1991), all for various incarnations of the Corporation's dwindling slots for one-off dramas. McGovern's reputation as a writer, forged on *Brookside*, was allowing him access to the so-called Holy Grail of the television writer just as the single play was about to become almost extinct as a format.

None of McGovern's single dramas of the period attracted a significant amount of critical attention and none survive as commercial VHS or DVD releases, despite his subsequent rise to prominence and the widespread availability of his later output. It is arguable that this is more of a reflection of the decline of the single drama form and its significance for the BBC than of the works themselves, but it nevertheless represents one of the few periods since he began as a writer when his work received comparatively little journalistic attention.

It is at this point in his career, after a period of writing single dramas, that McGovern began to display the versatility and adaptability that have become central to his success. From the outside *Cracker*, originally the brainchild of producer Gub Neal, looks a highly unlikely vehicle for the writer of the early radical *Brookside*. McGovern's interest in the police up to this point, at least on the evidence of his writing, would have been more likely to have featured their role in enforcing the punitive anti-trade-union legislation enacted by the 1980s Tory government. However, as will be discussed more fully later, *Cracker*'s attraction for McGovern lay in the opportunity to create one of a long line of deeply flawed 'heroes', one whose relationship to the police service that employed him was highly ambiguous. As was the case in *Brookside*, it was McGovern's radical approach to the problem of writing inside the confines of a popular television drama form that made *Cracker* the outstanding popular and critical success that it was.

It is perhaps the impulse to write *Cracker* after being granted the already rare 'auteur' accolade of being commissioned to write single dramas that defines McGovern. It is also a contributory factor to his exclusion from discussions of 'quality' drama (such as Nelson, 2007). For McGovern the enormous gift of being allowed access to the living rooms of a truly mass audience has always seemed paramount, something summed up slightly cynically, but tellingly, by *The Times* in a review of the one-off *Cracker* special in 2006:

> In truth it feels as though Jimmy McGovern had a lot of things that he wanted to say about terrorism, 9/11 and American imperialism – a lot of very inventive, valid and angry things –and he tried to find a way to massage them into *Cracker*. And I think he wanted to massage them into *Cracker* because that way ten million people – people who would normally read the *Daily Mail*, or give weight to the opinions of Jeremy Clarkson – would watch his comments on ITV 1. (Moran, 2006)

The point here is not to agree or disagree with the view of this version of *Cracker*, but to recognise the centrality of the popular audience to McGovern's most powerful work and, in the course of the book, to analyse the particularly potent ways in which he has gone about addressing this most difficult of problems for the television writer.

McGovern's journey as a writer has not, however, followed such a simple trajectory and throughout his post-Brookside career he has made a number of detours, often in parallel with his involvement in popular series. Alongside *Cracker*, for instance, he made the first of his infrequent ventures into feature film with *Priest* (dir. Antonia Bird, 1994) and another play (with co-writer, Paul Henry Powell) for a special season of one-off dramas on BBC1, *Love Bites*, called *Go Now* (1995). In between came *Hearts and Minds* (1995), a serial for Channel 4 which, whilst as accessible as much of his other work in many ways, tended to be defined as belonging to the Channel 4 audience.

Again there is the sense of McGovern's career partly following the evolution of television drama commissioning and, as his stock rises, beginning to shape it, though the latter came much later. *Priest* was to a large extent the product of the increasingly nervous and volatile commissioning process that had come to beset the BBC by the start of the 1990s. Originally an idea that formed part of a long series on the Ten Commandments, the shape of the series shrunk to four parts only to be shelved altogether before McGovern started on *Cracker*. The final version of *Priest* was commissioned for theatrical release, though within the BBC's structures this meant that it came from the same part of the organisation as single dramas. This latter point has, as Julian Petley (2008) says, 'long been a source of irritation for those who want the BBC to establish a theatrical arm to rival that of *Channel 4*'. As Petley points out, however, this has been impossible because of the commercial constraints under which the BBC operates, and in the end it inevitably contributes to the rather limited success of *Priest*.

Both in *Priest* and *Go Now* we find McGovern working with two directors who have come to be seen, to different extents, as significant figures in the British film industry, Antonia Bird and Michael Winterbottom. For McGovern, however, this was not the start of a film career and, with some notable exceptions, from this point onwards he became more and more strongly associated with the popular television series. Naturally the complex reasons for this will be explored in the relevant chapters, but for now it is worth signalling a number of interconnected possibilities: first the recurrent desire for mass audiences, but secondly the tendency of the film industry to privilege the sense of a directorial vision over that of the writer. In his later career McGovern has become one of the very few writers whose name is used to 'sell' a programme, and it is unlikely that his powerful presence on a project would ever have sat easily alongside most directors' aspiration to any kind of auteur status (as we will see in the brief discussion of *Liam* (2000) below).

Whilst *Hearts and Minds* never aimed to be the truly popular series of the kind that McGovern was soon to produce it was important in a number of key respects. First it established McGovern as a writer of accessible series outside the support of a clearly defined genre. Since then there has, in fact, emerged something of 'school' sub-genre through such offerings as *Teachers* (Channel 4, 2001–04), *Hope and Glory* (BBC, 1999–2000) and *Waterloo Road* (2006–), but at the time this was relatively untrodden territory, at least in the UK.

Moreover, *Hearts and Minds* saw a further development in the direction of what we might call the delicate balance of sympathies that surround his central characters. This represented a move away from what McGovern himself recognised as the 'mouthpiece' characters in his earlier work and towards writing that was equally committed to hard questions about the world but more open to moral ambiguities. In an interview in *The Times* Robert Crampton attempts an autobiographical explanation for the flaws that are very evident in the central character, Drew Mackenzie, played by long-term McGovern collaborator, Christopher Eccleston:

> Those readers who watched *Hearts and Minds*, which was about a former car worker who becomes an English teacher in an inner-city comprehensive, wants to change the world and finds he can't, will know the next bit: McGovern captured neither hearts nor minds, or not enough to make it worthwhile. His idealism dried up. Was teaching as bad – pupils cynical, staff decayed – as he depicted it on screen? It was worse, a lot worse. He tells one story by way of example, which *Hearts and Minds* viewers will recognise: 'I was out with my wife and kids, I think it was in the school holidays, and a load of kids started hurling abuse. I snapped, chased them, caught them all bar one kid, and he brought a guy round to my house. Big fella. Hard. A builder. Can you imagine, a Saturday afternoon, my kids all small, and there's this maniac knocking shite out of my door, wanting to come in and kill me?' (Crampton, 1995)

Here we can see clearly the link that McGovern has always made between his lived experience and the 'flawed' (sometimes extremely flawed) central characters that he has consistently created. Not only is Drew Mackenzie flawed, but so are the working-class families that the teacher sets out to help via the traditional escape-hatch of education. McGovern's first-hand experience leads him to a narrative of a kind that is a long way from liberal Hollywood accounts of the efficacy of committed educationalists in films such as the approximately contemporary *Dangerous Minds* (1995, dir. John E. Smith).

Shortly after *Hearts and Minds*, one of the most powerful episodes of *Cracker*, *To Be a Somebody*, became, on the face of it at least, an unlikely springboard for McGovern's first entry into the highly politicised world of drama documentary. One of a number of reasons that is often quoted as being behind McGovern's exit from *Brookside* was the refusal to accept his idea of a storyline that focused on the 1989 Hillsborough Stadium tragedy in which 96 Liverpool football fans died as the FA Cup semi-final between Liverpool and Nottingham Forest was being played. McGovern makes the connection between *Cracker* and these events in a much later interview:

> After I stormed out of 'Brookside' [the Liverpool soap refused a Hillsborough story-line] I went into 'Cracker' with such anger. I always say the thing about 'Cracker' was that it was post-Hillsborough, that was the key thing for me. The way contempt for a huge sector of humanity could lead to something like that. (Du Noyer, 2008)

Hillsborough (1996) and McGovern's very close relationship with the bereaved families will be discussed in the relevant chapter, but here it is worth noting once more McGovern's engagement with a particular phase in the history of television drama. Coming relatively late to what, in the UK at least, has come to be seen as a radical campaigning form, McGovern's first venture into drama documentary instantly placed him in a long line of writers and directors that have sought (and to an extent achieved) direct impact on public opinion and ultimately on public policy. It was, many felt, a form ideally suited to McGovern's uncompromising political position as a writer but also, crucially, to his growing stature as a writer brilliantly capable of creating flawed heroes. Just as *Cathy Come Home* (dir. Ken Loach, 1996) will always be linked to the founding of the charity Shelter, so *Hillsborough* was, at the very least, a significant factor in the decision to order a new public enquiry into the events in 1997.

To follow such expertise in the manipulation and reshaping of genre in *Cracker* with an important intervention in a highly specialised tradition was remarkable for a writer who very recently was known only for his work with a team on a soap opera. For him to then return almost immediately, to a popular form with *The Lakes* (1997–99) established clearly not only his versatility, but also a powerful unwillingness to be trapped within any kind of tradition, particularly one that might result in a degree of marginalisation as the writer of the kind of campaigning single dramas that were becoming less and less frequent on UK television.

The Lakes, according to Peter Salmon, then controller of BBC1, was originally conceived as a much longer series, even one of soap-opera proportions:

> I secretly hoped it would lead to a creative push for the BBC in the North and that together with *EastEnders* it might have done what *Coronation Street* and *Emmerdale* do for ITV every week. But sadly it didn't get beyond a second series, the debut of John Simm, notwithstanding. (Salmon, 2011)

In writing *The Lakes*, McGovern was, to some extent, returning to his roots in *Brookside* though, at least on the first series of *The Lakes*, with the autonomy and control that he could never have enjoyed on the production line of Mersey Television. As Salmon's remarks imply, this was a time when the continuing series became something of a Holy Grail for broadcasters and production companies keen to take advantage of the form's possibilities with regard to economies of scale, and *The Lakes* emerged into that tradition. It was, however, from the start, an extreme hybrid of the form, never sitting comfortably in the primetime Sunday evening slot that was allocated to it. *The Lakes*' particular engagement with McGovern's autobiography and its take on the everpresent Catholic guilt will be explored later, but again it is worth noting McGovern's early encounter with a format that he would return to more successfully in his later career. Whereas the four episodes of series one of *The Lakes* were all written by McGovern, he wrote only three out of the ten episodes of the much longer Series 2. The rest were split between three much less well-known writers who were being nurtured under the post-*Cracker* McGovern name.

For most people the second series of *The Lakes* was, at best, overextended and inclined to lurch into slightly desperate melodrama. How far this is directly attributable to the varied authorship is difficult to assess, but it is safe to say that the multiplying sub-plots tended to look somewhat like the product of a number of writers attempting to carve out their own distinctive space within the overall format of what was originally a tightly plotted family drama.

Nevertheless, the idea of a number of writers being nurtured 'underneath' the protective cover of an established name that could open commissioning doors would be something that McGovern returned to, albeit at a time when his overall producing control had increased considerably. Whilst this was not the first time McGovern had acted as a lead writer on a team (*Cracker* had quietly introduced the young Paul Abbott, for instance), it was the first time that his original idea had been extended and developed by younger and less experienced writers, a model that would, later in McGovern's career, go through a number of different mutations.

From the end of the second series of *The Lakes* in 1999 until the first series of *The Street* in 2006 McGovern's relationship with television became decidedly on–off, especially for someone who had now become one of its most recognisable and established writers. Whilst the second series of *The Lakes* had gathered mixed reviews, the programme as a whole had brought BAFTA nominations and relatively widespread popular acclaim that built upon the success of *Cracker*.

In the light of this McGovern's projects over the next few years look, at least from the outside, like something of a search for the right kind of framework for the work that he wanted to do. However, this becomes more explicable when it is understood that the history of television drama of that period was not only about the continuation of a path to extinction of the single drama, but also the obsessive search for the sustainable, cost-effective popular series that would ward off the threat of the ever-expanding number of cable and satellite channels. Lez Cooke's history of television drama (2003) refers frequently to a report on the quality of British television drama produced at this time (the late 1990s) in which the authors claimed: 'There's no long-term commitment to anything – no Lew Grade type character developing great pools of talent, nowhere for writers and directors to grow up. The quality end is a shrinking iceberg heading south' (Barnett and Seymour, 1999: 69).

In one sense McGovern's commitment to one-off projects such as *Heart* (1999), *Dockers* (1999) and *Liam* (2000) seem almost perverse, given the direction in which television was heading, but in another they are reflective of a writer finding it increasingly difficult to see a role for the kind of work that he wanted to do, whether in the single drama or the kind of popular series that still tried to take risks and deal with complex subjects.

Part of McGovern's response to changes in television during this period was to write two quite different feature films. Whilst the raw, potent melodrama of *Heart* is closer to much of his television work, the spare, unsentimental *Liam* is the closest that McGovern has come to art cinema. In one review the rather unlikely comparison is made between *Liam* and, on the one hand, the films of a Liverpool child made by Terence Davies, *Distant Voices, Still Lives* (1988) and *The Long Day Closes* (1992) and on the other with the more superficially similar work of Ken Loach:

> *Liam* is situated between, and obviously influenced by, some notable British films of a couple of years back that also draw on childhood memories of Liverpool. On the one hand, there is Terence Davies's trilogy, *Distant Voices, Still Lives* and *The Long Day Closes*, about a lonely, working-class Catholic boy with a brutal father growing up in the 1940s and 1950s in a world dominated by women and finding consolation in movies and popular music. On the other is Ken Loach's *Land and Freedom*. (French, 2001)

Both *Liam* and *Heart* are products of co-funding arrangements with broadcasters and are in that sense also representative of a particular period in the history of broadcasting, though at a time when such arrangements were in relative decline. In addition, *Heart* was also part-financed by the Merseyside Film Production Fund, one of a small number of UK schemes that saw local authorities enter the film business as a way of attracting production to cities and therefore contributing to economic development (Loach himself was a regular beneficiary of the Glasgow Film Fund).

Whilst *Liam*, in particular, earned respectable reviews and enabled McGovern to work with one of the key British film directors of recent times, Stephen Frears, there is the sense of McGovern not quite operating in territory where he is at his most effective. In a slightly tongue-in-cheek piece for *The Observer* McGovern even makes comic reference to the age-old authorial problems for any writer who ventures into cinema:

> Stephen shot the entire script (a rarity in the British film industry), took it to London and left me kicking my heels in Liverpool. But a week or two later I was able to see the first rough assembly. It was love at first sight: every scene beautifully shot, perfectly acted, and all in the order in which I had written them. In my ecstasy I didn't hear the ominous warnings from Stephen that further work was needed.
>
> Further work was done and I sat down at home and watched the result. Now look, nobody told me that this was work in progress. Nobody told me that this was Stephen trying things out. I just sat down in total ignorance and watched this latest cut. Watched with mounting horror. When it finished, I opened up a bottle and drank and drank and drank. Three-quarters down the bottle I phoned Colin McKeown, the co-producer. This is roughly what I said.
>
> That bastard Frears. He's tossed my script in the air, seen how it landed, and cut it accordingly. I spent years on that structure, Colin. Years. And he's chopping and changing it after two lousy weeks in the edit suite. He's a middle-class Jew (my ace, this; I'd played it repeatedly throughout the shoot) and this is a working-class Catholic film. Talk to him! (McGovern, 2001)

Despite the comic tone and the praise lavished on Frears in much of the same piece, its title is still resonant: 'Whose story is it anyway?' For all its McGovern trademarks, particularly the powerful Catholic guilt, there is inevitably a sense of this being a film most associated with a director of some eminence. Whilst any resentment of this on McGovern's part would be likely to have less to do with ego and more with a residual anxiety from his *Brookside* days of being unable to tell his story the way he wanted to, there remains a feeling that feature films were an interesting diversion for McGovern. At this particular moment in television history they could well have felt like a liberation, and McGovern's two efforts from this time for the cinema are far from being poor work. However, compared to the times when he is closest to the peak of his power and impact they do not feel like his natural home.

In some ways, even more remarkable than finding Jimmy McGovern working with Stephen Frears was McGovern's achievement in getting the project that became *Dockers* off the ground. This was not just because of its subject matter (though in the years of New Labour's pomp a long-running industrial dispute was not the kind of thing that played naturally with television drama executives), but because of McGovern's idea of writing it with the striking dockers and their families. Partly born out of expediency (McGovern was already committed to a number of projects), the idea of using a Worker's Education Association (WEA) class for sacked dock workers to produce a script on one of the longest running industrial disputes in British labour history was, if not unique, then incredibly rare in television history. That it should happen at a moment in the institutional history of television of the kind touched upon above is partly testament to the position that McGovern had established for himself, as well as the parallel bargaining power brought to the project by the Scottish novelist Irvine Welsh. The bare facts as described on the DVD of *Dockers* spell out the extraordinary detail of the arrangements under which the programme was made:

> Channel 4 had invited Jimmy McGovern to write a screenplay on the subject. Jimmy already had too many work commitments and recommended Irvine Welsh, author of *Trainspotting*, as an alternative. Unfortunately Irvine was also overstretched. Then it was suggested that members of the WEA class should do the writing with help from Jimmy and Irvine. Channel 4 liked the idea and commissioned the script . ...
> Then the historic moment came. Sixteen writers signed a contract with Parallax Pictures and co-producers the Initiative Factory, a co-operative set up by the sacked dockers. All the money was donated to the Initiative Factory. It was a unique event in the history of British scriptwriting. (Channel 4, 2001)

Whilst it would be false to suggest that *Dockers* reached the kinds of mass audience that most of McGovern's work has done, its appearance at all on one of the main UK terrestrial channels was remarkable, and it rekindled a relationship with Channel 4 that was to extend to McGovern's next project, *Sunday* (2002).

Sunday was the result of an approach from Gaslight Productions, a Derry-based company, who wanted McGovern to dramatise the events of Bloody Sunday to mark the thirtieth anniversary of the massacre in which British troops had opened fire on Catholic demonstrators in the Bogside district of Derry, killing a total of 13 people. According to McGovern: 'I had been asked before but always refused, arguing that it was a story that should be told by the Irish themselves' (2004). He goes on to explain that his mind was changed by the realisation that the story was also a British one and, on the same basis as *Hillsborough*, he agreed to work with some of those closest to the tragedy to dramatise what they saw as the truth of the events.

14 Jimmy McGovern

McGovern's take on *Bloody Sunday* was preceded by just over a week by another version of the events of January 1972, Paul Greengrass's *Bloody Sunday* (2002), commissioned by ITV. As Richard Kelly put it: 'You wait thirty years for a Bloody Sunday movie and then two come along at once' (2002: 81–2). The often fascinating contrasts between the two films will be examined in more detail later on, but here it is worth noting the way that, once again, McGovern's willingness to engage with documentary drama was driven by his strong personal relationship to the source material. His Irish Catholic roots and political background made *Sunday* as closely linked to his convictions as both *Hillsborough* and *Dockers*.

In terms of television history, at one level, McGovern's return to documentary drama made *Sunday* very much part of a relative boom in television's attempts to deal with the 'real'. As far back as 1981 Lesley Woodhead had been able to claim: 'To be sure there do seem to be an awful lot of the things about these days' (1999: 102), but by the time McGovern wrote *Sunday* television's negotiation with 'reality' had mutated and multiplied into a plethora of new forms in a trend that still dominates television. Many of these are ultra-cheap and easy to produce and have become the staple diet of the low-cost multi-channel era. *Sunday*, on the other hand, belonged to a more narrowly focused tradition which always courted exactly the kind of controversy that McGovern has found it difficult to avoid. Woodhead quotes Ian Gilmour, the Lord Privy Seal in the Conservative government in 1980, making one of a number of high-profile interventions by senior politicians on the legitimacy of this particular form of television: 'The so-called dramatisation or fictionalisation of alleged history is extremely dangerous and misleading, and is something to which the broadcasting authorities must give close attention' (1999: 101).

As Woodhead goes on to say, Gilmour's comments were made in the wake of one particular documentary that rattled politicians for the kinds of reasons that make writers like Jimmy McGovern turn to them in the first place. *Death of a Princess* (dir. Anthony Thomas, 1980) alleged uncomfortable truths about Saudi Arabia and caused an enormous international political row, including the expulsion of the British ambassador in Riyadh and, most seriously for the politicians, supposedly jeopardised a whole range of British economic interests in parts of the Middle East, including those in oil and arms sales. Work such as this and *Who Bombed Birmingham* (dir. Mike Beckham, 1990) were very much the antecedents of McGovern's forays into the tradition. Ironically though, it is possible to argue (see for example Bignell, 2010) that by the time McGovern wrote *Sunday* the documentary drama on British television as a whole had declined from its campaigning, controversial peak and had instead become part of the flight away from 'difficult' and expensive drama and documentary and towards the worst excesses of reality television.

Clearly such a polarity is too simple, and McGovern (and Greengrass's) work are testimony to that. What it illustrates again, perhaps, is the determination of McGovern frequently to work against the seemingly inevitable tide of television history. Moreover it is also evidence of his status as a writer who could, by this time, be commissioned to make prime-time television that also engaged with controversy and areas that were rarely seen by the broadcasters as fertile territory for mass audiences. Added to this, of course, was the fact that the Saville Inquiry into the events of Bloody Sunday was still proceeding, something which McGovern himself had been convinced would render the film untransmittable (see Hari, 2002). The fact that the film was made and shown is a clear marker of the growing status enjoyed by McGovern by the early 2000s and which would eventually give him more mainstream and critical success throughout the second half of the decade.

On the BBC's website, in a piece of background on McGovern's next project, Gub Neal, the originator and producer of *Cracker*, suggests that 'His writing, especially when one considers titles like *Cracker*, *Priest* or *Sunday*, is essentially Jacobean' (BBC, 2006). Without dwelling too long on how appropriate such an analogy might be, it goes some way towards explaining the relationship between McGovern and the four-hour drama that he wrote for BBC2, *Gunpowder, Treason and Plot* (dir. Gilles Mackinnon, 2004).

Originally two separate ideas, one on Mary Queen of Scots and the other on James I and the gunpowder plot, the BBC eventually agreed to combine the two into a two part, four-hour miniseries, giving McGovern scope and license to explore the historical underpinning of the gunpowder plot itself. Whilst the style and approach are very different from the core of the documentary-drama tradition, the length of the films and McGovern's instincts still gave *Gunpowder, Treason and Plot* a similar relationship to the idea of revealing historical truth. As McGovern himself said:

> I have written history before. *Sunday* was about Bloody Sunday in Derry in 1972. *Hillsborough* was about the 1989 football disaster and *Dockers* was about the Liverpool Docks' Dispute of the mid-Nineties.
>
> But the people affected by those events are still alive: so I did not dare to take any liberties with their stories. I could not impose clarity or simplicity upon them. The truth, no matter how messy or complicated, had to be told. (BBC, 2004)

McGovern here makes an understandable, though debatable, distinction between two approaches to the 'truth' and in so doing establishes a relationship with yet another television form that in itself has been liable to shift and change. At the time of writing the BBC's most recent large-scale investment in a drama series based upon history has been involved in conflict with academic historians about its interpretation of the past:

> 'Shame on the BBC!' yelled David Starkey when *The Tudors* began, outraged by what he saw as systematic inaccuracy. But as the Henry VIII saga reaches its final episode tomorrow night, fusty dons such as Starkey should be running scared – because the drama has exploded one historical bombshell after another, and has taught us that almost everything we thought we knew about Henry VIII was wrong. (Dugdale, 2011)

The *Guardian* blog is characteristically (in terms of responses to this much-derided series) tongue-in-cheek, but the debate has been a serious one and raises difficult questions about the relationship between television and history in general and drama and history in particular. The voracious appetite of the multi-channel era has meant not only an increase in relatively expensive historical drama, but also an increase in programmes about history in general. The fact that many such programmes contain reconstructions of various kinds means that many of the same issues apply to both.

In *Gunpowder, Treason and Plot*, then, we have yet another example of a McGovern intervention into a key recent question for television history. The nature of that intervention will be fully discussed in due course, but for now it is fascinating to note the approach of the production team on *Gunpowder, Treason and Plot* in relation to the dedication to particular ideas of truth that dominated McGovern's thinking on, say, *Hillsborough* and *Sunday*. In response to the usual discussions of authenticity that would inevitably surround such a comparatively expensive BBC historical drama, Gub Neale said: 'What history gives us is context ... It's a wonderful setting in which to tell a tale, but to be hamstrung by factual accuracy would be very, very, demeaning.' Leaving aside for a moment the myriad questions begged by the term 'factual accuracy', such an approach would surely have posed almost as many problems for McGovern as it solved. Whilst understanding completely Neale's position in relation to the historical epic, there are undeniable difficulties to be negotiated for a writer who took such a strong line on veracity in relation to other work.

After a relatively minor diversion into a one-off, feature-length *Cracker* comeback (which he later admitted was something of a mistake), McGovern's next work was to become his highest- profile success since the original *Cracker* began in the early 1990s. It also, crucially, in terms of his impact on the development of television drama, took the mentoring/producer instincts that had previously been evident as far back as the original *Cracker* into new territory.

The Street (2006–09) was produced by ITV at the old Granada studios in Manchester but commissioned and broadcast by the BBC as a prime-time BBC1 drama over three series. The idea and overall creative control were McGovern's, but to varying degrees all three series were part-written by voices either new to television, or who had previously worked in other genres. Whilst the overall effect was to foster and nurture new talent, the concept was also about getting fresh ideas, as McGovern has freely acknowledged:

> What we did was we had a trawl of writers actually. We put out the fact that we wanted good unusual stories. We got hundreds in but sad to say 85–90% of those were regurgitated TV stories, stories you're sick of seeing on TV. There were a few that were fresh and new but those are the ones that we picked up. (BBC, 2006b)

The relationship between McGovern, the totality of the series and the ways of working with the other writers will be explored fully in due course, as will the continuation of the idea into other forms such as his venture into daytime television, *Moving On* (2010–). Here, though, it is worth locating *The Street*, or at least certain aspects of its construction, within a tradition that Lez Cooke identified as 'the new social realism' (2005: 184). Cooke is writing primarily about *Clocking Off* (BBC1, 2000–03) written for the most part by McGovern's one-time collaborator on some of the episodes of *Cracker*, Paul Abbott. In the same piece Cooke proposes that Abbott has both inherited the social-realist tradition inherited from the likes of *Play for Today* and *The Wednesday Play* and adapted it in ways that are reflective not only of the constraints of contemporary television, but also of the changed landscape of working-class life in twenty-first-century post-industrial Britain.

It would be a mistake to equate *The Street* too precisely with *Clocking Off*, of course, and there are important distinctions to be discussed later, but there is little doubting that the latter demonstrated both an appetite for the kinds of stories of working-class life that *The Street* later offered, and also a model of a big-name writer able to oversee a series and bring new writers on within a safer institutional framework.

It is one thing to see an opportunity such as the model for reinstating the single-drama space by the back door, as *Clocking Off* managed to do, but quite another to capitalise on it in the manner that *The Street* managed to do over such a sustained period, and also to attract a cast of actors of the kind that helped retain a large popular audience. In its focus on the domestic space, rather than the workplace of *Clocking Off*, *The Street* is superficially closer to the soap-opera form that McGovern began his television life writing. In reality, however, *The Street*'s treatment of narrative and character is a long way from the rapid-fire of British soap opera in the twenty-first century with its voracious, four-episode-per-week schedules. *The Street* taps into an audience in which soap opera has developed an appetite for domestic drama and demands more from it and, in return, provides the rewards of something more substantial.

For most programme makers the very idea of daytime television connotes only the cheap and the second-rate, analgesic pap for an audience seeking mainly to pass the time when most of the active world is working. The announcement therefore that Jimmy McGovern was to produce a series of daytime dramas for the BBC under the overall title *Moving On* (2010) was, to say the least, startling. There is, though, some kind of logic. This is a writer that has not only taken on and subverted a whole range of popular genre and formats, but also one for whom the idea of producing genuine quality drama for mass audiences is reflective of his origins. If daytime television is indeed for the vulnerable, the elderly and the unemployed then, one can imagine McGovern asking, why are they not deserving of the best, or at least better?

It is, of course, true that *Moving On* has been, perhaps primarily, a test bed for new writers (and directors) nurtured by McGovern. On the other hand, this has not prevented a remarkable range of cast members agreeing to appear in a format that they would normally exclude themselves from. Among those appearing in the two series of *Moving On* that have been broadcast up until the time of writing include Sheila Hancock, Lesley Sharpe, Dervla Kirwan, John Simm and Anna Massey, whilst the directing team has included Dominic West, one of the stars of *The Wire*, making his debut behind the camera.

In a very real sense, then, *Moving On* shifted the possibilities of daytime television and was able to do so because of McGovern's name. Whether one sees this as an act of altruism on McGovern's part or not is, in a sense, beside the point. What is more interesting is the further extension of McGovern's willingness to keep extending the range of television's popular forms and in so doing reach large-scale audiences with work that he feels is worthwhile and has something to say. The scope for achieving any shift in audience perception and range of daytime television within the severe budgetary constraints will be discussed further in the relevant chapter, but the willingness of McGovern to be involved in such an intervention is part of a the strong innovative and risk-taking vein that runs through his work. Whilst one contributory factor to the lack of academic writing on McGovern is likely to be his perceived avoidance of aesthetic innovation of the kind that has seen Dennis Potter become so widely analysed, what *Moving On* suggests is someone who, like Potter, genuinely believes in the potential of television as a medium, but who is also willing to attempt to work with genre and, more unusually still, with parts of the schedule that are avoided entirely by those that see themselves defined by notions of 'quality'.

The focus of this book and the series to which it belongs on television authorship means that McGovern's brief return to theatre in the form of *King Cotton* (2007) will not be extensively discussed, but it is worth mentioning in this introduction because of what it adds to the picture of a writer's almost voracious appetite for a new direction and challenge. McGovern's early experiences of theatre were, he now says, alienating:

> My experiences in theatre back in the Eighties had made me realise that I simply fail to understand how it works or even necessarily what they were talking about. It was like there was this special coded language and you might have a discussion about a script and come away realising that you had no idea whether they liked it or not. (Ward, 2007)

Added to this, despite working on theatre that might have been made for his political instincts, McGovern's earliest professional work was mocked by critics, even those from his home city:

> A chorus of critical disapproval greeted his early '80s efforts for the theatre in his native Liverpool. As he recalls, the Daily Post's review of his first commission, a version of Dario Fo's *Can't Pay, Won't Pay* at the Everyman, began with the line: 'Can't pay, won't pay for rubbish like this', and continued in a similar vein. (Cavendish, 2007)

Despite such misgivings, both McGovern's powerful attraction to what he sees as a 'good story', combined with a desire to contribute to the Liverpool European Capital of Culture offering, albeit with mixed feelings, led him towards this highly unlikely venture into musical theatre.

The reviews varied, and McGovern has not yet repeated the experience, so the assumption must be that this is not a strong new direction. It is, however, perhaps a sign of a kind of relaxation on McGovern's behalf, particularly in relation to the close interconnection between class and the theatre. It is a relaxation that in this case enabled him to pursue an evident propensity to explore new territory, with the important proviso that the journey must lead towards saying something that he cares about. The following description of the historical source material for *King Cotton* makes its suitability for McGovern abundantly clear:

[it is set during] the Lancashire cotton famine of 1861–1865, when supplies of the raw material from the slave plantations of the Deep South in the US dried up as Union forces blockaded the ports of the Confederate south. The effect on Lancashire's mill towns was catastrophic: it is estimated that by November 1862, 331,000 men and women – three-fifths of the cotton trade labour force – were idle. (Ward, 2007)

McGovern's final completed project for television to date found him back on more familiar territory in that the BBC1 drama series *Accused* (2010–) was again a season of single dramas linked by a common thread. In fact the dramas are even closer to the single play than those in *The Street*, because each 'episode' is entirely separate, with no recurring cast of characters or common location to provide even the 'shadow' of a drama series. The one link that the individual dramas in *Accused* do possess is entirely thematic, namely to present a series of characters whose lives have led them to be on trial for a serious crime and to implicitly raise questions in its audience around questions of guilt and innocence. McGovern's own description of the series betrayed an impatience with aspects of the genre that he first subverted in *Cracker*:

> In the time it takes to climb the steps to the court we tell the story of how the accused came to be here.
>
> We see the crime and we see the punishment. Nothing else. No police procedure, thanks very much, no coppers striding along corridors with coats flapping. Just crime and punishment – the two things that matter most in any crime drama. (Conlan, 2010)

Implicitly though, alongside the criticism, is an acknowledgement of the power of the genre, and there is no mistaking *Accused*'s debt to the crime series. Once again, then, McGovern had returned to a popular form with very definite ideas of how it should be handled, ideas that in the end challenge the format itself.

In the case of *Accused*, as mentioned above, the key challenge to any notion of genre is the absence of recurrent characters or settings, making the series effectively an anthology of single dramas. However, the branding and publicity surrounding the programme worked hard to create a series identity, setting up an interesting tension between generic conventions and the freedom for each programme to begin again with entirely new characters.

In addition, *Accused* extends McGovern's work in the direction of using his own standing and reputation to bring on lesser-known writers under the protective umbrella of the linked series. In this case McGovern wrote three out of the six episodes of the first series with three other different writers used on the remaining three (at the time of writing a second series is in production).

Introduction 21

Whilst the critical reaction to *Accused* was not unfavourable, a disproportionate amount of the press coverage of the series became devoted to a single episode. 'Frankie's Story' (Episode 2, first broadcast on 22 November 2010) produced a storm of controversy when a number of senior British army officers publicly criticised its portrayal of life amongst soldiers serving in Afghanistan. According to a number of news reports, General Sir Peter Wall, the head of the army, went as far as asking the BBC to pull the episode:

> General Sir Peter Wall, chief of the general staff, said in a letter to the BBC director general, Mark Thompson, that the drama – part of a six-part series on the theme of crime and punishment – was 'deeply offensive' and 'distasteful' to serving soldiers and their families.
>
> Wall, who also called the drama 'misleading and inaccurate', said he would prefer the programme to be dropped. (Adetunji, 2010)

Once again, then, McGovern was back where he feels most at home. Just before the BBC started screening *Accused*, McGovern gave an interview in which he was critical of much contemporary television drama and made an assertion that has been a common refrain of many writers over the years: 'Why have a BBC complaints unit in the first place? They tell me, "Jimmy, it is in case you offend anybody," and I say, "I am a writer. That is my job." Just imagine if it said on my headstone that I had never offended anybody – I would turn in my grave' (Thorpe, 2010).

Despite the commonplace nature of such an assertion, in McGovern's case the long track record indicates far more than lip-service to the idea of the artist as principled outsider, prepared to 'cause trouble'. Again and again, often in ways that have actively worked against both the prevailing political climate and the interests of his career, McGovern has returned to controversy and the idea of telling uncomfortable truths. As one of his most frequent collaborators, Christopher Eccleston, put it: 'McGovern had so much power after *Cracker*, he could have done anything. What did he do? He went to the Hillsborough Family Support Group and said "I want to tell your story." That was an act of conscience. It's very rare. We should be proud of having a guy like that in our midst' (McGilliard, 2010: 23).

Characteristically, McGovern's account of the genesis of *Hillsborough* (mentioned above) is far more modest and, according to his account, was the result of an approach to him from the families. Nevertheless the essence of Eccleston's point remains true. Despite the centrality to his work of the popular and of the power of narrative, McGovern has managed to combine these with a relish for controversy and a willingness to adopt difficult moral standpoints. As we will see in Chapter 2, this is something which he has maintained throughout his career, whatever the commissioning climate.

In this, the first full-length study of McGovern's work, the intention is to examine this consistent courting of controversy alongside both the writer's impressive range of contributions to the recent history of television drama forms. In turn links will also be made to the thread of theoretical debates that underpin all of McGovern's work and his own commentary on his writing. On the issue of the representation of working-class masculinity alone McGovern's work would count as highly significant, but on broader questions of class, of the significance of the Catholic Church and of the nature of realism in drama he is, it will be argued, also a figure of genuine importance.

I would like to conclude this brief introduction to the book's scope with a brief note on inclusions and omissions. In McGovern's case this has been relatively simple because the vast majority of his writing has been for television and therefore vital to include in a volume to be published in a series on television authors. I would have also liked to include coverage of the small number of feature films for which McGovern has written the screenplay. This is primarily because the institutional context in which these films were made meant that their genesis was inevitably intertwined with British television in an era in which broadcasters, primarily the BBC and Channel 4, were one of the few significant sources of funding for the British film industry. In addition, in a number of cases, McGovern's work for feature films started life as television series and, in the case of *Gunpowder, Treason and Plot*, vice versa. However, the nature of this series and the restrictions on space have meant that it has been possible to include only brief mentions of McGovern's three screenplays that resulted in full-scale theatrical release: *Priest*, *Heart* and *Liam*.

The only other real omissions are any significant discussion of his early work for theatre and his single radio play, *Felix Randal* (first broadcast on BBC Radio 4 on 15 October 1985). The theatre work is mentioned a number of times in passing, primarily because of McGovern's suspicion of theatre's cultural position and its impact on his failure to break into it in the way that Willie Russell and Alan Bleasdale had managed to do to different extents. *Felix Randal*, in terms of any desire to write for radio, can be seen, on the one hand, as something of a minor diversion and part of a traditional 'apprenticeship' for British writers. On the other, the play's basis in the poem of the same name by Gerard Manley Hopkins is of some significance for the light it sheds on the rest of McGovern's career. Hopkins is not only the writer that Danny Kavanagh, McGovern's central character in *The Lakes* is reading, an act that marks him out as something more than the gambling-addicted scally we first meet, he is also someone whose writing McGovern has mentioned perhaps more than any other. In an interview that preceded the first broadcast of *The Lakes* McGovern urged everyone to 'read *The Windhover*. Best 14 lines ever written', and there is a sense in which the Jesuit Hopkins is at the heart of McGovern's sensibility.

Not only was Hopkins a Catholic priest who spent some time working in a parish in Liverpool, he is frequently cited as an example of a 'difficult' formal innovator in an age of relative conservatism for poetry. This combination of a man who was not born to a Catholic family, who many saw as struggling with the restrictions of the priesthood and who was also, as George Orwell once said, 'a writer's writer' (1941), was clearly of great significance for McGovern. Whilst *Felix Randal*, the early radio play, is not considered in this volume, the fact that McGovern's devotion to Hopkins both as a writer and a conflicted Catholic led him to make the poem the source for his first non-*Brookside* commission is surely worthy of recognition. It signals a seriousness about writing and, much more obviously, a seriousness about the religion that he was born to that he has placed at the core of his work even when his criticism of Catholicism is at its most severe.

Apart from the curiosity of McGovern writing a single episode of *Coronation Street* (ITV, 1960–) in 1990, all the rest of his work for television is covered in the volume. It represents, I would suggest, an almost unparalleled versatility and ability to range across the television drama forms that have changed so rapidly over the 30 years since McGovern began writing. It is hoped that bringing coverage of the work together in a single volume will not only stimulate scholars to undertake further work on McGovern, but also to reflect on the ways in which he has made a significant contribution to the development of British television drama itself.

Soaps, series and serials: *Brookside, Cracker, Hearts and Minds, The Lakes*

1

This chapter draws together work that is, in many ways, highly disparate both in terms of style and relationship to genre. All the programmes are, however, linked by belonging to a form that employs features of the television serial, particularly the flow of narrative across different episodes.

Though spanning almost a decade, the programmes provide a very full picture of the period of McGovern's development as a writer from his first break into television on *Brookside* up until the major popular success of *The Lakes*. As the Introduction makes clear, however, this is not a simple chronological account, and McGovern's other work from this period is covered in other chapters.

The central concern here is to chronicle McGovern's evolving approach to popular forms, both in terms of narrative style and content. During this period it is clear that McGovern moves from the relatively confining context of the writing teams on *Brookside* to the freedom of series such as *Hearts and Minds* and *The Lakes* in which his ideas are the central driving force. After *Cracker* in particular McGovern's name began to be the key factor in the commissioning and, eventually, the marketing of a series, and this status has an impact on the approaches that he felt able to try out.

After leaving *Brookside*, at least partly on a point of political principle, it is fair to say that McGovern's approach to politics in the series represented in this chapter gradually takes a more oblique turn. This is not say that even *The Lakes* does not have a clear relationship to contemporary life and that its perspective is clearly that of a writer for whom social class remains the one of the most significant factors in the formation of an individual. There is, however, little trace in these big popular series of the directness with which McGovern had managed to write, for example, for the radical trade-union leader, Bobby Grant, in the early days of *Brookside*.

Soaps, series and serials 25

This chapter, perhaps most significantly, chronicles McGovern's growing talent for negotiating a space within the popular. A space that required a different approach to political ideas, but which certainly never neutralised what remained, in the context of British television, a radical voice. In turn, though, this does not translate simply into a voice that always found favour on the British left, and in the following discussion of a number of the programmes we see McGovern's very honest and often troubled relationship with issue politics develop in ways that were almost unique for writers of his generation.

As the Introduction suggested, McGovern's career will be seen partly in relation to wider changes in the commissioning context of British television drama over the period in which he has been writing. In this chapter it will be argued that McGovern was amongst those that not only responded and adapted to this changing world, but who, in certain key respects, influenced thinking behind the commissioning of popular drama. The impact of *Brookside* on the development of British soap opera and the influence of *Cracker* on subsequent drama in which the role of the police became secondary to other forms of civilian investigation are just two of the ways in which this chapter discusses the relationship between British television history and McGovern's work.

Finally, it is in this earlier phase of his career that McGovern negotiates most clearly the role of autobiography in his work. Both *Hearts and Minds* and *The Lakes* contain some of the strongest and most direct correspondence between the events of McGovern's own life and the narratives that he creates. Perhaps only in *Hearts and Minds* does McGovern's engagement with his past approach an apparent exorcism of demons, dealing as it does with his deeply disillusioning experience of teaching in a comprehensive school, but with all the appropriate caveats there is no denying the power of McGovern's life as a Catholic, a working-class trade unionist and a young man seeking an escape from the prison of his background through education. This chapter seeks to examine some of the ways in which McGovern both earned the right to dramatise such experience but also to radically adapt it in pursuit of what he has also said is paramount, the 'good story'.

Brookside (1982–2003)

Given that academic scholarship on soap opera has tended to be something of a particular focus for feminist media scholars, it is somewhat ironic to begin this chapter by discussing Jimmy McGovern's work for the groundbreaking *Brookside* (Channel 4, 1982–2003).

This is not to suggest that McGovern's work for the soap opera (or indeed anything else) is unambiguously anti-feminist. However, what had been seen as predominantly a space for a female audience became, in McGovern's hands, also a powerful vehicle for the dramatisation of the experience of the white working-class male. This came in a decade when the forces of ideological conservatism were seen to be threatening everything that had previously sustained such a category, at least in the UK. The fact that McGovern also created some of the most memorable, if controversial, female characters in British soap-opera history is often highly contested, and his critical reputation is frequently called into question by referring to his focus on male experience.

The question of authorship should, however, be addressed, at least briefly. If McGovern has become perhaps the most prominent writer to have emerged from the *Brookside* experience, it is a mistake to allow his subsequent reputation to cloud the fact that he was always one of a large team of writers. A team, what is more, that operated under the strict regime run by Phil Redmond and his Mersey Television company. He cannot therefore be held entirely responsible for the representational issues that arise even from the episodes that he wrote, still less the ideological tone of the whole series. Nevertheless, McGovern himself has said enough about his preoccupations in the intervening years to give at least a framework upon which to base an analysis of his *Brookside* period and its continuing significance for British television, as well as the way that his own subsequent career is viewed.

McGovern's only previous experience as a writer before *Brookside* was in the theatre, where he looked for a breakthrough in a Liverpool whose theatre culture had, in recent times, fostered working-class male voices such as Willy Russell and Alan Bleasdale. McGovern was never to prosper in the same way in and, in McGovern's recollection of the time, there are glimpses of a class resentment of theatre that is altogether more hard-edged than, say, Russell's or Bleasdale's. In the Introduction to this volume I have already made reference to the review of his adaptation of the Dario Fo classic, *Can't Pay, Won't Pay*, which was headed: 'Well, we can't pay and won't pay for rubbish like this.' In an interview for the BBC McGovern develops the narrative around his stillborn career in theatre and describes how he 'escaped' from what looked like becoming a dead end and went straight into television on *Brookside*:

> I showed them a play I'd been working on, it would have been a studio play. Weeks later I'd heard nothing and I said, "What's happening?" The guy from the Everyman said, "Jimmy, I'm sorry mate, I got to page 20. Bleasdale got to page 22. Willy only got to page 14 but it's crap, Jim,

and I'm sorry, but the offer of the part-time writer in residence is now withdrawn."

I'm a writer, so I choose my words very carefully, but I was suicidal that night. This glittering prize had been offered to me and just snatched away. I was absolutely gutted. But what Chris Bond said to me eventually was, "Jimmy, they won't touch you upstairs in the studio", and then he said, "I'll give you a thousand pounds, go away and write a play and I'll put it on the main stage of Liverpool Playhouse." That's how I got commissioned. A working-class epic. ... Phil Redmond just at that moment – this is how lucky you've got to be – was looking for people to write *Brookside*. And fortunately again had done some deal with the council so he had to employ a fair proportion of people who were local. And so I was just lucky. (McGovern, 2009)

The 'had to' in McGovern's final sentence is a characteristic note. On the one hand, funny and refreshingly clear about why he got his break in the first place. On the other, defensive and prepared for the kinds of conflicts that did, inevitably, arise during the early years of *Brookside*.

McGovern's description of his stage commission perhaps summed up his approach to writing *Brookside* – 'a working-class epic'. This is also the characteristic of the programme that has most frequently been discussed by academics, many of whom saw the early *Brookside* as a clear departure from the British soap-opera tradition established by *Coronation Street* (ITV, 1961–) in particular. Christine Geraghty, in the book that has become one of the classic analyses of the significance of gender representation in soap opera, observed of *Brookside* that 'For the first time in British soap the viewer was offered a position for understanding a soap which was based on class and not gender', before going on to illustrate the point in more detail with reference to the Grant family, who are frequently the characters most closely associated with McGovern's contribution to *Brookside*:

> *Brookside* used soap's capacity to mull over problems and to take into account the nuances of a position in a way that had not been seen before by giving class issues the same weight as personal dilemmas. In one episode for example, Bobby's [Grant] decision to become a full-time trade union officer, potentially the slippery road to becoming a paid bureaucrat rather than an honourable activist, was subjected to the same careful scrutiny by his friends and workmates that would be given in other soaps to a decision to get married. (Geraghty, 1991: 152)

Geraghty's analysis of *Brookside*, whilst not being entirely negative by any stretch of the imagination, does focus heavily on what she and others saw as the contrast between its radical (in mainstream television terms at least) treatment of class and relatively conservative treatment of women:

> *Brookside* is normally deemed the most progressive of the British soaps, valued for the way in which it deals with social issues and recognises class as a major factor in the fabric of British life. It is somewhat ironic then to note that it is *Brookside* which has most consistently positioned women in the home and represented them through their relationship with their families. ...
>
> ... *Brookside* has thus continued the tradition of strong women in soaps but has tended to restrict their scope to the confines of the home. (Geraghty, 1991: 184–5)

From the very beginnings of his career, then, McGovern was associated with controversy around the representation of gender inside a broader 'progressive' framework. Such debates, at least in academic circles, were of course absolutely central to the formation of discourse in media studies from the late 1970s onwards. Soap opera (frequently the American versions, crucially broadcast during the day) became one of the key genres in debates that established an approach to the analysis of mass media that deconstructed formulations of high and low art alongside an embrace of ideas about gender and ethnicity. Tanya Modleski's formulation of the relationship between soap opera and the condition of women's existence is representative of a powerful strain in feminist thinking which, despite its origins in the USA, where the institutional position of soap opera was markedly different from the UK, became highly influential in Britain at the start of the 1980s:

> Tune in tomorrow, not in order to find out the answers, but to see what further complications will defer the resolutions and introduce new questions. Thus the narrative, by placing ever more complex obstacles between desire and its fulfilment, makes anticipation of an end an end in itself. Soap operas invest exquisite pleasure in the central condition of a woman's life: waiting – whether for her phone to ring, for the baby to take its nap, or for the family to be reunited shortly after the day's final soap opera has left *its* family still struggling against dissolution. (Modleski, 1979: 12)

Such a position self-evidently takes a particularly strong view of the social position of women at a historical moment, but it also describes soap operas that differed in certain key respects from the British model, even before the arrival of *Brookside*. Nevertheless the way that British soap opera before 1980 has been discussed by academics does have the clear underlying sense of the genre as being 'female' at its heart, something typified by this passage from a key essay by Christine Geraghty:

> Soaps have traditionally dealt with the fabric of personal relationships, setting up a network of gossip and support, conducted by women who were both the strongest characters in the programmes and their most

faithful viewers. It was the drama of personal relationships within a homogenous community which was the hallmark of *Coronation Street*, establishing a sense of geographical place so strongly that it over-rode the boundaries of the family. (Geraghty, 1992: 131)

As we saw previously, Geraghty and others saw *Brookside* as a clear departure from such a formula, but in this slightly later essay she goes on to develop the argument further, suggesting that not only *Brookside*, but also *Eastenders* were part of a strong move in the 1980s away from a focus upon 'personal relationships' and towards what she refers to as 'social issues'. This in turn took soaps away from the private and more and more towards the public sphere. As Geraghty goes on to discuss, one of the effects of this was to make the way that soap operas represented social groups a matter of wide public debate:

> In the 1980's then, British soaps became a matter of public debate and judgements about how they handle sensitive issues were continually being made, sometimes as a central point, sometimes as a casual remark in an interview dealing with something entirely different. In particular the soaps were felt to have responsibility for how they dealt with the new issues. (Geraghty, 1992: 134)

As Geraghty says, *Brookside*'s overt use of contemporary social concerns led it to be frequently cited by the popular press as a 'cause' of a particular public anxiety. One example was the way that a story about a gay man, Gordon Collins, was used as the pretext for accusing *Brookside* of, in Geraghty's words, 'increasing anxiety about Aids when Paul Collins, speaking as an anxious father and not an expert, gave the wrong information about the HIV virus'.

In Geraghty's reading *Brookside*'s trouble in the 1980s stemmed from an essentially noble aim, one which has always informed Jimmy McGovern's work, namely that of attempting to truthfully reflect contemporary social issues in a way that would still retain the ability to attract large audiences. In so doing, the argument goes, the programme leaves itself open to accusations of, on the one hand, tokenism (through the inclusion of 'minority' characters that are largely positive in the way that they are portrayed), and on the other of misrepresentation if a character is presented in a negative light.

The changes that were to overtake the production of soap opera in the UK during the 1980s were, then, ideally suited to what McGovern was to become as a writer. Working within established forms, but looking always to challenge their boundaries, McGovern initially benefited from the changing production climate pioneered by the likes of *Brookside* producer Phil Redmond and quite quickly became one of those at the forefront of change himself.

This leads, in the case of *Brookside* (and later *Eastenders*), to the perennial question of realism. Writing in Robert Allen's seminal collection of essays examining soaps as a worldwide phenomenon, Christine Geraghty identifies the negotiation of realism as the defining characteristic of post-1980 British soap opera:

> Realism is a key concept for these new British soaps and is called on as a justification or a rationale for the world which they depict. The claim to reflect reality helped the producers to combat those who asserted that the 1980s soaps were too outspoken and brutal in what they showed. 'We don't make life, we reflect it,' Julia Smith, the producer of *Eastenders*, told viewers who complained about the programme's direct approach. (Geraghty, 1995: 67)

If this leads to a picture of a brash, confident McGovern determined to use the new realist ethos to tell it how it is, then it is contradicted by the relatively few comments he has made about his first experiences on *Brookside*. To begin with, at least, he claims to have been somewhat overawed by the idea of writing for television and, as a consequence, tending towards strict observance of the perceived hierarchies and rules involved in writing as part of a team:

> I went into the world of television and I thought: oh my God, I don't know what I'm doing here. Here's Andy Lynch, Phil Redmond. These two were now gods to me; everything they did I followed slavishly. It took me months and months to dip my toe in the water and actually veer off slightly from the prescribed storyline. As writers you've got to invest a storyline with something of yourself but I wasn't doing that. It took me months to find that out. (McGovern, 2009)

Whilst there is little doubt that McGovern came to see *Brookside* as having a responsibility to provide doses of reality, in particular, the problematic realities of daily life for a working-class Liverpool decimated by the mass unemployment of the 1980s (something which will be discussed further in relation to the circumstances surrounding his leaving the soap), there is also ample evidence that he became quickly aware of the institutional realities of writing for television:

> McGovern worked on Brookside for seven years. He began with episode 14 when the houses in the close were still being built. There were 12 writers and each month only four would get the commission. 'You could always tell a Brookside writer because every fourth Friday they wouldn't go out. They'd sit by the phone, willing it to ring, and then it would ring and it would be some other writer saying 'Have you heard yet?' 'No, get off the line, they might be ringing!' The way to get the phone call, they all discovered, was to quote personal experience or make a big principled speech. (Butler, 1995)

Whilst the humorous cynicism of 'big principled speech' does not entirely negate the idea of McGovern becoming one of those who genuinely managed to push the boundaries of the form into area such as industrial politics, it is also a healthy corrective to a tendency to romanticise his role in a programme such as *Brookside*. In the same interview as the one cited above, McGovern's acute awareness of the imperatives of popular television come through at least as strongly as his politics:

> *EastEnders* had this timebomb. Who's the father of Michelle's baby? That was my big thesis. We need a timebomb. We need a timebomb. That's the body under the patio now. I was always going on about that. Timebomb. Timebomb. *EastEnders* had this beautiful timebomb. So it became 'Who Raped Sheila Grant?' not 'The Rape of Sheila Grant'. There were four candidates for the rapist, but it turned out to be a taxi-driver whom no one had ever seen. McGovern thought that 'a big let-down'. (McGovern, quoted in Butler, 1995)

What distinguished McGovern from others, perhaps, was the way that he combined these instincts for popular narrative forms with an unmistakable desire to write about the things and people he knew well. In *Brookside* this meant a strong focus on the Grant family. One of the bedrocks of *Brookside* in its earliest days, the Grants were staunch working-class Catholics whose arrival to live on Brookside Close at the start of the series in 1982 was itself a key marker of the changes in working-class representation to which *Brookside* made a significant contribution. The Grants were part of a shift to working-class home ownership, something greatly accelerated during the 1980s by the policy of successive Conservative governments of selling off local authority-owned housing via advantageous offers to council tenants to buy their own homes. The unease of the family's patriarch, Bobby Grant (Ricky Tomlinson), in his new surroundings is brought out through his relationship with a neighbour, Paul Collins (Jim Wiggins), whose family's social trajectory is the reverse of the Grants (Paul Collins has been made redundant from a lucrative management position and the family are forced to downsize).

Whilst the handling of the original Grant children, Barry, Karen and Damon (a fourth, Claire, was born later in the series) has been credited with the introduction of a wider range of youth-orientated concerns to the soap-opera form, it is really the potent mix of class and gender politics played out around the parents, Bobby and Sheila (Sue Johnston), that marked out the programme's key territory in its earliest days and it became the key territory most commonly associated with McGovern.

We will return to what McGovern called his 'timebomb', the rape of Sheila Grant, in due course, but first it is worth dwelling on what many felt was an even more transgressive act (in soap-opera terms), namely *Brookside*'s attempt to deal with detailed industrial relations issues through Bobby Grant's role as a staunch trade unionist and, later, union official. The inclusion of an article on a soap opera in *Marxism Today* was, at least in 1984, remarkable, and evidence of the way that *Brookside*'s approach to the dramatisation of industrial relations was taken seriously:

> *Brookside* probably signals most clearly its difference from other serials in the type of story it is willing to take on. It has consistently tried to use issues like strikes, redundancies, unemployment and union activity as a source of stories and character motivation. *Brookside* began with Bobby Grant's involvement in a strike at the factory and recent stories have centred on the fight to prevent the factory's closure. Such stories have been handled with considerable complexity and Bobby's role as an able shop steward who could take on a full-time union job has been both supported and criticised by characters within the programme. (Geraghty, 1984: 38)

In what is perhaps the apotheosis of *Brookside*'s direct engagement with not only trade-union activity, but also the struggles that were going on in the wider Labour movement in the 1980s, a 1987 episode, written by McGovern, shows Bobby Grant addressing a crowd of workers anxious about their job security after the union has asked them to walk out over serious health and safety problems in the factory where they work. Grant's speech, delivered with great power and passion by Ricky Tomlinson, is a classic defence of the principles of collective action shot through with emotional pleas to the men to remember their class loyalties and the struggles of those that had fought and made sacrifices in the past:

> *Grant*: Call yourselves red, eh? And you want to give away your trade union rights? Well, I've got news for yer! They're not yours to give away.
> *Man*: We want to feed our kids!
> *Grant*: They belong to your parents and grandparents who struggled and starved on them picket lines. Your parents and grandparents and their grandparents on top of them. And what about the trade union movement and the labour movement who have died in struggle throughout history? Do you want to give them rights away? You shower of scabs!
> (*Brookside*, Episode 450, 1987)

As Grant's speech gathers momentum one of the crowd begins to persistently heckle with a single taunt – 'Are you in the militant?' When Grant doesn't answer the man repeatedly asks the same question.

Finally Grant attempts to dismiss him with a joke, 'No, I can't afford the suits', and when that doesn't work he resorts to 'What has it got to do with you?' At this point, Grant's position looks impossible. He has lost the crowd, until one last 'Are you in the militant or not' tips him into a final passionate defence:

> *Grant*: What if I am? What harm has it done you, eh? All that they have ever done is build houses ... I've no need to be in it. Don't you understand? I am a militant with a small 'm' and I'm proud of it ... Anyone with the bottle to stand up and say 'I'm not having this' gets branded a militant ... We want good jobs, with good wages and good conditions, and if that's a militant then you can count me in!

At this point a little context is perhaps necessary. At the 1985 Labour Party conference in Blackpool the then Labour Party leader, Neil Kinnock, launched into a passionate attack on the so-called Militant Tendency, a far-left grouping within the party who, under the leadership of the controversial Derek Hatton, controlled Liverpool City Council. The argument was that Kinnock had to move against the 'extremists' within the Labour Party in order to give it a chance of becoming electable. The speech produced uproar on the conference floor as Kinnock was both heckled and cheered, with the veteran Labour Member of Parliament for Liverpool Walton, Eric Heffer, choosing to express his disgust by walking slowly out of the conference hall.

By the time of the broadcast of the episode of *Brookside* under discussion Labour had again been defeated at the 1987 general election by the Conservatives under Margaret Thatcher. Whilst Neil Kinnock retained widespread support there were some on the left of the Labour Party, especially in Liverpool, who remained angry at what they saw as misplaced attacks on activists at a time when energy could have been better expended fighting the Conservatives.[1]

Grant's words cannot of course be simply read as espousing any kind of position taken up personally by McGovern or any other contributor to the series. What is much more relevant to this context is that such a scene ever appeared at all within the format of a popular soap opera, something which McGovern himself still marvels at:

> You think you're watching a format and then suddenly you get hit with something, you get a Trojan horse in there. There were episodes of Brookside that were amazing in the content, this is meant to be a soap opera and we're discussing the militant tendency. So even within a tightly structured format you can say interesting things I think. (McGovern, 2009)

The Trojan horse metaphor is not unique to McGovern, but it has much to say, not just about his time on something as tightly organised as *Brookside*, but also his approach to so many writing projects later in his career. In the remarks above there is an unmistakable glee almost at getting away with and discussing complex, difficult things that have real relevance to the lives of many in the audience unused to seeing the details of their existence explored in popular television drama.

How far, then, does this willingness to engage with areas of daily life not traditionally associated with soap opera play out in relation to traditional questions about realism and television drama? There is clearly not the space or necessity to here fully rehearse a long tradition of critical anxiety about the incompatibility of any idea of 'radicalism' and the realist/naturalist forms that have dominated 'serious' television drama. However, given the emphasis on the 'real' in the early *Brookside* and its continuing importance in the subsequent career of Jimmy McGovern, it is important to discuss at least some of the key markers of such debates and where they seem to leave any claims that Channel 4's soap opera had to being groundbreaking or significant.

At one extreme of critical orthodoxy we are liable to find an approach to television drama that has its origins in a position that situates modernist art as the only response capable of sustaining a critique of the world with which it seeks to engage. Within such a frame of reference the number of television dramatists that have managed the almost impossible task of finding institutional space to create work of this kind is very small indeed and, within academic discourse, frequently confined to the work of Dennis Potter or, at a stretch, David Mercer. Dennis Potter himself defined the approach that he considered the most radical and powerful available to the aspiring television dramatist:

> The best non-naturalist drama, in its very structures disorientates the viewer smack in the middle of the orientation process which television perpetually uses. It disrupts the patterns that are endemic to television, and upsets or exposes the narrative styles of so many of the other allegedly non-fiction programmes. It shows the frame in the picture when most television is busy showing the picture in the frame. (quoted in Caughie, 2000: 152)

Potter's description follows one of what he characterises as the 'Loach–Garnett–Allen school' for which he professes some admiration, though he unambiguously, both in his analysis and through his own work, asserts the modernist position as the 'more valuable of the two approaches'.

Potter's views were originally expressed in the programme of the 1977 Edinburgh Film Festival and clearly drew upon what remains a pivotal moment in the history of academic responses to television in general, to television drama and, in particular, to the dramatising of history. This moment has come to be known and understood as the '*Days of Hope* debate'[2] which took place, for the most part, in the two years before Potter was writing.

The *Days of Hope* debate remains relevant to much of McGovern's work and we will return to it again in this book. For now, though, it is its pivotal role in defining the territory of progressive drama as being fundamentally anti-realist that I want to introduce briefly as way of engaging with both *Brookside* and the early McGovern's claims to any kind of radicalism.

In his book on one of the key figures in the history of television drama, Tony Garnett, Stephen Lacey neatly sums up the position of those that used the Garnett-produced BBC drama series *Days of Hope* (1975) as a vehicle for advancing a series of theoretical arguments about the 'classic realist text'. Foremost among these was Colin MacCabe writing in the leading film journal, *Screen*:

> The potential of realism to be a revolutionary form was first questioned by Colin MacCabe in the film journal *Screen* (MacCabe 1974) and returned to in later interventions when *Days of Hope* is the main issue. Using quotations from Brecht as his starting-point, MacCabe's argument was essentially that realism – or the 'classic realist text' – was best understood as a formal structure, rather than a historically variable practice, that derives from the nineteenth-century novel and which was linked to a particular, and fixed, notion of 'the real'. The classic realist text is a 'closed' discourse. Whilst it might be opposed to dominant ideologies (and MacCabe cites *Cathy Come Home* in this context) it is compromised by its form, since it is impossible 'for the classic realist text to offer any perspectives for struggling due to its inability to investigate contradiction' (MacCabe 1981: 225). The politics of the classic realist text is never more than social democratic. (Lacey, 2007: 101)

For Lacey though, 30 years on, MacCabe's arguments are limited by what he calls their 'brutal formalism' (2007: 101) and failure to recognise key distinctions between avowedly commercial and conservative forms and those such as work by the likes of Loach and Garnett. For the purposes of this book, too, his reference to Pawling and Perkins is of particular relevance:

> As Pawling and Perkins have argued, it was a particularly narrow position to take when popular television was under consideration: 'the refusal to countenance a progressive drama based on forms of emotional identification between audience and characters was debilitating in that it inevitably meant that vast majority of popular television drama was automatically categorised as reactionary' (Pawling and Perkins 1992: 47). (Lacey, 2007: 101)

It is important here to note, for those unfamiliar with the original debates, both that MacCabe's own position modified over time and also that it was challenged in the pages of *Screen* which provided an invaluable space within which to debate the vital question about the possibility of radicalism within the institutions of television. Most prominent of those who recognised the power of MacCabe's argument, but who also saw the need to challenge it, was Colin McArthur:

> My hunch is that we must think of Realisms and that a particular Realism will be progressive or conservative/reactionary not only to the extent to which its subject-matter is in contradiction with the dominant ideologies in that society, but to the extent to which its formal strategies mark a departure from the dominant film or television discourses of that society. (McArthur, 1981: 309)

To think of 'realisms' has indeed become a significantly widespread position since this quite polarised debate and such an approach has clear relevance to an understanding of *Brookside*'s early years and the involvement of McGovern in popular dramatic forms. I would propose that key aspects of early *Brookside*, whilst remaining within the scope of a particular kind of realist aesthetic, were radical in that they were introduced inside a popular form that had, up to this point at least, eschewed the kind of approach that it took. Christine Geraghty's view of such difference makes it very clear:

> Certainly *Brookside* is different from the other serials in its format, the stories it deals with and the characters it represents. Serials such as *Angels*, *Coronation Street* and *Crossroads* are very much based on the notion of a community – a street or a shared place of work – in which each character has a place. Stories often depend on disagreements and quarrels between characters but at times of celebration or distress the serials offer us a resolution through a community response which is generated across family, age or class divisions. When it started, *Brookside* resolutely set itself against this approach and presented us with a number of families which were clearly delineated in terms of class and whose men, at least, were mutually antagonistic. (Geraghty, 1984: 37–8)

Whilst *Brookside* would never have claimed to challenge the dominant realist discourse in the Brechtian mode that McCabe argued was an essential prerequisite for the 'revolutionary' text, its claims to radicalism do include a challenge to the dominant discourse within the popular serial form as it existed in the UK in the early 1980s. *Brookside* also, with McGovern centrally involved here, chose to tackle stories that, certainly at the time, were never dealt with in popular dramatic forms. We have already discussed one particular moment of industrial and attendant political tension in the speech made by Bobby Grant, but this was far from isolated, and industrial relations played a significant part in the early *Brookside* storylines which dealt with a range of redundancies, strikes, mass unemployment and trade-union tactics.

However, *Brookside's* claims to radicalism do not end with industrial relations, and before leaving the programme it is important to return for a moment to another significant story that became so closely associated with McGovern. For the *Independent* to headline a story with 'The man who raped Sheila Grant' (Butler, 1995) was, at best, in dubious taste, but it does draw attention to the extent to which McGovern became personally associated with this most famous and controversial of soap-opera sagas. As previously indicated it became, for McGovern at least, part of the everyday battle for ratings in which television is ultimately engaged, but it is also a key moment in the implicit debate that has always hung around McGovern's approach to gender and its relationship to issues of class that have always been seen as his more natural territory.

McGovern has always been very frank in interviews about his relationship to the battlegrounds of sexual politics that he wandered into as a new writer in the early 1980s. In answer to the very straight question, 'What about the sexual politics on Brookside?' he replies:

> That was 1982–89, a very confused time on Merseyside and I was sick and tired of the feminism of the 80s; this contempt for the white working-class male as racist, sexist, homophobic, so I put a lot of that into episodes of Brookside. For example, a white working-class trade unionist with a political agenda shifting to the right and not knowing where he is and everybody losing respect for him and everything he stands for. Also we had two great actresses and it was a joy to write for them. You know how dispiriting it is when you've written your heart out, you hand it over to a director who can't direct and actors who cannot act. But imagine the joy of writing for Sue Johnston, Amanda Burton ... (McGovern, 2009)

The polarity is unmistakable: on the one hand a visceral dislike for the contempt that he saw in a particular kind of feminism and on the other a relish of writing very prominent female roles for actresses that he admired and who went on to become some of the best-known faces on television (thanks at least in part to their roles in *Brookside*). It is a mistake, however, to take McGovern's open antagonism to what he saw as a very middle-class feminism as a more widespread misogyny. There is ample evidence that McGovern, like so many others at that time, was wrestling with unfamiliar ideas. The results of such struggles became powerful articulations of the contradictions that many on the left felt at this historical moment. In a study of the working-out of such tensions in a working-class 'writer's group', Tom Woodin quotes McGovern on the way he saw his particular position exactly at the time that he was writing *Brookside*:

> 1979–1989 was a bloody awful time to be a white working-class male ... The trade unions (built largely by white working-class males) were smashed. The factories and mines and shipyards (staffed largely by white working-class males) were closing. Feminists were telling us we were sexist pigs. Blacks were telling us we were racist bastards. Gays were telling us we were homophobic bigots ... The trendy left ... had a mental image of us: a foul-mouthed fascist skinhead with a tattoo on his arm and a spanner in his hand ... And quite a few people in the Fed thought something similar. ... I think that's why I packed the Fed in ... In the future, I decided, my identity would be 'white, working-class male'. I would still attack racism and sexism and homophobia, yes, but I would be a white, working class male and other decent, white working-class males would be my true brothers. (McGovern, 2001, quoted in Woodin, (2005: 1001)

There is also evidence that McGovern saw very clearly how this position could so easily be misinterpreted through his writing of the storyline around the rape of Sheila Grant (Sue Johnston):

> there was a danger that the script could be accused of fulfilling every working-class male's nightmare – if you let your women do an Open University course, some slick bastard's going to be at her – therefore keep your woman barefoot and pregnant' (Jimmy McGovern, scriptwriter, interview, August, 1990) (Coppock, Haydon and Richter, 1995: 123)

McGovern's tone here seems strong evidence to suggest that he was fully aware of the dichotomies involved in him writing the Sheila Grant story. Phil Redmond's care to foreground the thinking behind the portrayal of rape, even in a commercial 'companion' to *Brookside*, demonstrates at least some clarity of intention:

> The rape of Sheila Grant saw *Brookside* breaking more barriers with an unflinching portrayal of the aftermath of sexual assault. It also broke the dramatic 'code' of having awful events only befall characters that were either portrayed as victims or deserving of their own comeuppance. Sheila Grant was neither of these, and in fact for many she was *Brookside*'s 'everywoman' – the moderate character with whom the audience most identified. (Kibble-White, 2002: 41)

Of course the producer and writer's views are one thing and the complex interplay of audience and critical reaction quite another. There were many who were critical, not just of the treatment of this particular story, but also of the broader positioning of women in the *Brookside* storylines. As we saw above, a number of female academics saw *Brookside*'s claims to radicalism at least partly compromised by its formal moves away from the female-orientated spaces occupied by traditional British soap operas such as *Crossroads* and *Coronation Street*. The Sheila Grant rape story became, in this context, a fascinating case study for this debate. Even before the advent of this particular plot line Christine Geraghty's analysis both acknowledged *Brookside*'s progressive intent and argued that, perhaps despite its best intentions, it undermined itself:

> Why then does the presentation of Sheila seem to be so problematic? It is because Sheila, despite her strength, is continually a victim, a woman who knows that she wants more but is continually denied it. While the intention may be to present her positively, the effect of *Brookside*'s emphasis on both realism and class is to isolate her in the family without even the support of other women which is the bedrock of more traditional soaps. Sheila *is* defined as a wife and mother (when Bobby leaver her, she is quickly installed in the Corkhill household, once again mediating between father and children) and her protestations have the effect of reinforcing our sense of her inability to change anything. (Geraghty, 1991: 187)

Going on to discuss the rape storyline in particular, Geraghty is unambiguous in calling it 'highly problematic' and, in a more serious echo of McGovern's own words above, she argues that 'the logic of the narrative was that she had been punished' (on the night of the rape she has agreed to meet her evening-class tutor in a pub believing, incorrectly, that they were going to discuss aspects of her course).

This was clearly a key moment in the early career of Jimmy McGovern – building upon a reputation as one of the key instigators of the groundbreaking industrial relations stories that were so much part of *Brookside*'s claims to innovation, McGovern clearly relished the potential of writing an explosive story for one of his favourite actresses, one that would provide the programme with a new level of engagement with its audience. Even critics such as Geraghty are at pains to stress a belief that the combination of the painfully honest writing and Sue Johnston's performance provided the viewer with a searing account of the experience. What McGovern and the team behind the Sheila Grant rape story stand accused of seems to stem principally from the way that scholarship has positioned soap opera as being at the heart of a feminist approach to television (see for example Brunsdon, 1993; Brunsdon, D'Acci and Spigel, 1997). As *Brookside* led the way in moving UK soap opera from the territory led by *Coronation Street* and *Crossroads* it could not possibly remain satisfying within the theoretical construct proposed by Geraghty and otherwise. On the other hand, it began to play a different kind of role with mass audiences which many would argue contained a different kind of radicalism, even social responsibility.

Lesley Henderson's very detailed analysis of the production conditions of *Brookside* focuses more on a plot line that developed after McGovern left the programme. This concerned the Jordache family and the abuse suffered by the mother and two daughters at the hands of a violent husband and father. What Henderson's account highlights above all is the sheer complexity involved in creating storylines for a long running popular serial in which the demands of ratings, competing understandings of audience needs and production conditions all compete with an overarching aspiration to ideas of realism and social responsibility. (2007: 58–75).

For Jimmy McGovern, though always astutely aware of the ratings-attracting power of strong narrative, the need to be relevant and real was always paramount. According to most accounts, disputes over this priority were what led to his leaving the programme:

> He left the soap in 1989, frustrated with its perceived retreat from political comment and, specifically, by his producers' unwillingness to take on the fallout of that year's Hillsborough stadium disaster, in which 96 Liverpool supporters lost their lives as a result of failures in policing and inadequate ground safety procedures (itemised in the public enquiry by Lord Justice Taylor), but found themselves labelled by a hostile media as drunken football hooligans. (Duguid, 2010a)

McGovern's plans to cover Hillsborough included one of the young characters, Tracey Corkhill, organising a mass burning of the *Sun*, the newspaper that had provided the most negative coverage of the disaster, including claims of Liverpool fans urinating on the dying and on the policemen engaged in rescue attempts.

Characteristically, though, McGovern has stated his understanding of why *Brookside* under Phil Redmond had to repeatedly compromise on any vision he or any other writer might have had. Essentially, like many before him, he was grateful for the discipline and training that *Brookside* had offered, but he was now faced with stark institutional realities:

> Phil Redmond had loads of jobs. He had that burden to carry. If *Brookside* goes down the tubes a load of jobs go down the tubes as well. So every time he went down there [to Channel 4 in London] to talk about renewing it for the next period he wanted to go in from a position of strength, with the show doing well in the ratings, so he always went for ratings at certain times. In that commissioning process lay the seeds of our destruction. It was quite understandable that Phil would say 'OK, the show's doing well but if we throw in a car crash I can go to Channel Four with 6 million viewers.' The next time, 'Well, we've done a car crash, so ... a siege.' (McGovern, 2009)

After leaving *Brookside*, though he did initially manage to carve out just a little space for himself in the dying spaces of single drama, it was to be within another popular format that McGovern was to find his breakthrough success, and it is to McGovern's surprising move into police drama that we will turn to next.

Cracker (1993–96)

The idea for *Cracker* (1993–96) didn't originate with McGovern, but with producer Gub Neale, but in most accounts it is McGovern's distinctive authorial voice that defined the programme. This was doubly ironic because, as Mark Duguid has pointed out, *Cracker* emerged during a period that was particularly unwelcoming to both the television writer per se and particularly to the kind of writer that McGovern had announced that he was on *Brookside*:

> *Cracker* not only appeared in the middle of television drama's perceived decline but emerged from precisely the commissioning climate that was held largely responsible for it. And although the call was for a substitute for the stately *Morse*, what resulted was not more of the same but a drama, as Neale puts it, 'as noisy and as angry and as difficult and as awkward and as complex as we could have dreamed' … And he might have added, as *authored*. (Duguid, 2009: 9)

As Duguid goes on to discuss, arguably with a certain amount of over-reliance on biographical explanations, *Cracker* was a show born out of a degree of anger on McGovern's part. This was partly the result of his departure from *Brookside*, but also his subsequent frustrations at the BBC over a project that would later be completed as *Priest* (1994). Always the part-pragmatist, Gub Neale's approach to him (after seeing his single drama, *Needle* (1990)) was received voraciously by McGovern whose time on *Brookside* had left him with the ability to produce quickly and to rewrite ruthlessly.

However, if *Cracker* was partly seen as more steady work by a writer that still retained enough memory of life on the 'outside', the programme quickly became a means for McGovern to repeat the trick of the early *Brookside* and write about things that mattered to him within the vehicle of a popular form. This time, though, there weren't (at least initially) other writers, a weekly story conference and a dominating producer to wrestle with, and the result was arguably a stronger challenge to generic conventions than even his work on *Brookside* was able to present.

To begin with, *Cracker*, for a supposed replacement for *Inspector Morse*, did not have a policeman as its central character. This was not unique in the history of British television, but it was at least highly unusual and the first time that a popular series had employed the new(ish) profession of forensic psychologist at its heart. What this meant was that *Cracker*'s most prominent figure was an outsider, albeit an outsider who was meant to be on the same side as the police. Because of the nature of his profession he was also endowed, with a kind of innate superiority to the slightly clumsy officers that surrounded him (the male officers at least). He invariably out-thought his police colleagues in ways that were often startling and occasionally defied credibility.

Edward Fitzgerald, or 'Fitz', as he was always referred to in *Cracker*, as played by Robbie Coltrane, became one of popular television's iconic figures. As well as the strength of his intellect and accompanying sharp wit he also brought with him a collection of enormous and damaging flaws as the essential means of connecting with his audience. Fitz might have been an incorrigible smart-arse, but he was also a gambling addict, a heavy drinker and smoker and hopeless at sustaining trusting relationships. As Glen Creeber (2002) has pointed out, this is a set of characteristics that connects Fitz with a tradition that is more associated with the USA than the UK, namely the hard-boiled sleuth that had its origins in the detective fiction of Chandler and Hammett which, in turn, became key sources for film noir and the likes of *The Maltese Falcon* (dir. John Huston, 1941) and *The Big Sleep* (dir. Howard Hawks, 1946). However, as Creeber goes on to discuss, the British television police drama had already 'borrowed' from such a tradition in a number of different ways through the creation of maverick cops in series such as *The Sweeney* (ITV, 1975–82). What *Cracker* attempted was to take this generic mutation a stage further by setting up a version of the hard-boiled sleuth that not only had radically different features (an overtly well-educated background, a visible domestic hinterland), but who is also placed in a variety of narrative situations that call into question the traditional masculine power of the errant, but omnipotent, detective.

Creeber's foregrounding of the gender politics of *Cracker* provides a fascinating link to McGovern's work on *Brookside*, particularly his creation of the Shelia Grant rape story. The centrality of the same crime to a number of the episodes of *Cracker* makes it clear that McGovern saw storylines concerning rape and sexual assault as powerful vehicles to explore the rapidly evolving sexual politics of the late twentieth century. This is a narrative strategy that carried obvious risks, particularly given McGovern's outspoken comments about his encounters with the sharp end of sexual politics. In the section on Brookside I have already referred to Tom Woodin's study of working-class writer's groups, and in this extract from an interview with one of the workshop participants we can see again a key dilemma for McGovern and his search for his writer's voice and perspective:

> Well, it was slightly hard. Jimmy was a big deal in that stuff, and was a very heavy arguer ... I mean, Jen Jones from Stepney Books was an example of the kind of people who he was against, and you knew how much time Jen had put into things, you knew that she wasn't making much money out of it. It seemed unfair. Equally, you can understand why ... a low-paid, badly educated, working-class guy being told by a paid middle-class community worker that he was oppressing her ... hard to empathize with things like, 'All men, are keeping me down' [laugh] ... It didn't have to be as shouty as it was ... So it was a bit like, 'Yeah, but ...' I was a bit middle-of-the-road on it all really. (Woodin, 2005: 1010–11)

However, as something of a corrective, further on in the same article, in his own words this time, we see McGovern looking for a kind of accommodation with women that he admired: 'Rebecca O'Rourke, a lovely woman ... with whom I had one or two rows but I thought she was great ... And Anne Cassidy who always used to speak up for us poor misunderstood men' (Woodin, 2005: 1012). The persistent inclusion of rape in the storylines of *Cracker* following on from the Sheila Grant story in *Brookside* can, then, be seen as part of a process for McGovern of wrestling with the challenges that he felt feminists posed for a left-wing working-class man trying to give voice to the things that he felt mattered in the world, in ways that would reach the audiences he cared about. It is worth reminding ourselves for a moment that the story that he wanted to tell on *Brookside* when he left the programme involved a young working-class woman (Tracey Corkhill) organising mass political action in the form of burning the *Sun*. Whilst the principal motive for such action was the paper's treatment of Hillsborough, it is no accident that at the time the *Sun* was also a byword for pre-'lads'-mag' casual sexism in popular culture.

Perhaps the key moment in *Cracker*, as far as its engagement with sexual politics goes, occurs in the three-part story 'Men Should Weep' (1995). Detective Sergeant Jane Penhaligon (Geraldine Somerville) closes in on the fellow-officer, Jimmy Beck (Lorcan Cranitch), who raped her in a previous episode. Finally she confronts him alone in his flat and, in an act full of symbolic power, makes him lie on his bed while she forces a gun into his mouth, telling him to 'suck it'. For Mark Duguid this is a powerful moment which sees 'Penhaligon throw off any residue of passive victimhood in favour of an approach that explicitly mimics male sexual aggression and returns the kind of "low-level" harassment she has earlier endured' (2009: 66). Furthermore, he sees the scene as entirely satisfying for female viewers and one that 'recalls the rape revenge scenario of *Thelma and Louise* (1991), which had a huge cultural impact on its release for its celebration of female emancipation from abusive masculinity via the barrel of a gun' (2009: 66–7).

Glen Creeber, whilst acknowledging the moment's power and the fact that it 'subverts the conventional dynamics of the hard-boiled detective, forcing the traditionally "passive" women and "active" man to swap places' (2002: 179–80), is more inclined to cast doubt on the ability of the overall *Cracker* concept to sustain a serious disturbance of traditional narratives of male dominance. He argues, in fact, that the series wants it both ways: '*Cracker* may actually restore traditional notions of masculinity, radically disturbing but ultimately re-aligning gender constructions along surprisingly traditional grounds' (2002: 180–1).

The basis for this analysis seems to centre on what Creeber calls the series' 'obsession with its central male protagonist', resulting in all the female characters becoming vehicles for Fitz's own self-analysis. The climax of this line of argument results in the labelling of Fitz 'as part of an early manifestation of the more recent phenomenon of the "new lad"' (2002: 182), a social category that shifts the basis of masculinity without fundamentally altering the power relationships between the sexes.

Creeber's argument is persuasive, but is perhaps over-reliant on the idea that the audience are able only to identify with Fitz and that the narrative inevitably positions him as the most attractive and persuasive element in the show. Whilst Coltrane's performance undoubtedly makes the character endlessly fascinating, there seems a strong case for saying that we are not presented with a model for any new kind of masculinity, but rather a man in a perpetual state of struggle. Whilst the most obvious challenges for him are presented through the strong narrative threads around his addictions (gambling being the most powerful), he is also seen in a number of situations that force him to appraise his own masculinity and how it can fit into a world in which traditional gender boundaries are collapsing. Earlier in his article, Creeber in fact acknowledges this sense of struggle that is an important part of his identity as 'investigator':

> Fitz is clearly an example of how men may have reacted to the breakdown in traditional conceptions of masculinity, struggling to adapt to an increasingly 'post-modern' world in which all moral, religious, political and even gendered certainties have become inherently unstable ... Fitz's role in the narrative can be perceived as a psychological investigator of contemporary masculinity. (Creeber, 2002: 175)

Despite this, though, Creeber's verdict on the series' sexual politics remains, as we saw above, quite damning, particularly in its 'new-lad' analogy. Whilst there may be elements of wanting to have a cake and eat it in the creation of Fitz, it is surely the case that, as Mark Duguid concludes, he is not the only point of identification in the series, and audiences attracted to his intelligence and passion are invited to see the enormous cracks that open up in his ability to create a sustainable life for himself and those that he loves. In the first episode of *Cracker*, 'The Mad Woman in the Attic' (1993), McGovern allows Fitz an exchange that is surely full of all the bile that he seems to have accumulated during his encounters with middle-class feminists during his *Brookside* days. Fitz and his wife Judith (Barbara Flynn) are eating in a restaurant with another couple when the conversation turns to 'domestic help'. Fitz has been drinking heavily and his browbeating of his female friend reaches a climax with the following tirade:

> So you pay this woman three pounds an hour to clean your house so you can go out and teach 'women's studies' for twenty pound an hour. You don't think that's just a wee bit hypocritical? There's you up on the podium talking about equality, freedom, feminism and she's at home with her arm half way down your lavatory!

The relatively opulent surroundings, the multiple empty bottles of wine and the presence of a black waitress tend to create a sense of identification not simply with the slightly boorish tirade but with a wider class-based indignity about hypocrisy. However, the scene that immediately follows opens up the cracks underneath Fitz's already fragile moral high ground. The restaurant has not accepted his credit card and our suspicions are confirmed as we see Judith (inevitably driving) ask Fitz, 'How bad this time?' His response starts with 'Over the limit on both cards' and ends with 'I raised five grand on the mortgage. Told them it was for a new bathroom. I forged your signature.' Judith's reaction tells us, unmistakably, that this is not a surprise. Far from being the source of the series' morality, Fitz is a destructive mess who has driven his wife to wish that he had an addiction 'like heroin or cocaine' with the prospect of an end.

As the rest of this opening episode plays out McGovern gives us subtler ways through which to understand Fitz's relationship to masculinity. Called in by the police to assist in a stalled brutal murder investigation, one of Fitz's first interrogative acts is to tell a suspect how much he understands his impulse to kill and sexually assault young women and how he sees such an impulse as, in essence, an extension of masculinity itself. The process is taken further as the suspect is revealed as a 'Catholic grammar-school boy', 'same as me', says Fitz, adding, 'God help him.'

Whilst it is of some interest that this resembles a description of McGovern himself, it is not the main point here. The series' essential relationship to one of its dominant and recurring themes is being established and the point does not feel like a cynical 'lads'-mag' dissection of changing gender roles, a version that will ultimately revert to type and assert the continuance of the status quo.

Also central to 'Men Should Weep' and ultimately to the whole series is the establishment both of the character of Detective Sergeant Penhaligon and the beginning of her relationship with Fitz. At this point I am using the term relationship in the loosest sense, as it is a while later in the series when they begin a sexual affair. At the start of 'Men Should Weep' Penhaligon is seen very much in the background as the police investigation gets under way. Her unreconstructed colleagues, Detective Chief Inspector Bilborough (Christopher Eccleston) and Detective Sergeant Beck, treat her in ways that very pointedly emphasise the state of gender relations in the force at the time. She is, for example, always asked to be the one to deal with the mothers of murder victims because, as Bilborough says to her, 'you are good at that sort of thing'. Even more traditionally, she is the one asked to get a drink when a victim's mother gets upset. It is only when Fitz becomes involved in the investigation that her role changes to a more active one as she defies instructions to assist in Fitz's maverick deviation from the main line of enquiry.

It can be argued, of course, that Penhaligon is only 'active' in so much as she agrees to assist Fitz. She is only switching from one kind of male patronising dominance to another. Except that when Fitz works with her it is because of her skills, some of which, such as fast driving, are part of a traditional masculine domain (especially in police drama). Fitz sees not only a woman (he is clearly attracted to her) but someone intellectually capable of grasping his methods, a partner that can help him achieve what he needs to do. 'Men Should Weep', after a harrowing account of the brutal murders of young women, ends, as *Cracker* often does, on a comic note. The exchange between Fitz and Penhaligon, overheard by the viewer, as it were, with the screen showing only a long-shot of the car they are driving away in, is a clear indication of how their relationship will play out:

Fitz: Fancy a quick one?
Penhaligon: No.
Fitz: I'm talking alchohol, not sex.
Penhaligon: No to the former and you must be bloody joking to the latter.
Fitz: Do you get much, Panhandle?
Penhaligon: Tell me about your wife.

Fitz:	Did you ever cop off in uniform? Do men go for that sort of thing?
Penhaligon:	What made her leave you?
Fitz:	Do you know why uniforms turn women on? It reeks of death. Death, Panhandle, the finest aphrodisiac in the world.
Penhaligon:	What made her leave you? The gambling? The drink, or the fact that you are an arrogant, self-loathing, misogynistic slob?
Fitz:	The latter.

Here I would argue is a genuine tension and opening up of traditional gender relations within a popular television form. Yes, McGovern creates an attractive character with highly questionable views on a range of things. As a writer he would always argue that in such subversion of simplicities lies his job. On the other hand Fitz and his world-view are also ruthlessly exposed and the life that he is forced to lead as the result of his own stupidity is part of the programme's morality.

If from the start *Cracker* is a witty, often shocking extended essay on the evolving state of gender relations in the late twentieth century, it must not be forgotten that just prior to this McGovern had left a powerful position on a long-running programme because of the things he was not allowed to say. As Duguid and others have suggested, it is therefore surprising in some ways that the 'big P' politics of *Cracker* are for the most part not foregrounded at all. Apart from the occasional diatribe about sexual politics Fitz is not an essentially political character. On the other hand, McGovern's specific Rubicon at the end of his time at *Brookside* was the programme's refusal to tackle the Hillsborough disaster, an event which came to represent something even larger in McGovern's political consciousness.

We will inevitably return to some detail on the Hillsborough tragedy later in the book, during discussion of McGovern's drama documentary on the subject. However it is McGovern's storyline for *Cracker* concerning a relative of an indirect victim of the tragedy, Albie Kinsella (Robert Carlyle), that many people identify as his most powerful contribution to the programme and its generic distinctiveness.

For McGovern, beyond the personal tragedies of those who lost loved ones at Hillsborough lay a narrative of class-based indifference towards the event and its wider implications, not only for the policing of football matches, but for the way that the police force operates in Britain more generally. Taking this a stage further, Mark Duguid asserts that the Hillsborough tragedy and the subsequent official response marked the end of McGovern's faith in politics of the kind that had always been part of his life:

> For McGovern, the disaster would mark the final extinguishing of the faith in the ideologies of the left that he had been wrestling with throughout the 1980s; Hillsborough seemed, in retrospect, the consequence not only of police incompetence but of the left's abject abandonment of the white working class. (Duguid, 2009: 14)

Whilst there are things in such a definite statement that beg questions that we will return to in writing about *Hillsborough* itself, it contains sufficient force to be useful as clear background to the extraordinary venom (even for *Cracker*) contained in the writing of 'To Be a Somebody' (1994). The main character, Albie Kinsella, is indeed in full flight from the orthodoxies of the left that have, up to now, sustained his life as a *Guardian*-reading trade-unionist and Labour Party member. In the early scenes of the episode his bitter resentment at those who make assumptions about his tastes and level of education are the things that McGovern chooses to foreground in particular. The tipping point is the way a Pakistani shopkeeper treats him when he is four pence short when trying to pay for his paper and some milk. Kinsella's reaction, as Duguid points out, reminds audiences of the quasi-fascist rampage of the character 'D-Fens' (Michael Douglas) in *Falling Down* (dir. Joel Schumacher, 1992). 'D-Fens' went on the rampage, not because of any act equivalent to the Hillsborough tragedy, but because of his pent-up frustration at what he saw as the myriad acts of humiliation visited upon the 'ordinary decent citizen' by the conditions of everyday urban life – traffic jams, obscure bureaucracy and, the subtext implies, the impact of immigration on the white population.

Whilst it was undoubtedly brave of McGovern to make Kinsella's first victim a Pakistani shopkeeper, it does of course complicate the morality of the story in ways that McGovern would find wholly desirable, but which potentially compromise our understanding of Kinsella's motivation. For McGovern, though, there would no shying away from what he saw as exactly the kind of truths that the middle-class left would always shy away from in the pursuit of political correctness. In Tom Woodin's analysis of the working- class writer's group already referred to several times, McGovern's crumbling sense of the left-wing establishment and its attitudes to race emerges during an anecdote about one of his fellow-writers, referred to here only as 'Brian':

> Together we sat through a lousy story read by a black man. The well-meaning white liberals applauded it enthusiastically. Brian found this patronising and said so. 'They're only clapping like this because he's black,' said Brian ... An hour or so later, at the bar, nearly everyone is discussing Brian's remarks and declaring him racist. But Brian isn't around because he has come with his family and is putting his kids to

bed. Brian returned and there was a row. He tried to defend himself but no one listened. He had a skinhead, you see, and a lived-in working-class face and a thick Scouse accent. He was everything they secretly hated, secretly despised, and now they had a chance to put the boot in and they did so. (McGovern, quoted in Woodin, 2005: 1009)

Racism, in fact, plays little part in the creation of Albie Kinsella, but we can deduce that McGovern was determined not to avoid the awkward, ugly truths in the pursuit, not of the creation of a 'sympathetic' murderer, but a story that contained the real frustrations of working-class male existence on to which the injustices and humiliations of Hillsborough were heaped. When Fitz is belatedly brought on to investigate the series of murders that Kinsella commits he visits the murdered shopkeeper, Shahid Ali's (Badi Uzzaman) family. Whilst trying to persuade his daughter, Razia (Kim Vithna), of his desire to catch the killer, he takes up a line of argument that echoes the one he used in an earlier episode when he admitted to the potential of all men to be rapists: 'I'm a racist', he says, and then a little later, 'All white people are inherently racist – am I right?'

Above all, 'To Be a Somebody' is about uncomfortable truths, and McGovern is always at pains to include himself and his class within his revelations. That is what ultimately elevates his stories of injustice beyond the level of simple complaint. Neither Albie Kinsella nor any of the other working-class male heroes created by McGovern are sentimentalised. In fact they act as a plea to see the world in utterly unsentimental ways which makes them sometimes very uncomfortable to watch. Once Albie is caught, his long interview with Fitz slowly traces the origins of his murders back to Hillsborough. The tortuous rationale is that the tragedy triggered his father's cancer. Fitz dismisses the logic of this and any idea that a decent man such as his father or the families of the Hillsborough victims would want the terrible revenge that he is exacting. Less easily dismissed, however, is Albie's tracing of the disaster itself to class hatred. Hillsborough happened partly because of decisions made some years earlier to create pens or 'cages' inside football grounds in order to combat crowd trouble and pitch invasions. This meant that the surge of fans into the end of the ground occupied by Liverpool fans ultimately crushed 96 people. For Albie the real cause of the disaster makes for acutely uncomfortable watching for anyone on the liberal left:

Albie: People need to believe, people need to congregate, but there's nothing left to congregate for. Only football. They know that.
Fitz: Who's they?
Albie: The bizzies. The politicians. We go to the match, they march us along, they slam us against walls, They treat us like scum. We look

for help. We're socialists. We're trade unionists and we look to the Labour Party for help. But we're not queers, we're not black, we're not Paki. There's no brownie points in speaking up for us so the Labour Party turns its back. We're not getting treated like scum anymore. We're getting treated like wild animals. One or two of us start acting like wild animals. So the cages go up and ninety-six people die. The bizzies and the bourgeois lefties, they caused Hillsborough. They are going to pay.

Whilst the writing of 'To Be a Somebody' leaves us without any doubt that Albie's murderous rampage is wrong, it also understands not only how this happens, but also how working-class men turn towards far-right groups when the orthodox left desert them. Arguably the most radical thing about the episode, though, comes during its final seconds. Albie's attempts to murder more policemen using bombs are thwarted, but in the final frames Clare Moody (Beth Goddard), a journalist who has worked for the *Sun*, is seen putting the finishing touches to a tabloid story about Albie's capture, headed 'HUNTED'. She reaches across to her pile of post and the audience recognises the same kind of padded envelope Albie sent to the police. We cut to Fitz walking through Manchester city centre as the sound of a bomb exploding sends pigeons scattering into the air. Nothing else; then the credits roll. McGovern has been allowed his final encounter with the greatest villain of all as far as Hillsborough is concerned and, unlike most of the acts of violence committed by his anti-heroes, the understanding of motive is not followed by even an implicit condemnation. It is a remarkable moment in the context of a popular television series.

Charlotte Brunsdon has argued that 'crime fiction in this period [the 1980s and 1990s] speaks very directly to the concerns of a Great Britain in decline under a radical Conservative government with a strong rhetoric of law and order ... a privileged site for the staging of the trauma of the breakup of the post-war settlement' (1998: 223). This line of argument is a useful starting point for the final area of discussion around *Cracker* and its importance to the development of McGovern as a writer, namely its claims to have made both a strong contribution to the evolution of the genre and to have transcended its boundaries in a number of key ways.

Ironically, Brunsdon's article only mentions *Cracker* quite briefly, and only in the Conclusion (partly because its main period of investigation ends in 1993). Its argument about *Cracker* is that it was part of a trend away from the police themselves and 'towards the medicalization of crime within the crime series, with the focus moving away from the police as the solvers of riddles to pathologists and criminal psychologists'

(1998: 242). This is seen by Brunsdon as a departure from the robust interrogation of the very basis of policing in this country on a number of levels that had been undertaken by the likes of *Prime Suspect* (1991–2006) and *Between the Lines* (1991–93). *Cracker* gets bracketed somewhat pejoratively with the likes of '*Dangerfield* (1995–), *Silent Witness* (1996–), *McCallum* (1995–) and *Bliss* (1997–)' shows which Brunsdon suggests are part of a new trend, one which has become among the most enduring on British television: 'I would suggest that the dynamism of the questions about policing – who can police? who is responsible? has become diminished, and instead there is a detectable tendency towards a spectacularization of the body and site of crime' (1998: 242).

I would want to propose that such a reading unfairly diminishes the wider politics of *Cracker* and, in so doing, underplays the role that the character of Fitz plays in interrogating an older, highly masculinised culture of policing. In this respect *Cracker* sits more easily alongside *Prime Suspect* and *Between the Lines*. It shares certain positions with both series, but in key respects it is different and, through that difference, establishes its own distinctive contribution to the genre. Whilst *Prime Suspect* is rightly lauded for what Brunsdon describes as the revitalisation of a 'tired generic story ... given new life through the substitution of women for men' (1998: 233), I would want to argue that, as we have seen, *Cracker*'s engagement with the gender politics of the police force is also profound. Fitz's stumbling attempts to engage with the questions asked of him both by his wife and Jane Penhaligon reveal a class-related masculinity in crisis juxtaposed with old-fashioned police – officers who have not yet reached the point of even understanding that such questions are possible. There is no question that there is a part of Fitz that would like the world and its sexual politics to be as it once was, but he is also far too intelligent to think that is generally desirable or possible. The result is a rich vein of tension that runs throughout the very different storylines of all the series and can stand as a powerful compliment to the clearer sexual politics of *Prime Suspect* in which the leading protagonist is a woman.

In relation to *Between the Lines*, which foregrounds its stance on contemporary policing in the clearest possible way through its setting within a police complaints unit, *Cracker* also contributes in highly significant ways to a major question that came to the forefront in the period, namely, as Brunsdon puts it, 'whether effective policing can be achieved without a necessary blurring of boundaries between policing and criminality' (235). We have seen in the discussion above how very directly the programme attacked the role that the police played at Hillsborough specifically, in the policing of football generally and by extension the policing of working-class people. More widely though, as Mark Duguid argues, the series has the scrutiny of the modern police force at its heart:

> It comments on real cases: in 'To Be a Somebody' Fitz talks sarcastically of 'good old-fashioned British justice – where a man's innocent until proven Irish' ... in 'The Big Crunch', he compares the autistic Dean (Darren Tighe) wrongly suspected of the murder of Joanna Barnes (Samantha Morton) to Stefan Kisko. It returns repeatedly, particularly during the first two series, to questions about the assumption of guilt and the risk of a false conviction. And finally, it explores issues around the internal operation of the force, especially in relation to the position of women. (Duguid, 2009: 50)

Whilst there is no denying *Cracker*'s role in popularising the trend towards the inclusion of non-police 'experts' in the television crime genre, I would argue strongly that its roots not only remained in the mainstream of the genre but also that it provided a critique of the traditions of British policing from a highly original position. Subsequent television history has made the role of forensic scientists of all descriptions somewhat commonplace, but it was not Fitz's profession that made *Cracker*'s contribution to the history of television drama so much as the complex make-up of his background and individual failings.

As something of a footnote, at least in this context, it is worth noting that *Cracker* was, in a relatively minor way, the forerunner of a format that was to become so firmly associated with McGovern much later in his career. Whilst the writing of *Cracker* was strongly associated with McGovern, it is important to add that three out of the nine extended storylines in the original 1990s series were written by others. 'The Big Crunch' (1994) was written by Ted Whitehead, whilst both 'Best Boys' and 'True Romance' (both 1995) were written by Paul Abbott. Abbott also wrote a one-off special, 'White Ghost', in 1996, whilst McGovern himself was talked into a return in 2006 with 'Cracker'.

Whilst there is no suggestion of the explicit mentoring and nurturing of new writers that became a feature of several of McGovern's later ventures, the launch of what has become a very high-profile career for Abbott through a series that was well established and popular contains a trace of what was to come. Abbott was already very much part of the series when he began to write, having worked as a producer on two of McGovern's stories as well as the one written by Whitehead. His work, by most accounts, is true to McGovern's vision though, as Duguid argues, marked by a greater willingness to push at the boundaries of realist conventions through 'its sense of emotional excess' (2009: 122).

The strength of *Cracker* might perversely be measured by its reputation's ability to survive the programme's relative failures: in 1997 an American *Cracker* began screening on ABC in the USA only to be dropped early after it failed to find sufficient audience numbers to satisfy the voracious corporate appetite. In 2006 McGovern was persuaded to write a 'post 9/11' one-off return for Coltrane's character. Whilst the critical reception was not particularly hostile there was a consensus that it didn't approach the standards of the earlier work. On the other hand, by 2006 standards it reached a large audience, and the following extracts from a review illustrate that even reheated *Cracker* was seen as better than the contemporary competition, whilst not quite matching the power of the original:

> This is the bit where I say whether it's any good or not. Well *of course* it's good. It's an episode of *Cracker* written by Jimmy McGovern – whom one could fairly non-controversially call the best screenwriter in Britain – and starring Robbie Coltrane – an extremely charismatic actor who knew the role of a lifetime when he saw it, and ran with it, albeit quite slowly, and with a fag in his hand ...
>
> ... But. But ultimately, this *Cracker* doesn't feel as if it *had* to exist ... It dives in and out again, without ever stirring up the mud at the bottom. In one scene that's very pertinent, Fitz has explained to him the way that police procedure has changed in the last ten years. (Moran, 2006)

Though *Cracker* was ultimately a television series produced under industrial conditions like any other and with a powerful directing and producing team (the former included the likes of Michael Winterbottom), by and large, McGovern managed to make it his own. Even that more recent of benchmarks, the DVD box-set, has McGovern's name all over the cover. It was to provide McGovern with the institutional clout that he needed to avoid a repeat of his frustrations over the original idea for *Priest* with the BBC. For his next major project he returned to Channel 4 with the confidence to propose a series over which he would have even greater conceptual and creative control.

Hearts and Minds (1995)

As Robert Crampton says, in an interview with McGovern just after *Hearts and Minds* (1995) had concluded its run on Channel 4, the series 'was, unusually, advertised on the strength of its writer's name' (1995). Apart from anything else this is what the first two series of *Cracker* had done for McGovern, and it provided him with the freedom to work on a series outside the usual generic frameworks. This is not to say that

Hearts and Minds did not have a strong relationship to genre, but rather that its conception lay outside the generic norms that operated at the time.

The series also, as Crampton illustrates, generally worked hard to defy what many had somewhat lazily expected from a series by Jimmy McGovern about life as a teacher in an inner-city comprehensive in the 1990s. As briefly discussed in the Introduction to this volume, McGovern's own experiences as a teacher disabused him firmly of any easy liberal view of the way that education operates. This, in turn, in *Hearts and Minds*, met his ever-present determination to constantly question the certainties of his characters and to be truthful about his belief in flawed human beings and motivations. As Crampton says, *Hearts and Minds* 'was all set to be classic blame-the-Tories television', but for anyone who genuinely understood McGovern it was not surprising that the series was altogether more nuanced and interesting.

McGovern has, in fact, never troubled to hide what some (including him) would describe as somewhat reactionary views on education. In an interview just before the transmission of *Hearts and Minds* he said of his own time as a teacher: 'I saw lots of good teachers and some appalling ones. My line on education is really right-wing. Short-term contracts. Sack the lazy bastards' (Butler, 1995) and again in the *Times Education Supplement* in the same month:

> I've seen good teachers, but I've seen a lot more bad ones. As students they think 'I can't think of anything to do with my life so I'll be a teacher'. An awful lot of our schools are staffed with third-rate people with third-rate brains. They are boring, they have no enthusiasm. Our kids deserve better.
>
> If I was a head, I would have a core staff of five or six good and experienced people. I would pay maximum amounts but I would put most on short-term contracts. They would be young and enthusiastic. They would be exciting teachers despite mistakes. (Williams, 1995)

Based upon this and other interviews he has given, it is hard not to assume that of all his troubling life experiences it is those involving education that has left McGovern most unambiguously angry. The Catholic Church, the Labour Party, the trade-union movement – all come under fire in various ways, but the view of contemporary education that he offers both in interviews and in *Hearts and Minds* is in some ways the bleakest of all.

At one point in his life, McGovern opted for what has been a well-trodden path away from an endless round of low-paid manual labour by going back into education as a mature student and then into teaching. In interviews, his descriptions of both the experience of teaching and of his own education are shot through with disillusion born out of bitter experience. Initially a successful student who passed the eleven-plus, he became alienated by the severity and, according to McGovern, the snobbery of the Jesuit grammar school he was sent to. This ultimately led to his leaving at 16. After a long period in a variety of jobs his return to education and then his first job teaching were embraced passionately at first until a powerful sense of disillusion and exhaustion to set in:

> I went in there with boundless enthusiasm and energy. I loved it. It was the best job I had in my life.
> I coached football. I gave up all my Saturday mornings and I took drama, the school play. That could be a nightmare. When it was nice weather you couldn't get them in for rehearsals. The first thing I did was a satire on the school. The kids loved it, but the staff complained. But by the third year all that energy had gone. I just lost it. (Williams, 1995)

Even for a writer such as McGovern, who so frequently draws upon the cornerstones of his life *Hearts and Minds* seems particularly autobiographical. The central character in the series, Drew Mackenzie (Christopher Eccleston), comes late to teaching and pours himself into the job in a way that borders on the fanatical. Not only does it lead ultimately to disillusion, but it fatally damages his marriage when, after the years of training, his wife realises that teaching is a job that takes up evenings, weekends and all the spare time that she thinks his hard work has earned for them.

The disintegration of Drew's personal life is, though, secondary to the gradual disintegration of his identity as a passionate, committed teacher. From the start his animated, physical presence in the classroom presents a stark contrast to the other teachers, many of whom have the look of the utterly defeated. In one of the set-piece scenes of the early part of the series Drew takes over from an older English teacher who drones on about iambic pentameter as most of the class occupy themselves in their own worlds. Using the John Masefield poem *Cargoes*, Drew launches into a frenzied re-creation of its rhythms, beating on desk-tops, repeating over and over again in ways that connect the reading of poetry to rap or hip-hop. It is a triumphant moment as the lethargic class wake up and join in. The young teacher is exultant as he looks to a future of engaging young hearts and minds, liberating them from the torpor to which they have been consigned by poor teaching.

It is, though, a false dawn, as Drew encounters layer upon layer of the difficulties that we must assume ground down McGovern himself. These are most controversially expressed through a running battle that Drew has with a black teacher, Trevor (David Harewood), a part of the storyline that was inevitably highlighted by the educational press:

Drew makes a wrong move from the first with Trevor ... the school's only black teacher, when he mistakes him for the caretaker. Thereafter the two are at loggerheads. Drew's naiveté irritates Trevor, an irritation which turns to open hostility when Drew walks in to quell an unruly class, only to find Trevor playing cards with a group at the back. Later, after a skirmish in the shower, Drew suggests Trevor will face the sack for his behaviour. Trevor turns on Drew in Scouse: 'Look at me la, I'm black. I'm unsackable.' McGovern is certainly not afraid of contravening Political Correctness. (Williams, 1995)

This account foregrounds a number of issues. First Drew's initial mistake very honestly echoes McGovern's own self-confessed origins: 'My history was white. I grew up a racist person and it has taken education and travel to make me realise that I was a fool. We grew up racists, but it was not my fault' (quoted in Dugan, 2007). This in turn is part of a recurrent McGovern theme of subjecting his heroes (especially those that have large parts of himself contained within them) to the most intense scrutiny. We are reminded of Fitz's speech about the rapist inside him and all men or of Bobby Grant's descent towards an act of domestic violence.

Secondly, we see McGovern's endless wrestle with what he saw as the dishonesty of the middle-class left and its privileging of gender and race at the expense of class. In this case Drew despises Trevor for what he sees as his betrayal of children from backgrounds which mean that a good education would be their only hope of escaping lives of boredom and poverty. Just in case we should start to feel comfortable, though, as the series unfolds we, and to some extent Drew, are forced to see that Trevor, for all his casual manner, performs a difficult and vital function in the school. He might be cynical, but in a brutal world he forms a vital connection to groups of pupils who would otherwise become totally disconnected, and McGovern's vision is broad and subtle enough to embrace this.

Whilst *Hearts and Minds* is not primarily about the specific politics of the mid-1990s, McGovern did modify his original treatment to encompass the particular issue of what was then known as 'opting out'. In essence, this was one variant of what has become a policy of successive governments to allow schools to apply to become more or less independent of local authority control. To its opponents, this was an extension of a conservative ideology that believed in a doctrine of the privatisation of as many public services as possible, in the belief that only the entrepreneurial spirit of free enterprise could bring the energy required to revitalise the public sector. Again, though, McGovern is at pains to present the issue in its true, messy complexity. The idealist Drew is seen to support his headteacher's aspirations towards 'opt-out' status, not for ideological reasons, but because it is only through that kind of freedom of action that he can see any hope of reforming the complacent, cynical environment in which he finds himself. When, at the end of the series, his support for the head brings only distrust, any idealism involved in the notion of more independence is shown as a sham.

There is a case for saying that *Hearts and Minds* is one of McGovern's bleakest works. Its ending sees Drew cast adrift for what his colleagues see as his betrayal of them, mainly through his own mix of idealism and passion. He walks out on teaching, like McGovern, unable to cope with the demands that the system places upon him. If there is hope at all it is that his final act in the school is to stage one of the great plays about betrayal, *Julius Caesar*, not in the ossified manner that the school expects, but in a radical adaptation that is deeply critical of the head. It is not a sustainable victory, though, and McGovern leaves Drew in his garden, burning all his books.

The Lakes (1997–99)

If *Hearts and Minds* saw McGovern exercising his hard-won freedom in pursuit of some highly persistent demons (albeit shot through with characteristic black humour), *The Lakes* took him into much less familiar territory, even if elements of autobiography remained. Even at this stage in his career McGovern was clearly identified with inner cities and it was therefore something of a surprise to find him pitching a continuing drama for prime-time BBC1 audiences set in a Lake District tourist destination.

Part of the explanation for such an apparently radical change of direction, as is frequently the case with McGovern, does lie in autobiography and a 19-year-old McGovern looking for work in the Lake District and meeting his wife, Eileen. Not to mention the compulsive gambling and all-pervasive Catholicism. *The Lakes* can then at least partly be read as McGovern's return to his youth and a time before his decision to go back into education and ultimately to a career as a writer.

Ironically, considering his history, one of the criticisms levelled at *The Lakes* was its lack of an overt politics: 'As always with McGovern, there's some very strong writing – but was it too much to hope that his first major piece for the BBC, away from the commercial pressures of ITV, would have been more politically and dramatically ambitious?' (Cathode Ray, 1997). This of course begs a number of questions, not least that McGovern's work for ITV (*Cracker*) was ever lacking in dramatic and political ambition. For now, though, it is worth examining the production context of *The Lakes* for a moment, before going on to examine the work itself.

> To be honest, it was one of the several times I thought I'd get sacked when I ran BBC1. I had just worked with Jimmy at Granada on the searing *Hillsborough* drama, and *The Lakes* was a tough drama serial that I decided to schedule on Sunday evenings. Unsurprisingly, there was more than a little outrage and a bulging mailbag of complaints.
>
> It might not have been the kind of genteel drama that audiences normally expected on a Sunday evening, but it was classic McGovern. It was real, honest and a bit raunchy. I loved it but it was too much for mainstream audiences and the critics who felt it was too raw for Sunday evening viewing. (Salmon, 2011)

The point here is not to juxtapose this view of *The Lakes* with the one first quoted above, but rather to realistically assess the commissioning context of the time. Peter Salmon was, in 1997, the Controller of BBC1 and therefore responsible for commissioning *The Lakes*. Although he is here looking back over a long period, his view is a relatively accurate reflection of the time-frame during which *The Lakes* was broadcast. Not only was this a period of accelerated competition for the BBC, it was also a period of relative conservatism in terms of drama commissioning. Added to this is the specific history of Sunday-night BBC1 TV, one generally characterised by period drama and by a certain residual caution regarding religious sensibilities.

In this context, then, *The Lakes* can be seen as television that took clear risks. Its depiction not only of sexual encounters (the thing that it became most closely associated with in the popular imagination), but of emotional extremes in a broader sense, was particularly brave at this moment in television history and because of its scheduling at 9pm on a Sunday evening. As Philip Smith has implied, *The Lakes*' most direct contemporaries and comparators are further illustration that, contrary to the opinion of the *Sight & Sound* comment above (Cathode Ray), McGovern had produced a series every bit as transgressive of its context as *Cracker*:

> If religion in *Mind Games* [written by Linda La Plante] feels like a gimmick, in *The Lakes*, perhaps McGovern's most accomplished work, it provides an unexpected, brooding intensity which warps the pastoral form. At a time when *Hamish Macbeth* (BBC, 1995–7) and *Heartbeat* (ITV, 1992–) were pulling crime drama towards rural nostalgia, McGovern dragged the pastoral in the opposite direction, removing any sense of heritage or nostalgia from his depiction of the Lake District. (Smith, 2007: 223)

Soaps, series and serials 59

Though *The Lakes* is far removed from conventional crime drama in a number of ways its central narrative is close enough to bear comparison and, as Smith implies, particularly with the 'rural nostalgia' variant of the form as epitomised by the seemingly endless run of *Heartbeat*. In *The Lakes* the tourist idyll of the English Lake District and its genteel decaying hotels is opened up and its cultural and economic basis laid bare. Smith quotes one of the series' central characters, Gary Alcock (Charles Dale), or 'Chef' as he is known throughout, on the way that staff employed in the tourist industry see the reality of their lives. Talking to Danny Kavanagh (John Simm) on his arrival from Liverpool to work in a hotel he says:

> This is Wordsworth country, Danny, millions of people come here all looking for a bit of Nature. They clog up our roads. They stomp all over our fells. They pack our bars. They buy up our houses. Oh the hotels and restaurants spring up, but the mines, the quarries close down. The farms get turned into timeshare complexes. So for people like me Danny, *local* people like me, there's nothing left to do but look after this urban filth.

As the series unfolded the fractures and fault lines within the community open up and, unlike the reassurances of *Heartbeat* and its imitators, they expose divisions based upon class and power. The privately educated daughter of the local hotel owner is the catalyst for a sequence of events that bring simmering resentments to the surface, exposing some the fragility of any sentimental notions of community and village life.

The Lakes, far from being a retreat on McGovern's part from so-called 'political' drama, is shot through with the mid-1990s residue of Thatcherism. Danny Kavanagh only retreats to the Lake District in a bid to escape the suffocating lack of hope in his native Liverpool. His gambling addiction, which McGovern once referred to as 'working-class cocaine', is part of the same desire to escape, though as an ex-addict himself McGovern never sentimentalises gambling's destructive power. When confronted by his wife, Emma (Emma Cunniffe), Kavanagh tries the line that he is doing it to make her and their child's life better. Her retort that he never gambles for them but himself is unanswerable, and he doesn't even try.

There is another strain to *The Lakes*, however, and it surfaces in ways that brought a very mixed critical reception. From the series' first shots we see that one thing carried everywhere by Kavanagh is a copy of Gerard Manley Hopkins's poems. Some critics read this as an all-too convenient humanising device for a man whose habits were so destructive of those around him. McGovern, one suspects, would be scornful of such easy criticism of a young working-class man's higher aspirations. In one of many scenes in which Kavanagh's imagination is sent into new territory by the high peaks of the Lake District we hear, in voiceover,his internal recitation of Hopkins's *The Windhover*, a poem that McGovern himself has described as the 'Best 14 lines ever written' (Rees, 1997). There is also a visual flair to *The Lakes* which clearly owes much to director David Blair, but is also embedded in the writing, making it in many ways McGovern's most consciously 'poetic' script.

It is through the lens of the Irish Jesuit poetry of Hopkins, rather than that of the English romantic Wordsworth that we view the Lake District landscape and, in the same vein, *The Lakes* sees McGovern wrestle again with his Catholic demons. In some ways the series is, apart perhaps from *Priest* and *Liam*, McGovern's most explicit questioning of the Church, albeit whilst also offering a relatively sympathetic portrayal of one of its representatives in Father Matthew (Robert Pugh). In Bernie Quinlan (Emma's mother, played by Mary Jo Randle) McGovern offers a strong Catholic matriarch, almost in the mould of Sheila Grant, only to have her tempted by the attentions of her priest (Matthew), causing them both to ultimately question their faith. In interviews McGovern is often oblique about his attitude to the Church, and whilst one never gets a sense that he remains anything approaching devout, there are ties that he seems to regard as unbreakable:

> I can't imagine writing a script that doesn't have a Catholic element ... It's the moment of introspection I've always found valuable, and the guilt. As a source of material it's great ... By history, culture and tradition I'm still a Catholic. If you use it in times of need it seems more real than to simply go by rote. And if anyone dares criticise me for being a part-time Catholic, I'd say I have every right to use and abuse the Catholic faith, because it used and abused me as child. (www.crackertv.co.uk/youmagazineinterview.htm)

The Lakes' first series ran over four one-and-a-half-hour episodes, all written by McGovern. When a second series of ten episodes was commissioned McGovern was the writer on only three of them, and Series 2 of *The Lakes* became a further extension of the format of *Cracker*, with McGovern's story being taken up by lesser-known writers. To most critical eyes the series became drastically over-extended; in Philip Smith's words, 'it lost much of its predecessor's poetry, appearing crude in comparison' and, according to a BFI account of *The Lakes*, 'a second series in 1997 was, he [McGovern] later acknowledged, a mistake'.

Whilst such an account is probably close to the truth it runs the risk of overlooking something quite interesting both about the way that McGovern's work has been received and his own personal trajectory as a writer in relation to some of his near-contemporaries, especially Paul

Abbott. The main critical accounts of Series 2 of *The Lakes* invariably used words such a 'melodrama' and 'excessive', often coupling them with analyses that asserted that the programme had lost touch with its social-realist roots. We have seen already, though, that even in Series 1, *The Lakes* contained a strain of lyricism that was a strong counterpoint to the conventional social realism that inevitably characterised the depiction of Danny Kavanagh's origins in Liverpool. There was a sense that the central character's retreat to the Lake District did have something of the mythical about it and that there was a flirtation at least with some of the tropes of style less usually associated with McGovern.

In my view this makes the criticisms of Series 2 of *The Lakes* a little crude, even if they have some basis in reality. It is as if McGovern (even though he was not the writer on seven out of the ten episodes) was required to remain in his social-realist box and when Series 2 of *The Lakes* waded waist-deep in what at times became Grand-Guignol-inspired black horror it lost all claims to validity. A less critical echo of this kind of divide appears in accounts of the changes to the style of *Cracker* when Paul Abbott took over the writing. Of the first scene of 'Best Boys', Abbots first episode of *Cracker*, Mark Duguid wrote: 'Its a scene typical of Abbott – raucous, exuberant and celebratory of working-class sexuality' (2009: 121), whilst later on he identifies a 'sense of emotional excess' (2009: 122) as the defining feature of the Abbott *Cracker*.

It would be wrong, of course, to make too easy an identification between the changes to Series 2 of *The Lakes* and the kind of work that Abbott first started to produce on *Cracker* and which he went on to develop most famously in the numerous series of *Shameless* (Channel 4, 2004–). However, there is an unmistakable sense in Series 2 of *The Lakes* of the programme attempting something that may well have been ultimately flawed, but which in the context of its commissioning might well have been bold in its pushing of boundaries, particularly the relationship between horror, comedy and sexuality. Like many before him, McGovern has been parodied for what many have seen as his excessively pessimistic realism, only to be treated with even more suspicion on the occasions he strays outside such territory.

This is not in the end to make great claims for Series 2 of *The Lakes*. It is certainly flawed by its over-concentration on a number of sub-plots such as the headteacher's (Kevin Doyle) murder of his wife and increasingly comic attempts to conceal the body. However, it is worth re-examining the comparative boldness of the series and its attempts to work with the kind of treatment of both horror and sexuality that was, and still is, a rarity on British television. Whilst McGovern's relationship to a mainstream British social-realist tradition is undeniable, his stylistic range is also understated and in *The Lakes* there are clear attempts to push hard at the boundaries of what was possible at 9pm on BBC1.

The end of the 1990s, then, both saw McGovern involved in what, for him at least, was a critical failure. However, whilst even McGovern recognised the problems in the excesses of the second series of *The Lakes* it also took him in a direction that was to dominate the 'hybrid' forms that are the subject of the next chapter.

Working with a team of writers on the second series of *The Lakes* was not McGovern's first taste of overseeing the development of his original idea by others, but it took something that he first experienced on *Cracker* in another direction. The critical failure of the resulting episodes of *The Lakes* did not, however, put McGovern off the idea. In the next chapter we will see that, on the contrary, it led to a whole phase of McGovern's career in which he was to join the likes of Paul Abbott in moving towards a role that was part lead writer and part executive producer.

The 1980s and 1990s were a period in which McGovern became first frustrated with the constraints of certain kinds of popular television through his experiences on *Brookside*, and then learnt how to shape and mould their restrictions to his advantage in string of successes that firmly established him as one of the few British writers capable of 'selling' a show to an audience through his name alone. Such a trajectory inevitably involved a degree of compromise, certainly in political terms, and McGovern has always acknowledged the necessity of a certain amount of pragmatism when working in television. However such compromises did not, on the whole, blunt the power of McGovern's work, particularly when it is viewed in the context of the majority of television drama series commissions of the period.

By the time he came to *The Street* McGovern's work had bought him the power to propose work that pushed further at the generic and formal boundaries of British television drama. As the next chapter acknowledges, McGovern was not alone in pioneering a range of 'hybrid' forms that dominated the next phase of his writing career. Paul Abbott in particular has a strong claim to be seen in the same terms, but during the 2000s McGovern's sustained output confirmed his ability to both adapt to an ever-changing broadcasting environment and to influence it. Chapter 2 will attempt to chronicle this phase in McGovern's career and the way that he used his influence in British television to foster the careers of others.

Notes

1 For one of a number of very full accounts of the struggles within the Labour Party during this period see Eric Shaw (1994), *The Labour Party since 1979: Crisis and Transformation*, London, Routledge.
2 A full reprinting of the relevant articles in this debate, as well as contextualising material, can be found in Tony Bennett et al. (eds) (1981), pp 302–52.

'Hybrid' forms:
The Street, Moving On, Accused   2

The decision to create a separate chapter for these three programmes is designed to highlight McGovern's increasing tendency in his later career to both nurture new writers and push at the boundaries of television forms. All three programmes were made by independent production companies with McGovern acting in a producing as well as writing role, though as we shall see, he saw his contribution as being very much confined to the development of the ideas and the scripts rather than to production in any wider sense.

The Street and *Accused* took this evolution of McGovern's career a stage further still, in that they were both made by RSJ Films which was formed in 2009 by McGovern, Roxy Spencer and Sita Williams. At the time of writing this apparent move into independent production appears not to represent an ambition on McGovern's part to move towards exclusive control of his work, or even to develop the work of others without his involvement as a writer (although this is a stated aim on the company's website). *Moving On* was made by LA Productions and McGovern's next project after *Accused* is being developed with an independent Australian company.

In all three of the programmes considered in this chapter McGovern has challenged some contemporary norms, either in the structural composition of a popular television series or in his ambition of what is possible within scheduling norms. This is of course not to argue that, in all cases, the innovations that will be discussed in relation to the three series are uniquely McGovern's. In key respects he is building upon work from his collaborators and contemporaries, most obviously Paul Abbott. However, in terms of the sustained quantity and quality of output that McGovern has managed in the first decade of the twenty-first century, he can claim to have done as much as anyone to revise the ambitions of what is possible within the constraints of popular drama series. As we shall see below, for some he has effectively reclaimed the

'Hybrid' forms 65

space for the prime-time single play, almost by stealth. Whilst there is interesting territory to explore here, it is also too neat to suggest that McGovern's aim has been a simple return to any kind of 'golden age' of single drama. Instead we have seen something altogether more interesting – the development of hybrid forms that have enabled one of the lengthiest and most sustained careers among all television dramatists to continue to grow, develop and reach new levels of influence.

What is perhaps more remarkable is that McGovern's survival and, if anything, increased influence have been achieved against a backdrop of such abject pessimism on the part of industry commentators and, in many cases, writers and producers. The penultimate section of Lez Cooke's history of British television drama deals with the period 1991–2002 and is shot through with the despair of those who had witnessed the marketisation of British television in the 1980s and 1990s, with the particularly devastating consequences that it had for drama production. Cooke's account, as have those of many others, focuses on the figure of Dennis Potter and the almost symbolic significance that was attached to his death and its associations with the wider death of the writer as a figure of any significance in British television. Cooke quotes from Potter's 1993 MacTaggart Lecture at the Edinburgh Film Festival in which Potter launched into a vitriolic attack, with special ire reserved for the twin figureheads of the destruction of British television, Margaret Thatcher and Rupert Murdoch, as well as what Potter saw as the accountants in charge of the BBC (in fact one of the recent Director Generals of the BBC, Michael Checkland, was an accountant by profession):

> Our television has been ripped apart and falteringly reassembled by politicians who believe that value is a monetary term only, and that a cost-accountant is thereby the most suitable adjudicator of what we can and cannot see on our screens. And these accountants or their near-clones are employed by new kinds of media owners who try to gobble up everything in their path. (Cooke, 2003: 165)

Developing the logic of Potter's argument, Cooke terms the era about which he writes as 'consumer-led' in contrast to writer- or producer-led. In his view this was the death knell for the kind of work that became landmark drama of the fairly recent past:

> What the consumer-led approach to television drama produces is bland, audience-pleasing, undemanding drama, like *Heartbeat*, drama which is a pale reflection of the challenging, provocative, author-led drama of previous decades like *Cathy Come Home*, *Pennies from Heaven*, *Boys from the Blackstuff* and *The Singing Detective*, dramas which had made British television 'such a glory in British life'.[1] (Cooke, 2003: 166)

In a final chapter, though, Cooke's pessimism softens just a little and he concludes by seeing some tentative signs of hope in the television drama of the late 1990s and early 2000s. In Cooke's view, many of the successful models owe a strong debt to American television drama which had long had to adapt to a deregulated framework and had, according to Cooke's analysis, therefore become more adept at producing faster-paced 'flexi-narratives'[2] in the pursuit of holding an audience's attention in the face of multi-channel (and now multi-screen) competition. Amongst the British shows that Cooke singles out are Tony Marchant's *Holding On* (BBC2, 1997), Paul Abbot's *Clocking Off* (BBC1, 2001–4) and Russell T. Davies's *Queer as Folk* (Channel 4, 1999–2000). Though *The Lakes* was produced in the same year as *Holding On* and actually achieved what Cooke complains Marchant's series could not, namely appear on BBC1, it doesn't warrant a mention.

The essence of Cooke's position, writing in 2003, was that whilst there were was a reasonable quantity of drama produced in Britain 'to match the ambition, complexity and modernity of the best American television' (2003: 195) there were also causes for concern. These consisted mainly of anxiety about there being 'less original and innovative drama on British television than there once used to be', and what was produced had a greater tendency to be pushed to the 'minority' channels. Looking forward, there was also a degree of pessimism about the ability of television drama to survive as the multi-channel and internet age took an even firmer hold.

Whilst the following discussions of McGovern's work subsequent to the publication of Cooke's history are not designed to dispel such pessimism entirely, they do represent something of a response to such an overarching narrative of despair. Journalistic coverage of television drama broadcast in the UK is still much more likely to revere either recent work from the USA such as *Mad Men* or from Scandinavia such as *The Killing* or *Borgen* than anything produced in Britain, but I would contend that McGovern, whilst still writing for BBC1 rather than one of the minority channels, has managed to produce work that remains challenging both formally and controversially. It is hoped therefore that the following account will make some contribution to redressing an imbalance in terms of both coverage and recognition.

Essentially, then, this chapter aims to assess how, in three distinctive television series, McGovern contributed to the shifting of boundaries between the almost-extinct single play and the drama series. This shift is not identical over all three series, as we shall see below, and it is clear that *Accused* and *Moving On* are essentially composed of entirely separate single narratives with neither cast nor specific location in common.

The episodes are linked only thematically and, in the case of *Moving On*, such a link is very loose. *The Street* is much more genuinely hybrid in nature as the individual episodes include characters from other stories, usually in minor roles, as well as the eponymous location providing a much tighter structural framework.

Similarly, McGovern's personal role in all three series varies, though in all cases there is the essential aim of using writers that are either new to television or relatively inexperienced. In *Moving On* McGovern has gone as far as not to be credited as a writer on any episode at all, in all probability because of the constraints of a series for daytime television, whereas on *The Street* and *Accused* he has written some of his most memorable and distinctive work. In all three series, however, McGovern has some form of Executive Producer credit, though there is clear indication in interviews that this is a role confined to the shaping of ideas and to the production of scripts rather than the programmes themselves.

Finally, it is worth mentioning the particular case of *Moving On* and its contribution to the changing scheduling landscape of British television. As will be discussed further below, *Moving On* was commissioned by the BBC as daytime television, something eagerly embraced by McGovern as offering new possibilities for a woefully neglected audience. Once again it is possible to claim that McGovern has been part of the reshaping of the television landscape, and this is developed fully below.

The Street (BBC1, 2006–09)

It is in this context, then, that McGovern's interventions in the field of popular drama for BBC1 have to be assessed, starting first with *The Street*, the programme with arguably the strongest relationship to the pioneering work of Paul Abbott on *Clocking Off*. As was touched upon in the Introduction to this volume, *Clocking Off* was instrumental in reintroducing to the BBC what initially looked like an idea for an issue-based social-realist drama. Lez Cooke quotes Abbott talking to *Radio Times* about the thinking behind getting *Clocking Off* commissioned:

> 'I took the idea to the BBC because at that time, if you mentioned northern working-class textile drama to anyone else, each word knocked the budget down by about 50 grand an episode. I knew it had to be done on a large scale, otherwise the stories would look like soap'. (Naughton, 2006: 26, quoted in Cooke, 2005: 184)

As Cooke notes, even taking such an idea to the BBC at this time could not have been done with much optimism, considering the dearth of drama of this kind going back to the 1980s. Perhaps, though, the most significant thing about what Abbott has to say here is his description of the ambitions he had for the production values of *Clocking Off* and his desire to avoid the brand of social realism that had become the province of the soap opera since the advent of *Brookside* and *Eastenders*. However, it wasn't simply in terms of scale that Abbott wanted to avoid soap-style social realism; it was also through the whole range of production values and, most significantly for this discussion, structural and narrative strategies.

To begin with *Clocking Off* offered self-contained stories within each episode rather than any sense of serialisation. Running underneath those stories were longer-running narrative threads that played a greater or lesser role in each episode in relation to the main one-off story. Set in a factory, there was a permanent cast with characters coming to the fore and playing the lead in 'their' story only to retreat and become the fleetingly glimpsed background to another one. Because of the recognisability of many of the cast (Sarah Lancashire, Christopher Eccleston and David Morrissey, for example) the series offered the incidental pleasures of a Christopher Eccleston or a David Morrissey in the background of a scene with perhaps the odd line about putting out the bins.

Whilst such an approach has a relationship to the idea of 'flexi-narrative' used extensively by Robin Nelson (1997, 2007), it departs in key ways from a tradition that Nelson traces back to the American police drama *Hill St Blues* (1980) and the MTM stable more generally (1997: 30). This tradition, in Nelson's analysis, manifests itself most clearly in the UK through series such as the BBC's long-running hospital drama, *Casualty* (1993–). Whereas the approach of flexi-narrative offers a number of equally (or almost equally) important storylines within any one episode with the addition of long-running characters and narrative threads underneath, both *Clocking Off* and, later, *The Street*, focus on a single powerful narrative within each episode. They do, however, both have a stable set of recurrent characters and use traces of long-running or future storylines, though they are used quite differently in each case, as we shall see below.

The other important way in which *Clocking Off* was a forerunner of *The Street* was its approach to questions of social realism. Lez Cooke sees *Clocking Off* as a key development in which two variants of British social realism come together – on the one hand the tradition seen most frequently in the single play and on the other the more recent post-1980 soap-opera forms epitomised by *Eastenders* and *Brookside*:

Clocking Off can be seen as an amalgamation of these two traditions. On the one hand, the ambition to present 'good blue collar stories, told properly', the sort of stories that 'used to get the nation talking', locates the series in the Loach/Garnett/Allen tradition of The Wednesday Play and Play for Today. On the other hand, the 'domestic' qualities of *Clocking Off*, its emphasis on the camaraderie of the factory workers, the 'ordinariness' of the characters and their social situations, the element of serialisation that is present as a result of the personal relationships between regular characters, all suggest an affinity with the popular social realism of a soap opera ... a factor which may help to explain the popularity of such an unfashionable twenty-first century concept as a drama series set in a northern textiles factory. The blending of these two traditions in *Clocking Off* is indicative of a post-modern shift in the representation of social realism in twenty-first-century television drama. (Cooke, 2005: 188)

This persuasive account of *Clocking Off* can, in certain key ways, be applied to *The Street*, as can Cooke's analysis that the former managed to get commissioned and attract audiences through its skilful blending of traditions that had formerly been crudely characterised as 'serious' and 'popular'.

One of *The Street*'s structural differences from *Clocking Off* lies in the way that it uses its 'base community'. In the latter the textile factory in which all the characters work and around which the stories are set is itself a central feature of each episode. The public space of the street in McGovern's series is of course central, though the space is not of equivalent significance in each episode. There are also significant differences between the way the two series use characters that recur throughout, but which are not always central to a given episode. In *The Street* the focus each week is on a particular inhabitant, or set of inhabitants. At the same time we will see brief appearances by other characters who will themselves play a central role in one of the later stories. The content of these appearances will frequently acquire significance only when the character has played a central role in a later story. For example, in the first ever episode of *The Street*, 'The Accident' (dir. David Blair, 6 April 2006) we see Sean O'Neill (Lee Ingleby) fleetingly in an episode that focuses mainly on a child being run over and an affair between her mother (Jane Horrocks) and the man who runs her over (Shaun Dooley). O'Neill is seen performing two actions; one involves obvious disapproval of his wife singing karaoke at a local club; the other shows him expressing concern over some cases of whisky when the police are called to investigate the accident. In Episode 2, 'Stan' (dir. David Blair, 20 April 2006), Sean remains a minor character, but we see him arrested over the whisky, whilst it is not until Episode 6, 'Sean and Yvonne' (dir. David Blair, 18 May 2006), that the audience understand the full context of Sean's and his wife Yvonne's (Christine Bottomley) marriage. By contrast there was a tendency in *Clocking Off* to have longer-running threads that developed in every individual episode alongside the main one-off story of the week. Most prominently, especially in the early episodes, these involved the lives of Mac (Philip Glenister), the factory owner, his unfaithful wife and his secretary Trudy (Lesley Sharpe), who carries a torch for Mac.

Whilst these differences seem slight they tended to make *The Street* even closer to the single-play format, albeit within an 'anthology' framework. That this was very much in McGovern's thinking is borne out by his remark on the DVD commentary: 'I don't refer to this as a drama series. I see it as six films' (*Complete Series 1 DVD*). Whilst the multiple appearances of characters from other stories in minor roles make this not literally true, the fact that the central storyline of each episode is self-contained and can be watched independently from the rest of the series gives *The Street* the connection to the single play that McGovern clearly wanted. What the fleeting glimpses into other lives and stories still to come (or even that have already been told) provide is something of an extra layer, a bonus level to the reality of *The Street* available only to the regular viewer. It is almost as if McGovern is attempting to provide a kind of simulation of 'community' where the significance of minor actions can only be understood when one makes the effort to understand and become part of the places in which we find ourselves living. At some level, of course, this is true of serials and soap operas of all kinds, except that the formula of looking in depth at one story at a time offers the narrative depth of the single drama that serials cannot usually provide.

Structurally then, *The Street* tried to modify the attempt by *Clocking Off* to reinvent the single drama in a form that gave it a chance of survival in the commissioning environment of the 2000s. On the same DVD commentary McGovern makes comparison with two widely disparate narrative models, firstly *The Canterbury Tales* and secondly the US police drama *The Naked City* (ABC, 1958–63) which always ended with the voice-over 'There are eight million stories in the Naked City. This has been one of them.' *The Street*'s advance publicity had the tagline: 'Behind every door in every street, there's a story waiting to be told'. Whilst the two examples that McGovern cites are so wildly dissimilar, they also both suggest something in common that was certainly part of the construction of *The Street*, namely the idea of popular, oral narratives being transformed into collections that gave them some status and significance that it would be difficult for them to achieve separately. It is well-known that the producers of *The Street* (McGovern is a named Executive Producer) advertised for stories across the North-West (of England) and received an enormous number of responses (see Rampton, 2006). Whilst the stories are then shaped and constructed in all manner of ways, the device connects the series with the kind of tradition that sets it apart from the usual television commissioning process. *The Street*'s origins are at least partly connected, then, to the basic idea of oral narrative traditions. Traditions that generally survive only in ways that McGovern himself has summed up as 'Everyone has at least one story to tell ... I know that from bitter experience because every time I go into the boozer, someone comes up to me and says: "Have I got a story for you!"' (Rampton, 2006)

McGovern's view on this collection of popular narratives was not, however, in any way romantic:

> We got hundreds in but sad to say 85–90% of those were regurgitated TV stories, stories you're sick of seeing on TV. There were very few that were fresh and new but those are the ones that we picked up. We didn't go with established writers: we just said: 'we'll pick this story. Can the writer write? Well let's find out. And if he can't write, well it doesn't matter because we can work with him, you know? So the main thing was finding six great stories. And it's a very interesting way of working. (BBC, 2006b)

The story-gathering process was, then, not simply a matter of collecting ideas but also part of a new direction for McGovern's interest in working with new writers. Although he had been doing this at some level going back to *Cracker*, *The Street* took it in new directions by liberating the novice writer from working either within an established genre or an overall story arc (as in the case of *The Lakes*), but instead allowing them to originate the narrative and benefit from collaborating with an experienced writer and producer. The end result of this varies from a writer being commissioned to be the sole credited author of an episode, to being the co-writer with McGovern himself or, in one case, as the credit read, 'by Jimmy McGovern based on a story by Danny Brocklehurst'.

Such collaborations have the potential, of course, for all kinds of ethical dilemmas and disputes over intellectual property, but it is genuinely difficult to find any accounts of aggrieved, less-experienced writers feeling that McGovern has exploited their idea. What are common are accounts of the level of care and detail accorded to the work by McGovern, even if the process is not always comfortable. One of the least experienced writers to be allowed a single-author credit on *The Street*, Alan Field, said:

The biggest lesson I learned from Jimmy McGovern was a process he calls 'murdering your babies' ... A new writer will sit and convince you that this dialogue has to be in ... Jimmy will say 'well go and murder your babies'. It means taking a line out to see if the scene still stands. It's not about making the scene better, it's about you growing as a writer and realising that you shouldn't hold on to none of your dialogue. (Byrom, 2006)

Such accounts are commonplace when discussing creative writing retreats, but what is remarkable here is that Field is discussing writing an hour-long drama for a 9pm slot on BBC1 in the era of multi-channel, multi-platform competition. Through a combination of his own reputation and proven track record and the success of the format he was using, with *The Street* McGovern managed to find space on prime-time television to do what many claimed had gone forever with the demise of single-drama slots. That is, to find a space where strong storytellers could gain experience in trying to write intelligent work for large-scale audiences.

Glen Creeber, amongst others, has argued strongly that any hankering after the so-called 'golden age' of single dramas on British television is something of a mistake and that an alternative case can be made for the end of the single play marking a 'coming of age' in which television broke away from the 'aesthetic constraints' of the past (2004: 2). Creeber's argument is that the single play's key aesthetic relationship was with the theatre and that it may have simply run its course as televisual forms expanded and matured. In place of the single play, Creeber argues, has come the drama series and serial with their complex 'flexi-narrative' structures, reflective of what Raymond Williams once called the 'flow' of television (4).

Creeber's account is clearly an important corrective to the potentially reactionary tendency to deride the television serial in response to the loss of what many saw as the home of demanding, intelligent writing in Play for Today and other similar slots. He goes on to provide a convincing account of the increasingly hybrid nature of television forms in which traditional boundaries between soaps, series and serials become blurred both in terms of narrative structures but also in relation to the way that they deal with politics. In Creeber's view the newer forms of serial (he cites examples such as *Queer as Folk* (Channel 4, 1999–2000) and *Shameless* (2004–)): 'Offer examples of a new relationship between politics and the self (meaning that political issues are now increasingly centred convincingly around the domain of personal and private interaction' (2004: 12). Creeber's acceptance of this 'new relationship' marks a break with forms of traditional criticism that have usually equated the representation of history via the lives of individuals as lacking the potential to engage with ideas of radical change. These are clearly important arguments in relation to a writer such as McGovern (see the brief discussion on realism and the *Days of Hope* debate in Chapter 1) and his contribution to the evolution of the increasingly hybrid forms of television dramas through *The Street* increases such an importance.

First, as suggested above, I think it can be argued that *The Street* (which appeared after Creeber's book was published) is a further development of the series/serial form that Creeber quite rightly sees as at the heart of television dramatists' attempts to use the unique qualities of the medium to engage with the world. It certainly owes a debt to *Clocking Off* and others, but it takes the form even more strongly in the direction of the single play, whilst subtly and inventively retaining some of the advantages of the series/serial. This distinctive combination is important in relation to Creeber's point about a changed contemporary relationship between fictionalised personal lives and the political concerns of contemporary drama. I think it is possible to argue that *The Street* is able to take the detailed narrative and characterisation possible in a single one-off drama and interlace it with the ripples and ramifications of the characters' actions in the wider community. The individual stories are intensely personal, but they are also deeply rooted in the community and the wider society, and the form of *The Street* allows us to see this in the glimpses of other characters' lives.

This structural interlacing of the lives of the characters across the individual stories is not equally distributed across the three series, but is particularly true of the programme's early episodes. In 'The Accident' referred to above, Stan McDermott is a witness to the child being hit by a car and faints, perhaps from the shock. In court his testimony is pulled apart by a barrister intent on highlighting his age and infirmity. When the case against the driver collapses as a result, the family blames him. In the second episode, 'Stan', we see Stan forced to retire against his will and his life starts to disintegrate. His witnessing of the accident is part of a wider picture of rejection that is seen to be symptomatic of a cultural disregard for his experience and good sense. The awful leaving party and presentation of a carriage clock that he is forced to endure are grisly distortions of any ceremony to honour his life's work. He decides to commit suicide so that his wife and daughter will be better off financially, only for this to backfire and him ending up sectioned under the Mental Health Act. In a final indignity another neighbour, Sean O'Neill, berates Stan in the street for attracting the police to the neighbourhood, which results in Sean being arrested for receiving the stolen goods that we first saw in 'The Accident'.

Whilst the single play enables us to concentrate on Stan, the series as a whole makes the individual stories interconnect and become part of a wider social and cultural picture. Moreover, as Jane Horrocks suggested in an interview, Stan's story is not only that of an individual going through the trauma of retirement, but is representative of a youth-obsessed culture:

> Look at the second episode, where Jim Broadbent's character, Stan, is just left on the scrap-heap when he retires. These days you rarely see a mainstream drama about an older man who's made redundant and is contemplating suicide. It's such a youth-orientated market that it's great to see a story about a man in his sixties. Ageism so often prevails in television. (Rampton, 2006)

Stan's story undoubtedly becomes stronger in terms of its social and political engagement through the glimpses we see of the character in other episodes. There is a sense of the perception of Stan and, by extension, all elderly people, as infirm, not reliable, busybodies, and so on. Curiously, in a way, as is the case with most of *The Street* episodes, the choice is made to provide a happy ending of sorts. In one sense it is not a conventional one, as there is room for ambiguity, but it is one that contains such a degree of sentimentality as to take on a kind of mythical status. Contemplating yet another suicide attempt, Stan is shaken out of his morbid frame of mind by a drawing pushed through his letterbox by the young girl who he had seen run over in the street. It depicts Stan and the young girl holding hands, and he realises that he still has value in the world.

The ending of 'Stan' is not untypical of *The Street* and takes us into a consideration of the series' relationship both to realism as well as its politics. On the question of realism, the *Guardian*'s long-standing television critic, Nancy Banks-Smith, was unequivocal. Having started her review with the verdict '*The Street* (BBC1) by Jimmy McGovern was just about perfect', she goes on to discuss how 'realistic' the programme was, eventually concluding: 'I wouldn't say it was plausible. I'd say poetic' (2007). Although this is a relatively throwaway remark, it does raise an interesting and important issue, particularly because of the easy identification with social realism that many critics have made in relation to McGovern's work.

At one level, of course, *The Street* has a strong relationship to the central tradition of British realist television drama. Its setting is the kind of Northern working-class terraced street that has been at the heart of so much British television and which is a clear reference to the most prominent working-class drama of them all, *Coronation Street*. On the other hand this is a street that is both never named and which, as McGovern must clearly have understood from his *Brookside* days, the kind of place where fewer and fewer working-class people actually live. In setting his long-running drama *Shameless* on the sprawling Chatsworth estate, McGovern's one-time collaborator Paul Abbott signalled his own recognition of a changed working-class landscape, one altogether more anarchic in terms both of physical space and social relationships. By going back to the archetypal street of Victorian terraced housing and providing only a generic name ('street'), it is possible to see McGovern signalling not a traditional realist text, but a world that is at least partly raised to the status of myth or fable.

We have already seen in this chapter an allusion by McGovern himself to *The Canterbury Tales*. Elsewhere, on the DVD commentary on *The Lakes*, he lightheartedly refers to himself as 'the poor-man's Thomas Hardy' (Series 1, 2003). Whilst it may be contentious to take such a comparison too far, there is a definite sense of McGovern being conscious of the relationship that existed between his work and the varieties of realism to be found in some Victorian novelists. This kind of comparison is of course not new. The British Film Institute's official account of the concept of social realism makes specific reference to the idea: 'As in France, where the "actualités" of cinema pioneers the Lumière Brothers seemed to descend from the provincial realism of Gustave Flaubert, early British cinema picked up on the revelation of everyday social interaction to be found in Dickens and Thomas Hardy' (Armstrong, 2003).

This idea of the elevation of the status of 'everyday social interaction' into art is clearly at the heart of everything that McGovern has been associated with, but of equal significance, especially in relation to *The Street*, is the way that the work sometimes performs such a transformation. Rather than an 'abandonment' of social realism it is perhaps more accurate and productive to discuss *The Street* as another attempt to rework a social-realist television tradition. We have already alluded to Lez Cooke's argument that *Clocking Off* can be seen as one approach to the problem of classic social realism in a postmodern age. Cooke's analysis tends to emphasise the production values of *Clocking Off*, such as its use of primary colours, music, and so on to help distance itself from the traditional drabness associated with the form. *The Street* does not, on the whole, go in the same direction. However it does attempt its own variation, one I would argue that is based upon a self-conscious raising of the status of the ordinary through 'mythologising' storytelling motifs that in turn combine with many of the more traditional techniques associated with McGovern's work.

We have already seen, in the account of 'Stan', how a simple child's drawing restores to life an old man who sees only death in front of him.

In the first episode of the second series of *The Street*, 'Twin' (dir. Terry McDonough, 8 November 2007), we see another staple of myths and fables, the exchanged twin, put to devastating use when given a contemporary realist frame. David Thewlis plays twin brothers Harry and Joe Jennerson, the latter relatively affluent, free and successful; the former stuck in a dead-end job and marriage. When Joe dies in a freak choking accident while the brothers watch football, Harry attempts to take on his identity, pretending that it was Harry who died.

In the third and final series of *The Street* the individual episodes are not given names at all, but just called 'Episode 1' 'Episode 2', etc.. There is therefore something of an intensifying of the representative status of the stories as, in the titles at least, they become further removed from a simple playing-out of a single story. In 'Episode 2' (dir. Terry McDonough, 20 July 2009), Anna Friel plays Dee, a mother struggling to create a decent life for her young sons and turning to prostitution in her desperation to pay her way. The archetypal nature of the desperate woman having to sell herself and the fairy-tale ending of her sons getting into the good school that she has dreamed of again elevate a story full of the grim detail of Dee's life into the world of the fabulous.

McGovern's own notion of the 'poor man's Thomas Hardy' is also resonant in the strong sense of both morality and 'higher forces' at work in the tales that make up *The Street*. In the story mentioned above, Dee's final triumph comes about because a member of the school admissions appeals panel is a priest who has been amongst her clients. Instead of using the coincidence as an excuse for easy Catholic-bashing, McGovern and Jan McVerry (co-author of this episode) make him a priest with a smile and an understanding of irony. Dee gets her children into the school, but we are never sure whether it is to buy her silence or because the priest has seen the justice of the cause. When asked how she managed to get her sons into the school Dee simply replies, 'I shagged the Vicar!', once again allowing the writers to trade wittily on a particular kind of narrative trope.

None of this is to argue that *The Street* does not have a powerful connection to the realist tendency in British television drama. Its performances from some of the most experienced and lauded talents in British television (Broadbent, Thewlis, Horrocks, Timothy Spall) are detailed, plausible creations of fully realised characters. Each episode is shot through with the texture and detail of working-class domestic life in what are often subtle variations on a time-honoured theme. However there is a strong case for suggesting that *The Street* offers another variant on the social-realist tradition that is perhaps part Thomas Hardy, part soap-opera in which the extraordinary intervenes in the ultra-ordinary in ways that make for powerful attention-grabbing drama in the era of the three-minute YouTube clip. The relationship between *The Street* and ideas of 'the real' or 'realism' in any abstract sense are probably best negotiated via this kind of account of what such ideas can mean for television drama in the early twenty-first century:

> Realism, then, continues to reinvent itself, despite its own inherent contradictions and despite our increasing loss of faith in the ability of the camera to capture some fundamental social truth. Its boundaries are unclear, its conventions constantly shifting, and its terrain a contested. But if, as John Ellis writes, television now 'acts as our forum for interpretations of the world' (1999: 69), then realism, with its relentless search for 'the authentic', continues to be a means by which the 'truth' of those interpretations is both claimed and evaluated. (Thornham and Purvis, 2005: 73)

Both *The Street*'s relationship to realism and its political nature were brought sharply to the fore in 'The Promise' (dir. David Blair, 13 December 2007). The storyline concerns a young man, Paul Billerton (Toby Kebbell), who, as a young child, caused the death of a baby and its grandmother. Now a man in his early twenties he has been released from prison and is trying to make a stable life for himself only to be continually haunted by the enormous burden of his crime. His redemption comes at the unlikely hands of the baby's mother, Jean (Jodhi May), who tracks him to the tiny bedsit when he is on the point of committing suicide.

There are a number of things that work against the idea of 'The Promise' as social realism. First, the programme has little interest in the widely available detail about the way that the perpetrators of serious crimes in childhood are provided with new identities and the like. We find Paul living close to the scene of his crime and to the parents of the baby, his adulthood appearance apparently well known. At the scene at the end of Paul's trial, in flashback, we witness an intense embrace between his mother and Jean, both acknowledging that they have lost children. The scene is profoundly moving, though in practice the two women would be highly unlikely to be allowed to be in such physical proximity. Finally, a lengthy section of the narrative is structured around a long conversation between Paul and Jean on either side of a door that is only open a fraction because of its chain. During the conversation we see in flashback a number of the key events that brought their lives together. It is, of course, unlikely that such a conversation would ever take place at all, still less so that it would be sustained for so long through a crack in the open door so narrow that Jhodi May was, as Banks-Smith put it, 'acting half the time with only half her face' (2007). To cap it all,

Jean demands of Paul that he put away the idea of suicide and instead atone for his crime by falling in love, producing a child and loving it as she did hers. Almost the next cut is to a park with Paul and the young girl he has previously pushed away, afraid of getting close, pushing their child (we assume, the scene is wordless) on a swing. The whole scene is bathed in sunshine.

'The Promise' was one of the most critically acclaimed episodes of all three series of *The Street*. Banks-Smith, in her inimitable style, said that it 'was just about perfect, and there is nothing much you can say about perfection except: "Leave the washing up, mother. Come and have a look at this!"' (2007), and one suspects that its subject matter was particularly close to McGovern's heart (it was the only one written by him alone in Series 2). That he chose to tell such a tale in ways that strained every boundary of the genre with which he has become associated reveals a great deal about not only *The Street*, but the evolution of the idea of 'realism' on British television. The account of the narrative above, whilst admittedly not totally comprehensive, accurately represents its resemblance to a modern morality tale, stripped of the burden of police or hospital procedural accuracy that dogs what many people understand as realism. The representational energy is displaced as it were into the utter believability of the ordinary human beings that act out this extraordinary fable. McGovern's script is stripped back to the absolute essentials, with only the long confessional-style exchange between Paul and Jean allowed to become anything approaching a conversation. Instead we see moments of great intensity played out through the exchange of looks and glances brilliantly choreographed by McGovern's most frequent directorial collaborator, David Blair, as well as the writer himself.

'The Promise' tests what we mean when we casually use terms such as 'real' and 'realistic'. The idea of a child killing another child is itself not in the realms of the real for most of us. The same goes for the idea of confronting, forgiving and 'saving' someone who has killed a loved one. How, then, to find a form that reveals something real and truthful from such a situation, and how to show people that audiences can identify with coping with such extreme circumstances? McGovern manages to do this by drawing upon the strengths of realism in the creation of character and the active choice of working-class locations, but combining these elements with narratives and storytelling techniques that, when described in the abstract, seem to belong to another tradition altogether. McGovern and Blair's ultra-economical style enables the hour-long stories to contain moments of such intensity that even hard-bitten newspaper critics are given to use words such as 'unbearable', so that the breakneck speed of the narrative is suddenly arrested and we are diverted from the extraordinary events in order to witness their impact on people's lives. It is a variant on the realist tradition that reaches out for the profundity and dignity of earth-shattering events visited on lives so 'ordinary' that they are usually ignored or patronised.

As indicated above, 'The Promise' is also interesting in what it has to say about *The Street*'s relationship to politics. It is initially surprising to read the following review of a DVD set of *The Street* when reflecting on McGovern's history:

> Nor is *The Street* particularly political. It lasted from 2006 until 2009. Those were the last of the Labour years, before the banking bailouts, downturn and austerity. There is a recurrent awareness, granted, of the terminal mediocrity of the jobs market despite the supposed boom years of New Labour: this is a world of financial embarrassment and even catastrophe, shift work, petty criminality, call centres and muddling on perpetually uphill, a world in which no one is doing particularly well. But it's not quite Broken Britain. (Stubbs, 2011)

Leaving aside for the moment the fact that the critic appears not to have taken account of some of the truly extraordinary events that happen across the eighteen stories of the three series, this is a very narrow view of idea of 'political' drama. I want to argue, as an example of McGovern's approach to the series, that a Liverpool writer creating a drama about child murder in the decade following the James Bulger case is in itself a profoundly political act. This becomes even more the case when considered alongside the emotional investment made by McGovern in dramatising the Hillsborough tragedy, which is covered later in this book.

The abduction and subsequent murder of 2-year-old James Bulger from a Bootle shopping centre in February 1993 became one of the most reported crimes of the twentieth century. Whilst much of the coverage was horribly sensationalised, the case raised some fundamental questions about the treatment of young offenders, the jurisdiction of the European Court of Human Rights and, crucially in this case, the raising of children and relationships to questions of poverty and social class. As a result the case came to take on a status that went well beyond its immediate details and was eventually commented upon by two serving prime ministers, as well as the Home and Justice Secretaries of successive administrations.[3]

One strong line of tabloid reporting, both at the time and in the many years that followed successive appeals and other legal controversies, was an idea that actually prefigured the 'Broken Britain' cliché that appears in the quotation above. Not only were the parents of the two boys who committed the act vilified for producing children who became such 'monsters', in some cases, so were James Bulger's parents themselves. More significantly still, some reports cited the Merseyside area where the boys were brought up as lacking any sense of community responsibility, citing the fact that a young child could be abducted in broad daylight, taken several miles on foot to a railway line and then brutally murdered without anyone intervening. Writing on the tenth anniversary of James Bulger's death, Euan Ferguson summed up some of the ways that the case was exploited and used to vilify the Liverpool area:

> Even if the Bulger family had wanted to try to forget, it never had a chance; every twist in the legal wranglings prompted another call to elicit simplistic quotes such as the recent one from James' uncle, also James, that 'killing's too good for them', and the rest of us shake our heads again at Liverpool. Even politicians got in on it. Michael Howard extended the boys' sentences at the yelp of the tabloids. Tony Blair's speech at the time about 'hammer blows against the sleeping conscience of the country' went down particularly well; according to my Observer colleague Andrew Rawnsley, this episode as much as any other brought him first to public attention and was, in significant ways, the making of him. So we all got something out of it, something out of James. Except, of course, for Liverpool. (Ferguson, 2003)

Of course one of the tabloids most involved in the moral outrage was the *Sun*, the same newspaper so despised on Merseyside for its reporting of the Hillsborough tragedy. In such a context, then, it perhaps becomes easier to characterise 'The Promise' as a profoundly political piece of work. Admittedly written at a time when much of the visceral anger had dissipated, McGovern's drama does everything that the politicians, most of the newspapers and the lynch mob did not, and that is to invite his audience to experience the impact of such a cataclysmic event from more than one perspective. This was not done lightly, and the terrible loss of the mother is absolutely at the core of the drama, but one of McGovern's consistent beliefs is that human actions are always complex and never reducible to slogans or moral certainties. In 'The Promise' Paul's actions are seen as partly accidental and partly a result of a difficult life. It is a difficult life that itself is not easily reduced to moral simplicities.

Connected to this central narrative, which becomes a powerful corrective to the moral panics and calls for punitive measures that have become the norm surrounding real-life child-murder cases, are other threads that reinforce the politics of the piece. Paul's bedsit is in a house that also contains students, and the class divide between him and his neighbours forms an underlying theme that complements the main narrative. Even here, though, McGovern does not allow us easy certainties: Paul's speech about their privileged background and their keeping a cat against the rules of the tenancy is made to seem over-defensive, even if the students' attitudes to him can also seem patronising.

Of course, it is possible to argue that few of the episodes of *The Street* have such direct echoes of contemporary events. This, though, would be missing the point. Even 'The Promise' avoids too direct a comparison with the Bulger affair, making the details of the murder very different. What is apparent is a politics running through *The Street* that is not of the very direct kind that McGovern had to always fight hard to include in his scripts back in his *Brookside* days, but a politics expressed through the lives of working-class people living in an era of rapid decline in mass membership of political parties and trade unions. Characters in *The Street* are victims of a legal system in which they have an inadequate stake, are pensioned off without an adequate income when they remain fit and able to work, resort to dealing drugs or prostitution out of desperation, encounter racism and face the consequences of disability and ill health. They struggle with a world in which fundamental questions about gender, the role of faith and multiculturalism are changing all the time and they remain at the sharp end of such change without the buffer zone that reliable education and financial stability can bring.

Writing before the first series of *The Street* had appeared, Glen Creeber discussed what he saw as the development of a different kind of 'political' drama in the UK and the USA:

> the growth of 'soap drama' like *thirtysomething*, *This Life* and *Cold Feet* could actually reveal a growing interest in and awareness of 'micro' as opposed to 'macro' politics. In other words these 'soap dramas' reveal an explicit concern with the personal and private 'politics' of everyday life rather than concentrating on grand political issues and wider socio-economic debates. For while 'soap drama' may prioritise the 'personal' over the 'political', it could be argued that it does so in such a way that the political nature of the personal ... is explored and examined more powerfully and thoroughly than ever before. (Creeber, 2004: 116)

Whilst feeling that the term 'soap drama' would be an inadequate way to describe *The Street* there is clearly much in this account that applies to the series. What is missing, of course, is McGovern's powerful account of class, not simply as the 'subject' of his work, but as a key component of the ideological framework within which we operate. At the time of writing there are few others prepared to write in this way and in *The Street* McGovern not only reasserts the centrality of class to an adequate account of the world, he attempts an approach to telling stories of working-class life that afford such stories a different kind of status. It is an approach that at the very least brushes up against oral traditions that create enduring fables whilst populating such fables with characters as fully realised as anything on British television.

Finally, before leaving this account of *The Street*, it is important to return to the question both of McGovern's producer role on the series and also related questions of authorship and the creative contributions of other writers and directors. Though McGovern had, by this point in his career, worked in writer teams in various capacities as discussed elsewhere in this book, *The Street* represented a far more concerted attempt on McGovern's part to both nurture new writers and to use new voices as method of broadening the reach of the storytelling behind the series.

As we saw above, the process of creating *The Street* partly through advertising for stories is itself a rarity in mainstream television and it enabled the producers to put first-time as well as more experienced writers straight on to a 9pm series on BBC1. Elsewhere, though, McGovern is definitely at pains to stress the care taken to preserve both quality and an overall single authorial presence: '"I do a polish at the end of their scripts," McGovern explains. "It's not merely for the sake of it. It's to impose a single authorial voice on all six episodes. Otherwise, the series could be all over the place in theme and tone"' (BBC, 2007). Given that seven out of the eighteen episodes of *The Street* give single-author credits to other writers this is quite a strong statement of intent. In addition, the final series abandons single-author credits for anyone but McGovern, and instead he is credited as a co-author with five other writers (the sixth episode is credited to him alone).

This change to the final series suggests a slight tightening of the McGovern authorial grip, though there is no evidence of anxiety on the part of the production team, nor is there a perceptible shift in quality, with different episodes across all three series receiving only slightly different amounts of attention (though the 'The Promise', a McGovern solo script, was particularly singled out, as we have seen). What is likely to have been such a factor in keeping the appearance of a tight McGovern rein on the writing is his ability at this stage to attract other kinds of talent. We have already remarked upon the strength and status of the actors that were attracted to work on *The Street*, and this is reinforced by key members of the production team. McGovern's fellow executive producer praised his work with the actors, before going on to say, 'It is also testimony to Jimmy's writing that The Street will continue to attract the best actors in British drama today', something also echoed by producer John Chapman: 'Jimmy attracts the best people. People genuinely loved the first series, so you can go to anyone and offer them a part and they're likely to accept' (BBC, 2007).

'Hybrid' forms   83

Whilst all this concentration on McGovern might seem something of a distortion of a series with so many other writer credits, some of them belonging to experienced writers, it is undoubtedly the reality of the way that idea was sold in pre-production, when the programme itself was broadcast and on DVD, which has 'Jimmy McGovern's *The Street*' all over the covers. There is also evidence of the project being a clear bargain on both sides from the beginning, with McGovern's proven record of encouraging new voices (with *Dockers* being the ultimate example) being brought together with the BBC's need to develop talent within the constraints of the multi-channel, risk-averse environment. In this extract from an account of the genesis of Series 1 of *The Street* Sita Williams and John Yorke discuss the 'terms' under which everyone agreed to work:

> One of the attractive things about this project was Jimmy's commitment to getting new writers involved and giving them a voice on prime time BBC1. So he worked hand in hand with four new writers – honing and perfecting their stories into classic Play For Today like scripts. One of the things we are trying to do at the BBC is invest very heavily in the training of new talent. It's something we are doing in Drama Series with the Writers Academy, and to find another way of doing it through a writer of Jimmy's calibre is a huge boost to that cause. (BBC, 2006c)

Executive producer Sita Williams continues:

> Jimmy and I discussed setting up a series that he would be the principal writer of and we would bring in new voices – new writers to work with him in a very collaborative way. With Jimmy at the helm writing the first two stories and thereafter overwriting, where necessary, all the other scripts were the terms in which the writers came into the project.
>
> The writers felt that it was fantastic to be working with Jimmy, to be learning from him, and it was great to see less experienced writers working with someone who is so skilled at his craft. He hasn't done anything like this before and he really wanted to do it. (BBC, 2006c)

McGovern had, of course, done something similar before, on *The Lakes* in particular, but this represents a clear development and one which constituted a bargain worth making for all those involved.

Though McGovern is credited as Executive Producer, there is also a sense that, although his hand is everywhere in the writing, that is where it ends. He had commented previously about his own sense of how bad he is at casting (see Chapter 1 on *Cracker* and McGovern's initial objections to the casting of Robbie Coltrane), and it appears that he is seen as a writer passionate about the script but trusting of those in charge of the process after that. According to Sita Williams, 'He writes the script but doesn't get involved in casting. Yes we do run ideas by him, but his approach to the whole project is he is a writer and we're making it work for him.'

There is a little doubt that *The Street* is a writer-led series, but equally it would be remiss to end this discussion without some comment on the series' visual qualities, particularly in relation to questions of a social-realist aesthetic. Just as the writing has pushed at the boundaries of contemporary notions of realism, so too does the directorial approach, though the degree to which this is true varies from episode to episode. One of McGovern's most frequent collaborators, David Blair, directed ten out of the eighteen episodes, with Terry McDonough working on the rest. The ethos again is on consistency and a sympathy with McGovern's approach, one more complex than any idea of a so-called 'kitchen-sink' aesthetic. Whilst *The Street* does not attempt the contemporary swagger of *Clocking Off*, particularly in its soundtrack, there are moments throughout the series that veer, for example, in the direction of expressionist explorations of interior states, whilst others are clearly intent on capturing a visual poetry to match those tendencies in the writing.

An early moment in 'Twin' (Series 2) is illustrative of the way that *The Street* plays with the boundaries of social realism whilst remaining rooted in the lives and stories that are its source. The opening moments of the episode accumulate details of the deteriorating life of Joe Jennerson (David Thewlis). Mostly what we see is ultra-ordinary: unpaid bills, demanding children and, the last straw, suspension from a job. As Jennerson slumps onto the sofa after arriving home unexpectedly there is a cut to reveal his elderly mother sitting by him, dressed in a fairy costume. It isn't long before it is revealed that there is a party at the day-care centre that she attends, but it is long enough for there to be an arresting, almost surreal moment which underlines Joe's need for a fairy godmother. It is at once funny, strange and poignant in a way that relies both on the design and the pace of the cutting.

As briefly discussed above, 'Twin' is something of a surreal fable, even in its basic design, as a brother uses the opportunity of his identical twin's accidental death to take on his identity. But again, the manner of the death, choking on a sherbet lemon sweet, is treated as a powerful mixture of the banal and the terrifying. Harry Jennerson embarks on an endless rambling treatise on the decline of the sherbet lemon as the brand-new television in front of him changes channels of its own free will. When he chokes it is a while before his brother Joe takes it seriously, and then suddenly the number of edits increases rapidly as the camera angles gives us grotesque close-ups of the dying man and the brother who is trying to save him. The fact that they are twins, both

'Hybrid' forms 85

played by David Thewlis, heightens the sense of chaos and surreal fantasy. Moments later reality is back with us as the news of Harry's death is given to Joe's wife in a dingy Accident and Emergency waiting room – by this time the change of identity has moved from macabre fantasy to grim reality. We see Joe watching the effects of his own death on his wife as he sits playing the supportive brother.

'The Twin' exemplifies how *The Street*'s creative team takes the extraordinary stories that make up each episode and echoes their delicate balance of the everyday and the fantastical. It does this through a visual language that at times seems to freeze the characters in real time and then abruptly speed up as the headlong rush of fate takes us to the inevitable conclusions. This is heightened through a score that is anything but sentimental and at times powerfully discordant. At times these departures from the realist frame are much clearer and obvious, such as the moment in 'Old Flame' (dir. David Blair, 15 November 2007) when Margi McEvoy (Ger Ryan) is overwhelmed with the thought of her recently diagnosed breast cancer. She is sitting on a bus and all around her people seem to be discussing her condition as the passengers appear in huge close-ups and the colour drains from the naturalism of the scene. There are many such moments throughout all three series, but perhaps more fundamental to the impact of *The Street* is the tendency, alluded to above, which is to more subtly underscore the idea of the extraordinary appearing in ordinary lives through almost imperceptible changes of pace and the use of characters caught in the frame in ways that arrest the attention and imagination.

Stephen Lacey, discussing the BBC drama series *This Life* (BBC2, 1996–97), contrasts it with another series that was broadcast around the same time, *Our Friends in the North* (BBC2, 1996–7). For some he suggests the two represent the changing face of British television drama, with *Our Friends in the North* representing 'old style social realism' whilst '*This Life* embraced, and helped to define, an energetic and visually innovative narrative style tailored to the series/serial form' (Lacey, 2007: 159). I would suggest that *The Street* (and in different ways *Clocking Off* before it) attempted something of an accommodation between these two traditions. *The Street* certainly took the location of its narratives back to the more familiar territory of British social realism, but it did not represent an unthinking 'retreat' to the aesthetic of a different time and place. Through McGovern's close supervision and the use of experienced, long-standing directors who trusted and admired his work, *The Street* was able to partially re-create the space and freedom of the single drama, along with a certain freedom to push against the boundaries both of the social-realist frame and the traditional stylistic tropes that had come to characterise British drama series and the so-called 'flexi-narrative'.

Moving On (BBC1, 2010–)

Of all the risks and different directions that Jimmy McGovern has taken during his highly prolific career, arguably one of the most extreme has been his venture into daytime television with the series *Moving On*. At the time of writing the programme has entered a third series scheduled over a single week on BBC1, starting on 14 November 2011 and showing between 2pm and 3pm.

The BBC's publicity for all three series of *Moving On* makes frequent mention of McGovern's name, despite the fact that he is not credited as the writer on any of them. The series is billed as being 'created' by McGovern using up and coming writers and directors. There is also frequent mention of the fact that original daytime drama is a rarity and that, in UK terms, only the BBC is involved in new work for daytime scheduled slots. Ironically, under the radical cost-cutting measures announced by the BBC in 2011, the Corporation's ambitions to improve the image of daytime television through the likes of *Moving On* are likely to be curtailed. One commentator at least saw plans to cut daytime television as a clever idea that would produce the minimum of protest from the audience:

> New daytime programmes will largely disappear from BBC2, with a greater proportion of repeats on that and other networks outside of peak time. This is a smart tactical move because – given that the term 'daytime TV' has become pejoratively associated with low-budget, low-intelligence products – there seems unlikely to be a mass campaign. (Lawson, 2011)

Lawson's description of daytime television's image, whilst undoubtedly very generalised, is also close to the truth, making it remarkable on the face of it that a writer in McGovern's position should place his reputation at the disposal of a series such as *Moving On*. However, Lawson's other point about the unlikelihood of a 'mass campaign' to save daytime television is a clue to one of a number of potential motivations behind McGovern's motives for such a venture. During the BBC's cost-saving consultations in 2010–11 a number of proposals, or at least possibilities, reached the public domain, including the scrapping of Radio 6. This service was able to marshal a highly effective and ultimately successful campaign of protest largely because its audience included a high proportion of those skilled in using important channels of communication and with some access to public opinion.[4] The Radio 6 audience, it hardly

'Hybrid' forms 87

need be said, contains a high proportion of young, middle-class and relatively affluent people, the diametric opposite of the traditional audience for daytime television.

Part of McGovern's reasons for agreeing to be involved in a series for a daytime audience is, then, highly consistent with his career as a writer committed to giving voice both to unpopular truths and to those who are seldom heard. His attempts to include overt class politics in the storylines of his series may have faded after his disillusion with the organised left in the 1980s and 1990s, but his commitment to providing stories of what he frequently refers to as 'ordinary' lives for a mass audience has, if anything, intensified. In some ways the core demographic of the daytime audience is prime McGovern territory and an attempt to improve the quality of what such an audience receives is an entirely explicable McGovern mission.

Whilst *Moving On* does contain a wide variety of stories in settings across its three series to date, there is also a concern to write interestingly and originally about ageing that remains rare in television drama. This is not a new discovery for McGovern himself. From *Brookside* onwards McGovern's work has consistently not only dealt with age, but provided a genuine variety of roles designed to reflect the diversity that exists beneath the reductive category of 'elderly'. A number of the episodes of *Moving On*, then, appear to echo the concerns of 'Stan' from *The Street* in which, as we saw, a man's life and experiences were suddenly deemed to have no worth, only for the narrative to open up new lines of resistance and possibility.

In their study of the older audience's perception of their portrayal on British television, Tim Healey and Karen Ross comment on the lack of research that has been conducted in this area:

> It is a little odd, then, that interest in that most loyal of audience groups, the older consumer, has not been seen as an important segment for the industry to interrogate, although perhaps not so odd if we understand the strong thread that binds advertising and television together: advertisers are not interested in the older market and therefore media organizations work much harder at trying to attract younger audiences which they can then deliver up to advertisers in return for serious money. (Healey and Ross, 2002: 107)

Though of course the specific argument about advertisers is not directly relevant to the BBC, the general point about a widespread attitude to older viewers is well made and is, I would argue, important context for the way that *Moving On* was conceived. Healey and Ross's article was based upon fieldwork done with older viewers, and they describe their interviewees' sense of how they are perceived by broadcasters:

A number of viewers suggested that it was easy to see exactly what programme-makers think of them as a specific audience by the kinds of programmes they put on when they assume they have a large number of older people watching. 'They put on any old dross in the afternoons because they think we're too stupid to notice.' (Healey and Ross, 2002: 109)

In this significant study there emerged a clear sense of exclusion and, something that has always attracted the attention of Jimmy McGovern, a sense of injustice and unfairness about older people's treatment by television. As Healey and Ross go on to argue:

As members of the licence-paying public, older viewers have as much right to be heard as anyone else and can reasonably expect to see images and representations of themselves, in all their infinite diversity, across the spectrum of television programming. If television is a public space for us, the viewers, then strategies must surely be found to change those public spaces so that they become a bit more representative and accessible for television's many publics. (Healey and Ross, 2002: 118)

There is a clear case for reading *Moving On* partly as an intervention in the 'public space' of television, not exclusively on behalf of older people, as we shall see, but its scheduling and a significant proportion of its content is clearly aimed at providing drama that lies outside the negative stereotypes that older people have some to expect, particularly in daytime television.

One very clear strategy adopted by the production team behind *Moving On* has been to use the kind of casting rarely, if ever, associated with drama produced for the British daytime schedules. This has been particularly true of older actors, though the series contains a high proportion of well-known younger performers. The first episode of Series 1 of *Moving On*, 'The Rain Has Stopped' (dir. Gary Williams, first broadcast on 18 May 2009) centred on the new relationship between Liz (Sheila Hancock) and Damar (Bhasker Patel) and, in a number of ways, set a strong precedent for the series' approach, particularly to the representation of age. The casting of Hancock, who remains one of the most widely recognised of British actresses and someone still performing regularly on television, stage and in feature films, was itself of significance. Moreover the character she portrays, Liz, is seen starting a bold, adventurous and sexually active relationship with a man she has met on holiday. For her family, though, the principal significance of the relationship is that her new partner, Damar, is black and her son, in particular, cannot see beyond that.

Like most of the individual dramas that made up *Moving On*, 'The Rain Has Stopped' finishes by allowing the principal characters to move on and find some new kind of happiness. This sense of neatness is a clear concession to the constraints of the television schedule. However, along the way, there are subtleties that mark the drama out from the reductive nature of most daytime television. The portrayal of Liz is central to this. She does dote on her grandchildren, something which causes her enormous heartbreak when her daughter stops her seeing them as the result of their quarrel over Damar, but she is also someone with a job she enjoys and a clear sense of economic reality. She is also someone very clearly not about to give up on the full range of pleasures that life still has to offer which include travel, new friends and a properly physical relationship.

The tone set by 'The Rain Has Stopped' is taken up by a number of the other episodes, including 'Sauce for the Goose', which starred Anna Massey, almost as well known a face as Hancock, and 'The Test', with Corin Redgrave, in the last role he took before his death in 2010. In 'The Test' the idea of older people retaining ambition, a taste for new experience and a sense of daring is taken a stage further. Theresa (Hannah Gordon) falls for Gabe (Redgrave), who she first meets playing trumpet in a jazz band. Despite what Theresa admits is her inclination to caution, they sleep together on the first evening they meet, after which they smoke a cigarette together, their first for years. Aesthetically 'The Test' is more ambitious than 'The Rain Has Stopped', something that is generally true of *Moving On*'s second series, and the whole episode is lightly underscored with echoes of the jazz that Gabe plays as the couple talk against night-time backdrops of twinkling lights. At one point Theresa's best friend, Cyn (Maggie Steed), attempts to come between the couple and suggests a drive to the coast. Given the daytime budget the windswept, rainy Lancashire seaside is beautifully shot, reflecting Theresa's inner desolation and loneliness. Even the ending is slightly more complex than the earlier episode as we are unsure if the lifelong friendship of the two women will survive, though the romance between Gabe and Theresa is very much alive, as they dance together with the credits about to roll.

There is undoubtedly some sentimentality inherent in the narratives that make up *Moving On*, but the series also has, in the words of *The Times* review, 'the guts to disturb our afternoons' (Billen, 2010). 'The Test' is not only about a rather sensual romance, it also shows us two older women engaged in a criminal deception (Theresa agrees to take a driving test for Cyn who is a hopeless driver) and has Theresa drive a delivery van for a living. She also works for a boss whose every action tells us how dismissive he is of women that are no longer within his limited definition of 'attractive'. Her final pleasure in quitting her job is to tell him of his body-odour problem as a younger woman looks on, enjoying his humiliation.

Moving On is not, though, solely about the representation of older people. Whilst it avowedly attempts to do justice to this section of the likely daytime audience, it also attempts to contribute to a change in the perception of daytime drama that exists not only in an era of changing employment patterns, but also of an audience with a wide range of time-shifting devices at their disposal. Whilst the significance of television scheduling has not disappeared with the rapidity of the most extravagant claims, the advent of iPlayer and the Sky/Virgin/Freeview+ Box have all undoubtedly had an enormous impact on viewing patterns. In an article for the *Guardian* its ex-editor Peter Preston tells us that

> A full 10% of all UK citizens who switch on a set these days watch something pre-recorded they can summon back and speed through at the press of a button. In the wonderful world of personal video recorders (PVR) some 32% of drama series and 26% of soaps are watched this way ... (2011)

In 2010, the Controller of BBC daytime, Liam Keelan, was moved to respond to the BBC Trust's criticism of the quality of daytime television with a commitment to, among other things, more original drama. As the person who originally commissioned *Moving On*, Keelan cited the series as one of the channel's recent significant achievements and promised more of the same (Keelan, 2010). The responses to Keelan's blog were generally positive, including some who suggested that time-shifting enabled them to see series such as *Moving On* despite being out during the day. One viewer stated: 'Not being around during the day, I tend to do my viewing via iPlayer, and I must say, that increasingly, some of the best programmes are coming from daytime TV' whilst another website reported that BARB statistics were now showing that '20% of all drama viewing is now time-shifted' (Knowledge Bulletin, 2011).

> In this context, it is at least worth noting that, whilst commissioners have remain focused primarily on the audience traditionally associated with the broadcast time slot, *Moving On* emerged at a time when the BBC showed signs of thinking of daytime drama in different ways. To an extent this is confirmed by the BBC's continuation of the trend through the commissioning of dramas such as the *The Indian Doctor* (BBC1, 2010–) and *32 Brinkburn Street* (BBC1, 2011–).

Moving On is not, though, entirely the product of the era of time-shifting. Employment (and unemployment) patterns have evolved in such a way as to disturb the settled idea of the daytime audience, and this is reflected both in the diversity of storylines in the series and in the kinds of talent that the programme attracted. Through a combination of McGovern's name being so firmly associated with *Moving On* and changing perceptions of the role of daytime drama the series has continued to be able to attract very high-profile actors, something which in turn makes the likelihood of an extended audience much greater. In Series 2 of *Moving On*, the fourth episode, 'Malaise', not only featured the actors John Simm and Ewan Bremner but was also directed by Dominic West, who had achieved international acclaim for his role as Jimmy McNulty in *The Wire* (HBO, 2002–8). In the context of the history of British daytime television this represented a remarkable collision of contemporary talent whose ability to attract roles both on television and feature films was decidedly undiminished.

Despite the casting and the production history of the director, 'Malaise' does not have the pretensions to be groundbreaking drama, but it clearly possesses more of a sense of moral ambiguity than is customary for daytime drama. Simm plays Moose, recently released from prison and keen to be reunited with Tina (Susan Lynch) and his daughter Jess (Olivia Poole). In a familiar trope, Tina is now living happily with Adam (Bremner), who is the antithesis of Simm. Adam works hard at a job he dislikes and is adored by Jess. At first Moose looks every inch the villain, trying to muscle his way back into a settled life and promising the earth on the money he is owed from criminal friends. Over time, though, a different story unravels and, recognising what is ultimately best for Tina in the long term, Adam not only walks away, but encourages Jess to accept her father back into her and her mother's life. The final shot sees Adam, a hooded, isolated figure, walking off into the distance. Neither writer nor director attempt to put an idealistic gloss onto Adam's sense of loss. Whilst there is happy ending for Tina, Moose and Jess, the blameless Adam is abandoned.

It would be unwise to make too great a set of claims for 'Malaise', but its level of ambition in terms of cast and director and the resultant playing-out of a narrative that is, in the context of daytime television, morally challenging, make it a real indicator of what *Moving On* was trying to do. Through McGovern's reputation, and his willingness to take a risk through involvement in a deeply unfashionable area of production, the series was able to make a significant contribution to a small, but perceptible shift in the television drama landscape.

Finally, it is also worth noting another clear motivation on McGovern's part that informed his role in the series. As we have already seen, particularly in relation to *The Street*, *Moving On* was not the first time that McGovern had used a popular format partly as a vehicle to bring on a team of less well-known writers. It was, however, the first time that he had worked in a purely supervisory role. His credit throughout *Moving On* is purely as an Executive Producer, with all the episodes being written by other writers. Some of the latter are those who have collaborated with McGovern before, such as Esther Wilson and Alice Nutter; others, such as Dale Overton, are new to collaborations involving McGovern, but experienced writers in some way or other. Overton's experience in fact had been overwhelmingly on other daytime dramas, suggesting that McGovern's involvement was, to some extent, an attempt to encourage an increase in ambition. For McGovern himself, there is a clear long-term commitment to developing writing talent, but in the case of *Moving On*, the home of the independent production company, LA Productions, was equally significant. Though always retaining his personal home in Liverpool, McGovern's most significant work up to the time of *Moving On* had frequently been based in Manchester. McGovern had even once remarked that he found it easier to work away from the intense scrutiny that he sometimes felt in his home city. Talking about The Street he said:

> It's actually set up here in Manchester but I had thoughts initially of a street off Kensington – that's Kensington, Merseyside NOT Kensington, London! But there are always problems on Merseyside because if you portray a character on screen who's a thief say, then you're compounding a stereotype. Our city is very sensitive about how Scousers are portrayed. So it's a lot easier to do it in Manchester. (McGovern, quoted in BBC, 2006b)

This 'burden of representation' is often referred to by writers who become very strongly identified with a place, in the way that McGovern has with Liverpool. However, *Moving On* seems to signal something of a change of attitude on McGovern's behalf, seeing it as a fresh opportunity to offer the chance of work to writers and production crew based on Merseyside. Before the series was produced McGovern gave an interview suggesting his pleasure at being back making programmes in his home city: 'Part of the attraction is that we'll be making the programmes in Liverpool, our home town, a city full of talent' (Holmwood, 2008). In another interview, whilst reiterating his point about the problems of portraying Liverpool, he suggests that *Moving On* was at least partly about remembering his own struggles to get a break as a writer in the 1980s and realising that, again, there was a recession with a similar lack of opportunity: 'Basically, we knew such a huge number of writers who weren't getting any work, particularly after the demise of Brookside. We knew the head of daytime drama, Liam Keelan, was a Scouser and he was looking for some good stuff to play Monday to Friday in the daytime.'

'Hybrid' forms 93

McGovern has shown enough times that he is at least part pragmatist, and one suspects that he would be the first to dismiss the idea that he would lend his name to a series in the spirit of pure philanthropy. However, by the time of *Moving On*, McGovern was a in a position to be extremely selective about the projects that he chose to work on. *Moving On* can then be seen, at least partly, in the same vein as, on the one hand, *Dockers*, in which McGovern worked to allow others to speak for themselves, and on the other *Hillsborough*, a project to which he felt an overwhelming obligation. One suspects also that there was a certain delight in challenging the idea that daytime drama could not be taken seriously, in the same way that he had previously offered challenges to generic conventions in both *Brookside* and *Cracker*. If, on the face of it, *Moving On* is much safer fare than the majority of McGovern's work, in the context of daytime television it deserves to be seen as altogether more groundbreaking and ambitious.

Accused (BBC1, 2010–)

Accused, the second series that McGovern developed with RSJ films (in which he is a partner) was, in many ways, his firmest step of all in the direction of a return to the out-and-out single drama. As we have seen above, all three series covered in this chapter involve episodes that are to greater and lesser extents single dramas, with the parts of *Moving On* only connected by a loose thematic thread. To a large extent *Accused* is structurally very similar to *Moving On*, but this time McGovern was able to return the single drama to the original Wednesday Play/Play for Today prime-time audience on BBC1, where single drama had become such an endangered species. In an interview, given a few years before *Accused*, Tony Garnett, perhaps the producer most closely associated with the great single dramas of the 1960s and 1970s, felt able to declare that 'what used to be the single play or single drama was pretty well dead by 1990' (cited in Lacey, 2007: 131). On the face of it, there has been little since to contest such a view, but to some extent in *The Street* and more fully in *Accused*, McGovern has managed to reintroduce the form on BBC1 in prime time, but in the guise of a linked series. The factors involved in such a coup and the way that these dramas both echoed and differed from the single plays of the so-called 'golden age' will be discussed below.

Accused saw McGovern return to an active writing role, though other writers are also involved in some of the episodes. The other writers in this case were, perhaps significantly, all people with whom McGovern had already collaborated, namely Danny Brocklehurst, Alice Nutter and Esther Wilson. Each of the other writers is credited as a co-writer with McGovern on one episode each. In short, *Accused* can be said to represent something of a return to a greater level of creative control for McGovern, though advance publicity for the Australian series that McGovern is working on at the time of writing suggests that this is not an irrevocable about-face.[5]

McGovern's own assertions about the unifying element of *Accused* can be seen as something of a statement about his current thinking around genre and his relationship at this stage of his career to popular television forms:

> In the time it takes to climb the steps of the court we tell the story of how the accused came to be there. We see the crime and we see the punishment. Nothing else. No police procedure, thanks very much, no coppers striding along corridors with coats flapping. Just crime and punishment – the two things that matter most in any crime drama. (BBC, 2010a)

McGovern's take on the crime or police series was never conventional, of course, and *Cracker* was itself a programme that pushed hard at the boundaries of the police procedural. Here though, McGovern seems impatient with the limitations and, as he sees it, tedium of the attempts at verisimilitude that traditionally surround police series. Far from being a whodunit or a show valorising expert detection, *Accused* tells us who did it in the opening moments and is instead interested in motivation and moral judgement. As an audience we are presented with enormously complex moral judgements to make and, if Christopher Eccleston's account is to be believed, such judgements are presented as so finely balanced as to leave even those in the cast of the episodes divided as to the correct 'verdict'. Eccleston appeared in the first episode of *Accused*, 'Willy's Story' (dir. David Blair), and was asked whether his character, Willy, should be seen as guilty of the crime of which he is accused, to which he replied 'By the letter of the law he should be ... But when we had the read-through there was a vote afterwards – should Willy be found innocent or guilty? The vote was split between those who wanted to send him down and those who wanted to set him free' (BBC, 2010a).

As well as the series being set largely outside the world of the police, it also avoids focusing on the habitual criminal. Just as *The Street* set out to place 'ordinary people in extraordinary circumstances', so *Accused* is built upon the idea of people caught up in a crime through choices they have made. Esther Wilson, who co-wrote Episode 5, 'Kenny's Story' (dir. David Blair, first broadcast on 13 December 2010), focuses on this and the resultant moral ambiguity as the heart of the appeal of the series:

'What I love about the idea is that it's not people who are gangsters, it's not people who are criminals or who live in that world and know the world of criminality,' she explains.

'It's ordinary people like you and me who through circumstance, or tragic circumstances, or something happening, they make a wrong choice, or the right choice that the law doesn't account for.

It's always morally ambiguous with Jimmy, that's the work he likes, he's quite philosophical in that way.' (Jones, 2010)

Wilson's enthusiastic description of *Accused*, together with the rarity of its ability to effectively provide space for the reintroduction of the single drama, draw attention to the enormous changes that had taken place in television since the heyday of the single play in the 1960s. Whilst it is undoubtedly true that McGovern retains a reputation for what most see as a broadly left-wing radicalism, *Accused* was only received as a 'political' series when Episode 2, 'Frankie's Story' (dir. David Blair, first broadcast on 22 November 2010), included a storyline about bullying in the army. The furore around 'Frankie's Story' will be discussed more fully below, but for the moment it is worth dwelling upon the way that *Accused*'s moral ambiguity, and the form it chooses to express that position, relate to debates about the traditional power of the single play on British television.

At one level *Accused* is a continuation of the tendency discussed in relation to *The Street* and described by Creeber (above), of all contemporary television drama to represent a new relationship between politics and the personal. On the other hand, the form of *Accused* is different. By making all six stories unconnected in time and space and linked only by their thematic concern with crime and punishment, McGovern moves even more firmly into the territory that raises questions about how far such personal, individual narratives can ever be seen as part of a wider political debate.

Strikingly, I think that *Accused* needs to be treated somewhat differently to *The Street*, because the greater freedom that McGovern has allowed himself and the other writers means that each individual episode has a different relationship to contemporary politics, particularly in relation to class, but also in a wider sense. *Accused*, appearing as it does just after the end of the deep disappointments of a long period of successive Labour governments (surely felt particularly bitterly by someone from McGovern's background), seems far less inclined to reflect the traditional oppositions of working-class realism, both in terms of form and content. Instead we seem to be offered an extension of McGovern's lifelong tendency to disturb our sense of easy judgement, not least of his own work and beliefs.

'Willy's Story' centres on a man who both possesses ultra-traditional McGovern tendencies – he gambles, smokes, drinks and is an uneasy Catholic – but also has qualities that make him difficult to like on most levels. For Rachel Cooke these were enough to make the drama too deeply flawed to be judged against McGovern's best work: 'McGovern supposedly specialises in decent Everyman figures, but this one was a bully, a loudmouth and a misogynist, and I felt no pity when he was sent down' (2010). As the rest of her piece indicates, Cooke's feelings about McGovern in general are at best ambiguous, so her judgement here needs to be seen in that context; nevertheless the character of Willy does demand a huge stretching of the audience's sympathies.

This is not, however, something which in itself is particularly inconsistent with McGovern's lifelong project. McGovern's 'heroes' – from Ricky Tomlinson's Bobby Grant through Robbie Coltrane's Fitz to Eccleston's Drew Mackenzie in *Hearts and Minds* – have all, to greater or lesser extents, tested the tolerance levels of most viewers, and Willy Houlihan as played by Eccleston is no exception. In fact, it is as if McGovern was determined to open the series with the kind of character that would deliberately fly in the face of any sense that *Accused* would be about working-class heroes who had fallen foul of a system of state justice consistently biased against them.

Willy Houlihan is, to begin with, more ambiguous in his class position than most of McGovern's central male characters. He is a plumber, but one who has clearly prospered over time and who lives in the kind of semi-detached house, complete with conservatory, that recalls *Brookside* days (though looming over the house are two gasholders, which act as kind of reminder of the precarious nature of the family's relative prosperity). Though McGovern is at pains to reveal Houlihan's aggressive opposition to Britain's involvement in the wars in Iraq and Afghanistan, his life looks somewhat like the prosperous lower-middle classes that supposedly brought Margaret Thatcher to power and who continued to preoccupy Blair's governments. Houlihan is a self-employed plumber whose successful business is derailed, not by his own profligacy, but by the bankruptcy of a major client.

If this makes Houlihan look more sinned against than sinning, McGovern also provides him with an impressive series of opportunities to demonstrate not just his frailties, but also his boorish contempt for the feelings of others. Near the start of the episode Houlihan is seen making a pact with his (much younger) lover that they will both tell their respective spouses that they are leaving them at the exact same moment. The precision and chilling banality of this arrangement is captured in telling McGovern fashion as Houlihan's lover, Michelle (Emma Stansfield), chooses the moment: '... half-six. When the woman says "Now it's time to join the BBC news teams where you are."' Houlihan seems to enter the pact with something approaching callousness but, in a moment of spectacular dramatic surprise, at around 6.29, Houlihan's daughter comes in with her boyfriend to announce that they are to marry.

This wrecking of Houlihan's plans by what seems to be malevolent fate is just the first of a series of similar moments in 'Willy's Story' that remind us of the interweaving of social realism and a storytelling that, in relation to *The Street*, McGovern himself likened to Thomas Hardy. Throwing himself into his daughter's wedding plans whilst postponing his flight with his lover (until the evening of the wedding!), Willy's testosterone-fuelled pride leads him to book an expensive venue and insist on paying for an expensive dinner for his future in-laws only to discover that his client's bankruptcy has left him with almost nothing.

The fable-like structure of the narrative becomes more and more overt as the episode proceeds. At one point Houlihan visits his bank manager to plead for some grace. He starts his plea with: 'There's this Western, I think it's a Western, I'm not sure. Anyway, there's this bloke who walks into a bank and asks for a loan ...'. After recounting the story he ends with: 'I know it's not Hollywood but ...', tailing off as he sees the bank manager's blank expression. In this moment McGovern's narrative technique is allowed to surface as we see the grim reality of Houlihan's situation played against the extraordinary events that are buffeting him. The obstacles that are put in front of him remind him of some the great popular myths of the twentieth century and he casts himself as the John Wayne-like anti-hero able to battle his way out with the use of his fists and his heart. Sadly, though, there are no happy endings and resolutions, as Willy discovers that any fragile status he has inside a bank in front of a man in a pinstripe suit are entirely dependent on his continuing prosperity.

Willy is undoubtedly unlucky, but in writing surely one of his least sentimental leading roles McGovern works very hard to make him repel us. This is most telling not so much in the deceptions and hubris of his long-term plans, but in the coldness and bullying that characterise his daily human transactions. He doesn't so much speak to his sons as bark at them; when he meets his in-laws he browbeats them with his tastes and opinions in a relentless onslaught that has his wife (Pooky Quesnel) dying from embarrassment, and even his sympathy for his lover's blackened eye (the result of telling her husband she is leaving) is expressed not through tenderness but by 'sorting him' with his fists. Willy's natural discourse is the relentless harangue, even when he is in a good mood, and even without trying hard he comes over as a bully.

As he has always done, McGovern then sets himself the challenge of engaging our sympathies for Houlihan whilst not asking us to forgive him his very obvious failings. I would argue that he and the director David Blair attempt this by an even more radical disruption of the realist base of the story than even those we have discussed in relation to *The Street*. This occurs in a number of ways, including the use of a score that is frequently highly emotive, camera angles which at one point show Houlihan as a tiny figure dominated by the tower blocks that he feels he has worked so hard to free himself from, but most of all through the appearance in the narrative of a priest who proved very divisive amongst critics. Houlihan encounters the priest when, at rock bottom, he is walking past the Catholic church where he and his wife were married. He decides to go inside for 'a bit of peace' and to make a deal with the God that he stopped believing in many years ago. Instead he is engaged in conversation by a sardonic priest who appears to know all about the background to his bargain and appears to promise Houlihan a way out of his troubles if only he gives up his mistress. For Rachel Cooke the appearance of the priest was a deep flaw in 'Willy's Story', commenting that 'you could practically see his halo' and going on to say that 'The thought occurs that McGovern, a cradle Catholic, is in the process of returning to the church, as cradle Catholics are often apt to do once liver spots begin appearing on their hands' (Cooke, 2010). In an otherwise more positive assessment Howard Male still identified McGovern's use of the priest as a mistake:

> This irritatingly cheery priest, whose uncanny instincts could only be credible if he were omnipresent, seemed a highly unlikely McGovern character ... He came across like cuddly Clarence the angel in *It's a Wonderful Life* as he smiled knowingly while telling Willy some home truths (and simultaneously pissing him off by inexplicably knowing about his mistress). (Male, 2010)

The appearance of the priest in 'Willy's Story' appears to be a heightened example of the way that McGovern's later work has approached questions of realism. It is perhaps significant, to begin with, that the credits list the character as 'Priest' (Rod Arthur) rather than by name, despite his involvement in a lengthy conversation and being identified by Willy as having officiated at his wedding. At the same time the lighting of the scene in the church is highly suggestive of a moment that is somehow out of time, perhaps even the product of Willy's fevered consciousness, though this is very definitely not made anything close to explicit. Finally, the priest makes other appearances in 'Willy's Story', all of which are at best ambiguous in their relationship to conventions of realism. The most telling of these is during the delivery of the verdict in the courtroom as the episode closes. Willy looks around the room at all those whose lives are being damaged by his actions and sees the priest sitting among them, though nobody else appears to acknowledge his presence.

Cooke's view that 'Willy's Story' is part of a rather hackneyed 'cradle Catholic' writer's return to the Church is surely too easy and somewhat simplistic. What is more credible is that Willy Houlihan is represented as a deeply flawed and passionate individual whose life tends to be structured around powerful mythologies that he struggles to negotiate. In some ways the most powerful of these is the least dramatic and centres on his faith that hard work will bring him and his family their just rewards. Just as the 1930s brought another Willy (Loman), Arthur Miller's 'Salesman', face to face with the reality of who has to pay when capitalism is in crisis, so 2010 confronts Willy Houlihan with his real place in the recession economy. Powerless to resist the economic forces that are about to ruin him (beyond smashing up some bathrooms that he has installed and will not be paid for), Willy's consciousness turns almost unwittingly to the myths that he was brought up on, first the heroic Westerns of his childhood and then the harsh, but sustaining morality of the Catholic Church. Willy's scene in the church is less about faith and more about desperation, and the priest functions at a similar level of reality to the gunslinging heroes that have helped form the way that Willy sees the world.

Ultimately it is probably futile to question just how 'realistic' the appearance of the priest is in 'Willy's Story'. This is a story that functions through the central character's consciousness in a number of ways and the ambiguity of the priest's status in such an aesthetic framework is part of the point. Moreover, the way that McGovern and David Blair have framed the key scene in the church is clearly designed to elevate the moment to a status that is mythical without the pretension of any kind of spiritual awakening.

Willy Houlihan, the ultimate control freak, is presented, like so many other McGovern characters, in the terrible throes of realising that his life is not in control. Late McGovern is undoubtedly more ambivalent about such control being wrested from working-class people solely by the forces of economic power, but they are undoubtedly still there and playing an enormously significant part. Also omnipresent, and perhaps more so in Willy's case than ever before, is human fallibility, expressed most powerfully through those appetites most designed to hurt others if indulged. In this context those brought up in the Catholic faith are bound to return at least to the ghostly traces of its teachings, though this is very different from 'returning to the church'.

Whilst McGovern has chosen, albeit playfully, to allude to Hardy in relation to his own writing, one review of 'Willy's Story' made another telling literary comparison: 'A man on the edge of total breakdown ends up bargaining with God. It is classic Graham Greene territory' (Chater, 2010). This is not the place to argue the very different relationship between Greene and his faith and McGovern's own spiritual position, but it is undeniable that both writers tap so powerfully into the hold that a Catholic education and upbringing have on the consciousness of those that receive it, especially at moments of crisis. In McGovern's late work we don't so much see a writer turning back to Catholicism, but rather someone who sees the residual power of lapsed faith in people's lives, especially in an age of profound disaffection with political certainty. A key McGovern theme is the powerlessness of ordinary people and 'Willy's Story' (and to some extent the whole *Accused* series) is a prime example of the way that such a feeling can lead to desperate measures that fatally compromise a moral code.

Before turning to the episode of *Accused* that attracted more press attention than the rest of the series put together, 'Frankie's Story' (dir. David Blair, first broadcast on 22 November 2010), it is worth reflecting on the way that the thematic concerns that have always preoccupied McGovern play out across this series of six single plays, in which, at least theoretically, he was as artistically free as he had ever been. To begin with, despite two of the stories centring on a female leading character, there is little doubt that the series is a profound, kaleidoscopic meditation on masculinity. In all six episodes a key part of the narrative revolves around a man's sense of his role as provider or protector being fatally compromised. In all cases there is a man who sees himself to a greater or lesser extent as a failure in such a role, something which leads the character to behave in ways that are ultimately very destructive.

Leaving aside 'Frankie's Story' for a moment, perhaps the most controversial and raw exploration of masculinity and its contemporary context was played out in the final episode of Series 1 of *Accused*. The story ostensibly focuses on Alison Wade (Naomie Harris), a teacher of children with learning disabilities whose husband David (Warren Browne) becomes the main carer for their two children because he is out of work. At first McGovern avoids the usual tropes of such commonplace stories, as David seems both content with and good at being a full-time parent. However, subsequent events suggest that beneath the relatively cosy domestic surface of their lives some extremely primitive feelings exist. They are revealed in relatively conventional fashion when Alison has a brief fling with a work colleague, producing a reaction in David that is shocking in its barbaric ferocity. David's rape of his wife is brutal enough, but his subsequent chilling observation that 'after battle there's always rape' completely shatters any remaining illusion that there may be substance to the attractive and well-lit surface of their relationship.

'Alison's Story' represents something of a return to an old McGovern battleground as David's old-school policeman father, Detective Sergeant George Wade (Tony Pitts), enters the fray. The territory of the conflict is all too clear as Wade stands on the doorstep of his small house towering over Alison, every inch the macho bully, but with the self-righteousness of white working-class anger behind him. First of all he uses that most reductive of contemporary terms of abuse of women, 'slag', and then follows it with an unsolicited diatribe about his views on contemporary gender politics: 'I grew up with women like you, always spouting about their rights, equality, feminism. Shall I tell you what I know about women like them? Give them the same rights as men and they start acting like men. Using, abusing, shagging.'

This is a clear echo of a common McGovern refrain, of course (see Chapter 1), and his suspicions about 'middle-class feminists' are well documented and discussed elsewhere in this book. However, just as the uneasy feeling that an act of rape is to be closely followed by a devastating verbal humiliation, he has Alison retort with, 'Must stop you reading that *Guardian*, George!' The script at once becomes both self-reflexive and restoring of some element of power to Alison. From here onwards, the narrative becomes perhaps the most conventional and police-procedural of all the episodes of *Accused* as George resorts to that age-old staple of wronged policemen, the planting of evidence, resulting in Alison being charged – somewhat unbelievably, given the way that the character is set up – with supplying Class A drugs.

Whilst the ending of 'Alison's Story' appears morally unambiguous, with Alison reunited with her children and George and David arrested for conspiring to pervert the course of justice, there remains, as is the case with all the 'villains' of the *Accused* stories, an invitation towards some trace of sympathy for two men whose fundamental masculine instincts have been unleashed by circumstances not of their making. The major portion of such sympathy is undoubtedly reserved for David, despite his brutal act. Before he rapes his wife you see a man terrified at the thought of losing Alison (in all senses – in one typical McGovern moment he fears that she has died in a train crash, whereas it transpires that she was not on the train at all because she was with her lover) and dedicated to the care of their children. Whilst his unemployment is a source of distress, the early sections of the episode show David working stoically and creating a caring environment for his children and his bewilderment when his wife deceives him is genuine. His character is made sympathetic to the point where his attack on his wife comes close to feeling like a slightly mechanical device. It is one of McGovern's missions as a writer to continually unsettle our easy moral assumptions, and this is clearly at play in 'Alison's Story', though this time its strategy is at least a little undermined by the introduction of rather thinly motivated behaviour.

In terms of its contribution to *Accused*'s take on contemporary masculinity, 'Alison's Story' certainly feels very bleak, and there is little to counterbalance the brutal resort to violence and coercion that are eventually practised by David and George. In comparison to some of the other episodes there is also a dependence on narrative devices that sit uncomfortably within a narrative approach that is closer to being realist than, say, 'Willy's Story'. To some extent it is unfair to judge a story centred on a woman on its representation of masculinity, but despite the convincing portrayal of Alison by Naomie Harris the episode does feel defined by what the threat posed by her independent behaviour unleashes in the men.

The other episode that focuses on a woman, 'Helen's Story' (dir. Richard Laxton, first broadcast on 29 November 2010), contains a more complex and ultimately sympathetic portrayal of male behaviour under extreme duress. Helen (Juliet Stevenson) and Frank (Peter Capaldi) lose their son in an accident at work. While Helen responds to the apparent incompetence of the workplace in ensuring her son's safety by vigorously pursuing the company in every way she can think of, Frank slowly disintegrates until they fight over what he sees as her inability to accept her son's death. Capaldi's portrayal of Frank is a wonderfully moving account of a man's sense of impotence in the face of the worst tragedy imaginable. He is finally set free by his wife's arrest for burning down the factory where her son works, after the Crown Prosecution Service refuses to pursue the company and a verdict of accidental death is returned in the Coroner's Court. As his wife's trial begins we first see Frank at home putting on clown make-up and clothes. It appears to be the act of a man on the edge of a breakdown until he charges into the courtroom declaring that the outfit is a protest against the 'joke' that is the legal system. Frank has discovered a kind of courage through his wife and, as he sits alone in the cell he has been taken to from the court, we hear him singing at the top of his voice, a poignant coda to a moment earlier in the episode when Helen asked him to sing to her, but he could manage only a few croaky bars before his voice failed him.

Not only is Frank a less conventional portrayal of masculinity, but 'Helen's Story' also retains the mixture of powerful, grounded realism coupled with the extraordinary and fantastical that is at the heart of McGovern's later work. As Frank walks to the court through a crowded shopping centre, dressed in full clown's outfit and make-up, he becomes a more potent visual symbol of rage, defiance and grief than any more conventional fist-waving father and husband could hope to be. At this moment what is already a powerful story of grief and injustice takes flight to another, almost mythical, level in a way that we already seen happen in a number of other instances from McGovern's late work. Frank's voice, singing 'Desperado', echoes down the corridors of the cells beneath the court and acts almost as a lament for all those in the series who have either sought justice, or who have become entangled in crime through the extremity of their situations.

In a way that undoubtedly unbalanced the critical coverage of the series overall, 'Frankie's Story' received more press attention than all five of the other episodes put together. In some ways this returned McGovern to the territory that he had so often relished in the past as a substantial element of the British establishment and the right-wing press turned on him for having the temerity to write such a story. As always, context is everything, and a large section of 'Frankie's Story' is set amongst British troops in Afghanistan at a moment when the political sensitivities surrounding Britain's part in the long-term occupation of the country were being compounded by reviews of defence spending, as well as the increased prominence of the sight of soldiers' coffins on their return to Britain being paraded through the streets of Wootton Bassett, a town in Wiltshire close to RAF Lyneham, the air base to which soldiers bodies were being repatriated at the time.

Despite these contextualising factors, the scale of the row surrounding 'Frankie's Story' was remarkable and, as many speculated at the time, was not entirely unrelated to McGovern having written another drama highly critical of the behaviour of the army in *Sunday*. The hostility of the coverage of 'Frankie's Story' appears to have been initiated by a piece in the normally uncontroversial *Radio Times* by Colonel Tim Collins, who retains a pivotal symbolic place in the British imaginations because of the coverage of his address to British troops during the build-up to the invasion of Iraq in 2003.[6] In an article before 'Frankie's Story' was broadcast, Collins alleged that the episode 'fails the soldiers on the front line', going on to say, 'Having served in the British army for 23 years I can unequivocally say this has absolutely no basis in reality ... There is no point to *Accused* except to try to shock' (BBC, 2010b). Collins's preview in a relatively low-key publication soon became a media 'event', with first General Sir Peter Wall, Chief of the General Staff, writing to the BBC's Director General, Mark Thompson, requesting that the programme be withdrawn (Adetunji, 2010) and then General Sir Richard Dannatt, a former Head of the Army, appearing on radio and television to denounce the programme and support Wall's call for it not to be shown. Dannatt's contribution was summarised on the British Forces News website as a forthright challenge to the BBC:

> General Dannatt told BBC Radio 4's Today programme: 'Accused portrayed bullying that has got no place in fact or fiction in the 21st century, it portrayed a warped loyalty that is completely unrecognisable in the Army.'
>
> Asked whether the BBC should treat the Army differently from other institutions in society in works of fiction, Gen Dannatt replied: 'You could make a case to say that, while the Army is conducting difficult and dangerous operations on behalf of the nation.'
>
> 'If this sort of thing continues, I worry about so-called public service broadcasting in this country. I think BBC1 has got a real issue it has got to deal with, and deal with it it must,' he said.

Significantly, Dannatt's attempt to attack the programme broadened into a debate about the role of the BBC and public service broadcasting at a moment when the BBC's vulnerability had been highlighted by the Coalition government's spending review and a draconian round of cuts in programme funding. It was, in short, a clear attempt to browbeat and intimidate the broadcaster, on the part of a figure who had officially retired from the military, but who remained an influential public figure.

To its credit the BBC did not waver in any way, though the manner in which Jana Bennett, BBC 'Director of Vision', chose to defend the programme was attacked by some as confusing the real issue. Bennett's intervention initially took the form of an interview on BBC Radio 4's *Today* programme, in the same edition that contained the interview with Dannatt referred to above and later reported in the *Guardian*:

> 'This isn't in any way a docudrama or a documentary, nor a campaigning piece,' Bennett said. 'It was a piece of fiction written about ... moral issues like loyalty, guilt and not being able to kill.'
>
> She added that audiences were able to distinguish between drama and factual programming. Bennett described the programme as 'thought-provoking' and said the six-part Accused series is 'a set of morality tales'. She said: 'It was a very extreme situation which I don't think purported to be docudrama.'

Whilst it is an understandable stance to defend the programme by reasserting its fictitious nature, there is also the wider question of the appropriateness, in a democracy, of a senior serving member of the armed forces putting pressure on a public service broadcaster to censor programme content that has nothing to do with questions of national interest. Predictably enough, Bennett's defence did nothing to defuse the row and instead gave sections of the tabloid press another reason to denounce the BBC in language that sometimes defies parody:

> She [Jana Bennett] is a characteristic specimen of the cosseted, woolly-thinking, metropolitan types running the BBC who have no notion of what it is to risk one's life as a soldier, and no understanding and little concern for those who are doing so. It appears not to have occurred to her that families of soldiers, or servicemen themselves, might be distressed by the drama – or, if it did, she doesn't care. But the sheer, callous irresponsibility of the BBC does take one's breath away. And also its double standards.
>
> It is fashionable in Leftist or liberal circles to oppose the wars in Iraq and Afghanistan, and so any drama that depicts those conflicts in a discreditable light can find itself on television even while our troops are still risking their lives. (Glover, 2010)

Interestingly, McGovern himself appears to have been upset by the criticism, not because he didn't stand by what the programme had to say, but because of the implication that his writing was critical, in a general sense, of the working-class men and women who make up the vast majority of the armed forces. Proving (in a way that McGovern himself would approve of) that the world is not a simple place, the right-wing *Daily Telegraph* was among those defending 'Frankie's Story' and who allowed McGovern space to defend his position on the army:

> 'I come from a part of the world and a socio-economic group that feeds the Army' he [McGovern] says. 'If our young men and women are going to die for it, then it's got to be a good reason. One definition of a just war is having an achievable aim. I don't think we have got that in Afghanistan. It's a war of retribution or a war of mad pique – it doesn't have a point where we can declare victory of defeat.' (Cumming, 2010)

A close examination of 'Frankie's Story' makes it entirely consistent with the idea that the army contains large numbers of brave and honourable people, but also that the demands made upon young men (especially) also have the capacity to unleash forces that can be brutally destructive. In this respect 'Frankie's Story' has much in common with 'Alison's Story', for all their differences in setting. Whilst David in the latter episode inhabits an entirely domestic world, he still unleashes rape as a weapon and, moreover, makes its military history as a weapon of oppression explicit. In 'Frankie's Story' Lance-Corporal Alan Buckley (Mackenzie Crook) believes that only utter humiliation and degradation are suitable deterrents to prevent others from following the example of one of his men, Peter MacShane (Ben Batt), who finds himself unable to cope with his first experience of being under enemy fire. MacShane is subjected to a relentless campaign of bullying and torture until he finally commits suicide in an incident that was an uncomfortable reminder of the real-life spate of suicides amongst young soldiers at the Deepcut barracks between 1995 and 2002.[7] There seems little doubt that the echo of the Deepcut incidents was another factor in the army's very defensive stance over the broadcast of 'Frankie's Story'.

Ultimately, 'Frankie's Story' has far less to say about the army itself (and still less about Afghanistan) than about *Accused*'s biggest preoccupation, which is with justice and its close relationship to human vulnerability. Apart from some brilliant exceptions that we have already discussed, that vulnerability is most often played out through working-class men becoming prey to their instincts in moments of great stress and pressure. In setting 'Frankie's Story' in Helmand Province in 2010 McGovern chose perhaps the most extreme example of that pressure imaginable, at least for those who have been brought up in the West.

There is a case for seeing Alan Buckley as the least redeemable of McGovern's creations in *Accused*. The casting of Crook in the role was brilliant in the way that it played against the well-established types that he had become internationally famous for in the British situation comedy *The Office* (BBC1/2 2001–03) and the feature-film series *Pirates of the Caribbean* (2003–). In 'Frankie's Story' Crook retained the slight, rather feeble physical appearance of both of these characters, but McGovern's writing created a terrifying, relentless bully capable of intimidating all those around him including, in subtle ways, his superiors. That such a character had Crook's natural appearance added to the disturbing impact. However McGovern is rarely, if ever, content to allow his audience to settle into unambiguous moral judgements and the narrative is partly about the extremes that a career soldier thinks are necessary in order to protect the reputation and discipline that he sees as being at the heart of his identity.

At the start of 'Frankie's Story' we see two young men, Peter and Frankie Nash (Benjamin Smith), join the army to avoid prison after a violent fight in a pub. They are both ill-disciplined and selfish and Buckley sees it as his job to make them into soldiers who will not let down the people that have to work with them. This is perhaps McGovern's glimmer of understanding for Buckley, whose very appearance reinforces the idea that without the status that the army has given him he would be nothing. This is an age-old story of working-class men, of course, and McGovern's remarks about the area he comes from being the one of the army's prime recruiting grounds is telling. He doesn't flinch from the horror of Buckley's actions and the eventual consequences, but he is prepared to acknowledge the logic of his motives.

Reflecting on the overall shape of *Accused* its most significant achievement remains, as I said at the start, to get as close as anyone has done for a considerable time to reintroduce a modified form of the single drama slot in prime time on BBC1. Though its ratings were modest for the channel, at the time of writing its second season has just begun filming, with a very strong cast including Anne-Marie Duff and Olivia Colman. Whilst McGovern himself saw *The Street*, to all intents and purposes as single drama, the increased freedom in terms of location and background afforded by *Accused* did result in a wider variety of thematic concerns and, to some extent, aesthetic approaches.

In terms of authorship McGovern's hand is firmly on all of the episodes of *Accused*, though it is important to recognise the joint authorship of some of the episodes, perhaps particularly that of the comparatively inexperienced Alice Nutter on the outstanding 'Helen's Story'.

There is little doubt that McGovern earned his out-and-out single-play slot through sheer bankability, a quality that has not cost him his right to cross swords with the establishment and, in his particular way, to take chances in terms of formal and narrative structures. This has partly, it must be acknowledged, been achieved through partnership and it is notable how McGovern's late career has involved tighter circles of collaboration. Most obviously this has resulted in the formation of RSJ films with Roxy Spencer and Sita Williams, but also the ever-more frequent use of David Blair as a director.

Finally it is worth discussing for a moment whether McGovern and his collaborators' achievement in carving out such precious territory in the schedules has resulted in a 'return' to the values of what some have glorified as a golden age of television drama. In some ways such a question misses the point and a more nuanced approach to the recent history of British television drama has begun to emerge. Prominent in publicising such an idea was a season run by the British Film Institute that opened in May 2010, entitled *Second Coming*. Without in any sense denigrating the work of the Play for Today generation in the 1960s and 1970s, this season sought to counter the myth that the decade up to 2010 had witnessed quality drama on British television only in the form of American imported series epitomised by *The Wire*. As the curator of the series, Mark Duguid put it:

> far from being an age of stagnation, the last decade has witnessed the maturation of a generation of dramatists every bit as talented as their 'golden age' forebears. Writers like Russell T. Davies, Paul Abbott, Jimmy McGovern, Guy Hibbert, Tony Marchant, Abi Morgan, Peter Moffat, Dominic Savage, Rowan Joffe, Donna Franceschild, William Ivory, Jed

Mercurio, Peter Bowker and Neil Biswas have all grown up with television and produced highly distinctive work that restlessly explores its possibilities (even if, yes, there is still too much unchallenging, formulaic work churned out by less able, less ambitious or, perhaps, more constrained writers). (Duguid, 2010b: 50)

The point here is not so much to engage in the kind of debate over value judgements that Duguid implies here, but rather to assess the importance of McGovern's role in carving out a particular space for television drama at a time when many critics remain pessimistic as to the seriousness of the broadcasters' commitment to all but the most 'bankable' of products. Among those who have signalled what some have seen as a dangerous slide towards mediocrity in the drama-commissioning process is one of the chief architects of the 'golden age', Tony Garnett, whose argument is referred to by Duguid later in the same article:

Last summer, in an email that ricocheted around the industry, esteemed television veteran Tony Garnett charged the BBC with 'stifling creativity' in drama writing. He painted a bleak picture of an organisation riddled with management consultants, in which power had migrated to the top of a tall pyramid, leaving hapless writers fending off 'totalitarian micro management' and reduced to 'executives' scribes'. Garnett's email eventually found its way into the broadsheets, where it usefully slotted into the prolonged BBC-under-siege narrative alongside Sachsgate, the salaries crises and the relentless Murdochian crusade.

The pressures may be real. But the more astute observers, including Garnett, recognise that whatever problems British television faces, it's not a deficit of writing talent – a point dangerously obscured in the less-nuanced debate in the press. I'd go further: what if, despite difficult circumstances, a new golden generation of writers had emerged but we were failing to notice it? (Duguid, 2010b: 50)

As Duguid notes, someone as steeped in television drama as Tony Garnett would never become over-romantic about the idea of a golden age and would be likely to understand that writing talent is present now as it ever was. The article then goes on to identify a surprising degree of optimism amongst at least some television writers who have seen an upsurge in commissions at what many still refer to as the 'quality' end of the market. There is less coverage, though, of the kind of spaces that McGovern has carved out, in different ways, through all three series covered in this chapter. McGovern is mentioned, but mainly as part of the introduction into the UK of the 'showrunning' concept, whereby a named writer works also as the Executive Producer on the series. It is however Russell T. Davies and his work on *Doctor Who* and *Torchwood* who is seen as the pioneer with the greatest success in this field.

I would like to argue that McGovern's work (and that of his collaborators) on the 'hybrid' series covered in this chapter has attempted something more radical still. Not only is his work firmly aimed at the large popular audience that many have now dismissed as too fragmented or else too preoccupied with reality television to consider watching demanding drama, but it has also created space for the one-off drama idea that lies outside the usual idea of 'showrunning'. Structurally this is most apparent on *Accused*, where the stories are connected only by the fact that we meet all the central characters in the dock at the start of a court case, though the episodes of *Moving On* are also linked only by a thematic device.

At the time of writing it is impossible to tell whether the kind of space that McGovern has managed to establish will be sustainable over time and transferable in different ways to other writers. He is unsure himself whether it is possible because the BBC and others have not yet grasped the investment that is needed at the 'front end', the writer:

> 'You end up subsidising independent production companies or maybe even the BBC,' he says, noting that the Americans devote a far larger proportion of the budget to scripts: 'The showrunning approach should be much more expensive than it is [treated as being in the UK], and the BBC have yet to grasp that nettle.' (Duguid, 2010b: 54)

Despite McGovern's formidable versatility and current power with commissioners the situation is clearly fragile. Even the press release announcing a second series of *Accused* made clear mention of the slightly disappointing ratings for the first series before going on to the usual process of talking up the excitement that was felt in anticipation of a second. This said, McGovern's most recent work has made clear inroads in the pursuit of excellence on the mainstream channels aimed at the largest kind of popular audience there is in the multi-channel age, and in so doing may just have signalled a direction for other writers who can see, as McGovern has always done, what an enormous privilege it is to write for a medium that can still reach the largest number of people that it is possible to address at any one time.

This chapter has sought to examine McGovern's most recent work, mainly from the perspective of the ways that they have tested the conventional boundaries between the television drama series and the single play and, in so doing, helped to re-establish a space for individual closed narratives within broad thematic frameworks of different kinds. Whilst this links McGovern's work with other pioneers of the 'flexi-narrative' such as Paul Abbott, his output has been sustained over a decade and through a number of variations.

It is through working within such hybrid forms that McGovern has been able to write in ways that also extend the boundaries of the social realist frame that is most commonly assumed to be his natural territory. In *The Street* and *Accused* a number of McGovern's narratives have drawn on suggestions of magic realism and fable whilst remaining, ultimately, grounded in a contemporary material reality. It is perhaps the hybrid form that has become McGovern's most natural territory, enabling him to work with the extended space of the television series alongside using the sharp focus of the single play and the fully developed central character.

Notes

1 Here Cooke is quoting from Potter (1994: 38).
2 The term flexi-narrative was coined by Robin Nelson (1997: 30–49) to describe what he saw as the emergence of new narrative forms in television drama. Such forms were characterised by a faster tempo and a more rapid editing style, but more significantly in this context by a tendency to include a number of different stories within episodes of a series and to move fluently between them. Some stories continue over a number of episodes, whilst others are concluded within a shorter time frame. Nelson's account traces the origins of flexi-narratives to American television of the 1970s and 1980s and attempts to write drama suited to what was perceived as a decreasing attention span amongst audiences. An example of a key American series of this type is *Hill Street Blues* (MTM/NBC 1980–87).
3 For an incisive account of how the Bulger case was used by politicians and the media in ways that went well beyond its immediate ramifications see Cohen, 2002.
4 For an account of the campaign to save BBC Radio 6 see www.guardian.co.uk/media/2010/mar/03/bbc-6-music-protest (accessed February 2012).
5 For a brief account of the collaborative nature of McGovern's Australian adventure with the working title of *Redfern Now* see www.tvtonight.com.au/2011/11/indigenous-jobs-on-redfern-now.html (accessed November 2011).
6 Lieutenant-Colonel Tim Collins became famous during the build-up to the 2003 Iraq conflict after a *Daily Mail* journalist recorded in shorthand a speech that he made to the 1st Battalion of the Royal Irish Regiment before they went into battle. For an account of the speech see the BBC news website at http://news.bbc.co.uk/1/hi/uk/2866581.stm (accessed November 2003).
7 The BBC News website contains the following sentence, which is a bald description of the facts of the Deepcut Barracks incidents: 'Geoff Gray, from Durham, Sean Benton, from Hastings, James Collinson, from Perth and Cheryl James, from Llangollen, north Wales, died from gunshot wounds at the Royal Logistics Corps HQ between 1995 and 2002.' For a fuller account and links to a range of opinion on the cases go to http://news.bbc.co.uk/1/hi/uk/3528839.stm (accessed November 2011).

Documentary and historical drama: *Hillsborough*, *Sunday*, *Dockers*, *Gunpowder, Treason and Plot*

3

In deciding how best to categorise some of Jimmy McGovern's work, one of the most difficult decisions related to *Gunpowder, Treason and Plot* (dir. Gilles Mackinnon, first broadcast on BBC2 on 14 and 21 March 2002). Structurally it resembles a miniseries, but with only two episodes, each two hours long, it does not provide the same kind of narrative space as most work of this kind for television. In other ways it has much in common with McGovern's single films. It has a recognised independent auteur as director in Gilles Mackinnon, who shot it using many of the stylistic conventions commonly employed by the contemporary historical epic. It uses a cast of recognised film actors, including some with international 'star' status, and it grew from an out-and-out film project on Mary, Queen of Scots, that McGovern had originally begun with BBC Northern Ireland.

However, something that McGovern himself was quoted as saying in the BBC press information seemed to offer the best sense of his approach to the combined stories of Mary and James I: 'I have written history before. *Sunday* was about Bloody Sunday in Derry in 1972. *Hillsborough* was about the 1989 football disaster and *Dockers* was about the Liverpool Docks' Dispute of the mid-Nineties.' For McGovern, then, *Gunpowder, Treason and Plot* was very much about finding the right storytelling approach to both engage an audience and get at what he came to see as the essential truths of an episode in British history that continued to have powerful contemporary resonances.

McGovern was, though, clearly aware of the essential differences as well as the similarities involved in writing *Gunpowder* in relation to the other three films that are considered in this chapter. Discussing his previous work on real events, he said:

> But the people affected by those events are still alive; so I did not dare to take any liberties with their stories. I could not impose clarity or

simplicity upon them. The truth, no matter how messy or complicated, had to be told.

Writing about the early Stuarts is much easier. They have been dead for 400 years. Nobody is going to get hurt by what I write. And nobody knows the truth ... There are some established facts, of course ... And where the facts are established, I have stuck to them ... But where there is room for embellishment, I have embellished. That is what a dramatist does. (BBC, 2006a)

McGovern's position on a dramatist's relationship to truth and 'facts' here has resonance, not just for the relationship between *Gunpowder* and the rest of his work, but for all his involvement in documentary drama. It is, of course, only appropriate to acknowledge the strong ethical stance that he has consistently taken up in relation to all three of the contemporary dramas discussed in this chapter, and it is understandable that for him this changes the imperatives behind what is included in a dramatist's account of real events. However, in trying to draw a distinction between his contemporary work and the historical epic that is *Gunpowder*, he has tended to obscure some of the very real questions that are common to all work that is based largely on 'real' events.

The first of these concerns the question of selection. Even given McGovern's very real and exhaustive engagement with the families of the victims of the Hillsborough tragedy, it is obvious that difficult choices have to be made about what can and cannot be included in a time-limited television drama. This includes choices about whose faces are seen, whose voices are heard and which parts of a tragedy that spans a number of years (and is still going on many years after the film was complete) are given the job of representing the whole on the screen. In other words, the creation of a narrative structure using a sequence of real events.

The second question is perhaps best encapsulated through the title of an Arts and Humanities Research Council Project run by the Department of Theatre, Film and Television at the University of Reading called 'Acting with Facts'. The project interviewed a large range of theatre, film and television actors about the process of portraying real people and concluded that there were significant differences for the actors, including what they often referred to as a sense of responsibility for what they were doing and also a stronger compulsion to research the role.[1] This was of course less so in relation to famous people, particularly historical figures, when the 'facts' are virtually always contested. Nevertheless, this idea of portraying a sequence of events that have a strong relationship to 'facts' or reality suggests both a continuum within McGovern's works that are included in this chapter, as well as important differences. This is particularly the case bearing in mind McGovern's remarks above, and also the series' clear links with the present, which will be discussed further below.

Finally, it is worth engaging for a moment with McGovern's use of the term 'embellishment'. As will be discussed further in relation to *Gunpowder,* there is one sense of the term that comes through clearly in the series' use of generic conventions and its apparent relish in the Grand Guignol dimension to the Tudor Court. However, McGovern implies a greater distinction between *Gunpowder* and his work in more conventional documentary drama. He suggests that in the latter he has been able to remain in some sense 'pure' in his approach to the stories that he attempts to tell and that the resultant works simply provide a window into the lives of those that are represented.

Given his approach to the work, no one would seriously doubt McGovern's ethical integrity in relation to *Hillsborough, Sunday* and *Dockers.* They are all models of their kind in the way that they work with the people who were available to tell the stories that form the core of the film. However, the very act of constructing dialogue and a narrative structure are of course themselves 'embellishment', albeit in a different sense than McGovern had in mind when he discussed *Gunpowder.*

The point here is not so much to rehearse some of the basic tenets about the representation of the real through drama, but to suggest that placing discussion of the apparently anomalous *Gunpowder* alongside that of more straightforwardly classifiable drama documentaries tends to help us make sense of what is a less-than-typical McGovern project. In addition, such a juxtaposition raises questions about the boundaries of a form that has, more than any other, brought McGovern at least some limited attention in academic work. That this should be the case amongst his formidable range of output is itself indicative of a need to examine the form, and McGovern's varied contribution to its history, particularly carefully.

Hillsborough (1996)

In one of McGovern's rare mentions in the authoritative academic studies of British television drama, Lez Cooke places *Hillsborough* (dir. Charles McDougall, first broadcast on ITV on 5 December 1996) 'in the campaigning tradition of *Cathy Come Home* and the more recent *Who Bombed Birmingham*' (2003: 172). Cooke's intention is not to imply equivalence in any formal or aesthetic between these three very different dramas, but rather to suggest that they were all primarily concerned with assisting campaigns of some kind, whether for broad social policy change or more specific legal cases.

In the case of *Hillsborough* there is ample evidence that the relationship between McGovern's impulse to write a drama about the events at the Hillsborough stadium on 15 April 1989 and a campaign to uncover the real truth of what happened and to get justice for its victims was a very direct one. In an article for the *Guardian,* some time after the film was broadcast, McGovern wrote very clearly about the genesis of the script as far as he was concerned and, in so doing, made a strong moral argument about the ethics of documentary drama as a form:

> A rule I stick to: you don't write drama-docs to further your career. You write them because the victims or their families have asked you to write them.
>
> In 1995, after the success of the film *Priest* and the drama series *Cracker,* I was one of the hottest writers around. I could have done anything. But the two women who had lost children in the Hillsborough football disaster turned up on my doorstep and asked me to write their story. I said yes. (McGovern, 2004)

McGovern's characteristically direct and personal 'rule' may not be literally practicable or desirable for even the most principled writers or film-makers, but the underlying point is a serious one and something which informed not only McGovern's impulse to write *Hillsborough* but also his approach to the necessary research:

> I began by interviewing the families of the dead in their homes. Long, gut-wrenching stuff. The more I heard about the lies and incompetence of the South Yorkshire police, the angrier I became. So angry, in fact, that I didn't trust myself to be fair to them. So we brought in Katy Jones, a *World in Action* veteran, as a factual producer.
>
> Jones checked every word I wrote, challenged every assertion I made, interviewed scores of independent witnesses and unearthed new evidence. The result, *Hillsborough,* was hailed by the families as an utterly truthful account of their experiences and even the South Yorkshire police, portrayed throughout the piece as the chief culprits, praised our accuracy and attention to detail. (McGovern, 2004)

Whilst there is absolutely no doubt about the integrity of both McGovern's approach and the final result, the idea of a factual producer becoming the arbiter of veracity does beg a number of questions about the relationship between drama and documentary, questions that have been at the heart of a number of controversies surrounding the documentary-drama form going back to at least the 1960s. In one of the most thorough accounts of the form in both the UK and the USA, Derek Paget frequently emphasises not the clear distinction between

Documentary and historical drama 115

drama and documentary, but their close relationship, a relationship that becomes vital to recognise in any sensible discussion of the documentary-drama form:

> All televisual forms and genres offer resemblances/explanations of elements in a society and culture, some of which are problematical. As well as offering a resemblance between what is depicted and some aspect of anterior reality dramadoc/docudrama offers an intertextual relationship between two forms that elsewhere are kept separate. The programmes, crucially, 'point towards' their anterior realities in an altogether more urgent way than either the contemporary drama or the history play of old. Additionally, we can see them as suggesting an equivalence between drama and documentary that is provocative in audience terms (asking, sub-textually, in what ways any drama can be 'documentary' and any documentary 'drama'). (Paget, 1998: 134)

The point is not to deny the importance of accuracy in McGovern's terms, but rather to emphasise the complexity of the relationship between dramatised and documentary versions of real events and, of course, between any constructed version for television and the event itself. What Paget very usefully suggests here is the power of documentary drama to raise 'sub-textually' key questions around ideas of truth and veracity and their relationship to any narrative form. In the case of *Hillsborough*, all of McGovern's and his collaborators' efforts to not only carefully research all the available evidence, but also to gain the trust of the victims, is vital in terms of making a programme that can be read as credible and ethical in its conception. However, there is also an argument to be made that an over-emphasis on the purity of its factual basis denies the reality of the way that documentary drama actually works. One review that was full of praise for McGovern's work still opened with the sentence 'Was *Hillsborough* (ITV) prejudiced? Did it matter? No' (Sutcliffe, 1996). Whilst one might quibble with the pejorative tone, it is hard to disagree with the key idea, which is that, as the review itself puts it, *Hillsborough* is 'a passionate piece of advocacy' and therefore highly selective in what it does and does not present on screen. This is not at all at odds with something that sets much store by accuracy and a commitment to the truth.

It is entirely understandable that McGovern should be more than usually particular, in interviews, to stress the care taken over the research behind *Hillsborough*. As a Liverpool citizen, a passionate fan of Liverpool Football Club and, most of all, as a writer whose work was so deeply rooted in working-class life in the city, it was inevitable that he would have approached any reference to the tragedy with the utmost respect, as well as personal passion. As we have already seen in Chapter

1, it was a thwarted desire to have *Brookside* make proper reference to the events at Hillsborough that, by his own account, partly led to McGovern leaving his job on the soap opera and to move on eventually to *Cracker*, where he would place the aftermath of the tragedy at the heart of one of the most powerful of the stories.

In important ways, then, events at Hillsborough had been central to the formation of McGovern as a writer and, probably, as an individual, making the writing of *Hillsborough* among the most directly personal of all his works. An article in *The New Statesman* written to coincide with the broadcast of a later work, *Sunday*, suggests that Hillsborough was a key political landmark for McGovern:

> It was the moment at which he [McGovern] realised that the hard left 'didn't care about us or our class. They hated us ... I firmly believe that if you say to people on the left, 'white working-class male', they picture a football supporter with a spanner in his hand about to riot. But if you say to me, 'working-class male', I think cultured trade unionists – not fine culture, but, you know books and music and internationalism ... White working-class males aren't a sexy cause to champion. (Hari, 2002)

Alongside his passionate championing of the Hillsborough victims' families McGovern also felt, then, that his work on the tragedy had the power to give voice in a wider sense to a class that had been abandoned, not only by the Conservative government in power at the time of Hillsborough, but also by elements on the left, at a time when the Labour Party was about to take power in Britain. In the case of the Hillsborough tragedy the need for a 'voice' had been made particularly acute by the fact that, in the immediate aftermath of the events, some sections of the media had reported them in such a grossly distorted way. This aroused feelings that were so strong that over twenty years later there remains an active boycott of the *Sun* newspaper in Liverpool. The *Sun*'s coverage was particularly resented because of its portrayal of the behaviour of the Liverpool supporters and the consequent initial attribution of blame for the 96 deaths that occurred to 'hooliganism'. On a website that at the time of writing is still dedicated to a boycott of the *Sun* there is a full account of the source of the continuing resentment of the coverage, something which fuelled McGovern's writing on both *Hillsborough* itself and 'To Be a Somebody', the *Cracker* episode centred on a Hillsborough 'survivor'. The account contains a reproduction of the headline and sub-headings from the *Sun*'s front page on Wednesday 19 April 1989, four days after the events at the FA Cup semi-final:

> The Truth.
> Some fans picked pockets of victims

Documentary and historical drama 117

> Some fans urinated on the brave cops
> Some fans beat up PC giving kiss of life. (http://dontbuythesun.co.uk/site/)

The website follows this account with an impassioned plea not to buy the newspaper for the following reasons:

> So just four days after their loved ones had died, four days after they had narrowly escaped death themselves, Liverpool supporters were confronted with those headlines. People actually believed those headlines. Those who were there did not believe the headlines of course, nor did those who knew people who had been there. Unfortunately though a lot of people did believe those headlines; people who were not Liverpool supporters, perhaps supporters of another team or people who did not follow football at all. The headlines sowed seeds in so many people's minds that the 96 supporters died at the hands of their own kind. All lies, all proven to be lies, yet never put right by that publication.

As discussed in Chapter 1, McGovern's idea for a *Brookside* story that was never made involved one of the characters becoming involved in the newspaper-boycott campaign and organizing public burnings of the *Sun*. His approach to *Hillsborough* is therefore undoubtedly strongly informed by the need to counter the kind of impression that had been created by the *Sun* (and to a lesser extent other sections of the media) at the time. The opening sequences of the drama are therefore dominated by the relative tranquillity and normality of the domestic lives of the three families chosen by McGovern to represent all of the victims of the tragedy. It is no accident that the families are all different, as one of the main complaints of the Hillsborough victims concerned the idea that all football fans were being categorised in the same way – an undifferentiated hooligan mass. Those depicted in the film are therefore seen as individuals, albeit as part of strong families with lives that are easy for the majority of the audience to identify with. They worry about work, squabble over minor domestic details and are united in their love of the game of football in general and Liverpool FC in particular.

It was a difficult decision for McGovern to adopt a dramatic approach that allowed only three families, the Hicks, Glovers and Spearitts, to occupy the screen for any significant proportion of the film's running time. To begin with it involved him in an agonising process of selection from a large group of people to who he had come to owe the strongest allegiance, something of which McGovern was acutely conscious:

> He was desperate to honour everybody's story. 'Awful things happen when a loved one dies en masse' he says, 'but one of the worst things is anonymity. I wanted to name as many people as possible. It ended up

a total mess. The first draft, nobody could make it out. I was arguing: "Don't cut a thing." The second draft, they were still in. The third one, I cut them out.' (Crampton, 1996)

In theory there are many ways to tell a story such as that of Hillsborough, and there is no particular inevitability about a narrative technique that focuses in depth on the emotional plight of three families out of the many affected. However, it is important to consider the context of the production, both in terms of McGovern's qualities as a writer and the position of the production company who offered him the commission. McGovern was approached to write the drama for good reason, namely because of the combination of his emotional relationship to the tragedy and his growing reputation as a hard-hitting, but also popular, television dramatist. Although he had written single dramas for the BBC his reputation had been made through work on *Brookside* and, more recently, *Cracker*, both series reliant on traditional virtues of strong storylines and fully developed characters. The programme was commissioned by ITV, the terrestrial network with the greatest need to appeal to a very broad audience. There was therefore an inherent requirement to build a narrative approach to the events around the structures of strong popular drama with characters developed to the point of clear identification.

The choice of the actual families that were significantly represented was, in part at least, determined by the kinds of roles that they originally played in the Hillsborough Family Support Group. Trevor Hicks (Christopher Eccleston) chaired the group and played a very prominent role in the early days of the campaign, whilst John Glover (Ricky Tomlinson) eventually became a prominent dissenting voice in relation to the tactics that the group employed. The third family that is extensively featured in *Hillsborough* is the Spearitts, who lost their son, Adam. The Spearitts were also strong voices in the Support Group and in addition were amongst those for whom the long-term impact of the trauma was to be the most painful. Eddie Spearitt (Mark Womack) is also the one character who features extensively in the film who actually survived the crush in the central 'pens' at the Leppings Lane end of the stadium, and is therefore a vital source of the way that the drama attempts to convey the events, of which more below.

If the choice of which families to portray was a difficult one for McGovern, so too was the way that they were represented, particularly in the period following the tragedy. On the whole McGovern treads very sensitively and lightly on a key issue that remains a source of conflict over twenty years after the events, namely, differences around the way that the families should conduct themselves in relation to the official processes that were under way to investigate the causes of the tragedy.

McGovern's film shows these differences surfacing relatively late in the film and in such a way as not to denigrate either side, but subsequent years revealed some bitter disputes between members of the Support Group, one consequence of which was the forming of the generally more outspoken and radical Hillsborough Justice Campaign. This is of course not the place to discuss these disputes in any detail, but the seeds of them were clearly of importance to McGovern's script in that they became one means of connecting the central tragedy of Hillsborough to a wider social frame of reference. The actor who played John Glover in *Hillsborough*, Ricky Tomlinson, helped Glover found the Justice Campaign[2] and, in a newspaper article ten years after the disaster, he clearly articulated what McGovern's film tends only to hint at:

> Tomlinson believes that the conflict is partly to do with class. 'I don't mean this in a derogatory sense, but people in the [Hillsborough] Support Group are mainly working class, and Trevor Hicks comes in with a collar and tie, he's a businessman, and immediately they think that whatever he says is right.' (Hattenstone and O'Sullivan, 1999)

The portrayal of Trevor Hicks in *Hillsborough* is a complex one and, whatever the rights and wrongs of subsequent events, the access that McGovern must have had to painful family testimony suggests a great deal of courage on Hicks's part. Under the strain of events Trevor Hicks and his wife, Jenni (Annabelle Apsion), separate, with Jenni becoming the first to criticise her husband's leadership of the family campaign as too respectful of authority. Later, especially near the end of the film, as the coroner records a verdict of accidental death on the victims, the split in the group becomes more open as the Glover and Spearitt families' anger spills out into open rage whilst Trevor Hicks looks on in despair at what he sees as the disintegration of a 'dignified' response. McGovern's script and Christopher Eccleston's performance as Trevor Hicks have to tread a fine line between hinting at a person perhaps too conscious of his place in 'respectable' society whilst also bravely and honestly working hard to seek the truth in the most demanding of all possible circumstances. At the time of the tragedy the Hicks family lived in Pinner, on the outskirts of London, and one marker of Trevor and Jenni's separation is her determination to move to Liverpool to be near the graves of her two daughters. It is a difference between the couple that symbolises some of the film's underlying tensions and which perhaps hints at the splits and conflicts between victims' families that were yet to come. For Trevor, his instinctive response to the devastating loss of two children is to try and remain rational and dignified in order not to allow the justice system any scope for the kinds of accusations that we have seen so graphically in the *Sun*'s reporting of the events. For many of the others, including his wife, this comes to seem cold and over-cautious, and their sense of naked class and regional prejudices leads them to respond far more emotionally. In terms of the drama this makes the late stages of *Hillsborough* agonising as McGovern makes what could have been very formal verbatim accounts of coroner's proceedings into scenes of grief-stricken chaos.

Though many have characterised *Hillsborough* as outspoken because of its unambiguous attribution of blame for the tragedy, there is also a strong case for suggesting that it is also amongst McGovern's most restrained pieces of writing. His closeness to the tragedy and desire to speak for the families in as honest a way as possible, within the institutional confines of popular television, resulted in a script that is frequently about denial. If Ricky Tomlinson's remarks about the role that class played in Trevor Hicks running of the Family Support Group are right, then one suspects that McGovern's instincts may possibly have drawn him into a more direct portrayal of the divisions in the group. However, whilst Eccleston's performance suggests a man ill at ease with open displays of emotion and therefore not always easy to empathise with or even like, his desire for dignity is portrayed as something more substantial than middle-class manners. He is seen as, above all, a 'doer' whose response to his awful loss is to look for constructive action rather than what he sees as the 'luxury' of open displays of feeling.

A moment near the start of the film is indicative of the economy with which McGovern and Eccleston create a portrait of Trevor Hicks, a man whose loss of two middle-class daughters was so much part of giving the lie to any myth of Hillsborough as a tragedy of drunken hooliganism. As the family walk to the stadium in bright sunshine on the morning of the match, Hicks, his wife and daughters exchange friendly banter over who amongst them should have the one ticket they have that is in a seated area. This develops into a light-hearted discussion of feminism, ending with Hicks threatening to buy the rest of his female-dominated household 'broomsticks', whilst they make noises suggesting the male chauvinist pig that he undoubtedly is. The tone, however, is anything but harsh and, as the group splits up to go their respective parts of the ground, the last time Trevor and Jenni will see their daughters alive, the overriding impression is of a man who might be something of an anachronism, a prisoner of class and history, but also essentially good. The representation of Trevor Hicks is an important and complex addition to McGovern's gallery of tortured masculinity.

The most important dimension to *Hillsborough*'s restraint, however, is in its approach to the details of the tragedy itself. Any film that centres around the violent deaths of large numbers of people has to face the

Documentary and historical drama   121

crucial problem of how to represent the details of such appalling events. In the case of *Hillsborough* this problem was still more acute because of the very recent nature of the tragedy and McGovern's personal relationship to the victims and their families. Also, although there is no evidence to suggest that this was the primary factor in this particular set of decisions, there was the question of finance. To create anything approaching a credible re-enactment of events would have required a budget well beyond what ITV were offering. However, there is little question that the handling of the tragedy itself was governed principally not by production constraints, but by ethical questions, questions which McGovern in fact turns to dramatic advantage. The latter is something that Lez Cooke comments upon when referring to the way that an advertising break happens just after Eddie Spearitt and his son Adam (Kevin Knapman) disappear down the dark tunnel that was to lead to Adam's death on the Leppings Lane end of the football stadium. Quoting from a *Guardian* review of *Hillsborough,* Cooke emphasises how both McGovern's moral sense and his experience of commercial television come together to sensitively handle a key moment in the film:

> When the first ad break arrived, halfway through the match-day narrative, it felt initially that the momentum, so carefully built up, had been destroyed. But McGovern was freeze-framing the action to consider the key moment in the disaster. After the break, an actor playing a father of one of the dead said to camera: 'All they had to do was close off the tunnel like they normally did and we would have all had to go round the sides into pens with plenty of space. They didn't. And we all went down that tunnel into two pens that were already chocker and no way out.' This device served both McGovern's didactic end of indicting the senior police officers responsible for crowd control that day, and denying us what perhaps we expected and feared – the dramatized representation of the crush against the defence. (Jeffries, 1996, quoted in Cooke, 2003: 173)

In some ways this account slightly underplays the handling of the moment. As Eddie and Adam make their way across the entrance to the ground they look slightly anxious for a moment, mainly at the length of time that it has taken to get into the stadium, but then a chant starts and Adam raises his hands, clapping and joining in. At this moment sombre music plays in over the chant and the screen gradually darkens, staying that way for longer than usual. The sense of what happened next is chillingly and economically conveyed.

As Stuart Jeffries's review goes on to suggest, the morality of McGovern's decisions to stay away from any representation of the events inside the spectator pen can usefully also be seen in the context of the way that the tabloid press covered the day. We have already discussed the much reviled *Sun* coverage, but a number of other papers, including the *Daily Mirror*, published photographs on their front pages the next day that could be called distasteful at best. By contrast, as Jeffries put it:

> McGovern ... insisted on the dignity of the dead. The drama didn't even attempt to represent the crush of bodies at the bottom of the Leppings Lane end in which 96 people died. It was an astute, deeply moral omission, one that should have governed tabloid picture editors' decisions on the days after the disaster. (Jeffries, 1996)

The restraint of the film is further reinforced by the film's use of a structuring device that involves the actors playing the main adult roles speaking direct to camera at key moments, such as the one involving Eddie Spearitt described above. These interludes punctuate the dramatic reconstruction of events either at the football ground, or, later, at the inquest. They are performed, in strong contrast to the highly charged dramatisation, as if the person is giving evidence in as cool and detached a manner as is possible, given the circumstances. This is of course the point, to put into the wider public consciousness evidence that would counteract the impression, given in the *Sun* and elsewhere, that Hillsborough was a tragedy caused by impatient, possibly drunken, football fans.

If *Hillsborough* became a drama of restraint in pursuit of credibility and truth for the victims and their families, McGovern was clearly conscious of what this had to mean for him as a particular kind of writer. Elsewhere in this volume I have discussed the heightened reality in which McGovern so often deals, even at times resorting to an almost operatic mode, but in the case of Hillsborough there is a sense that any writerly 'excess' has been sacrificed in the pursuit of respect, something that McGovern hints at here: 'It was never going to be creative. Usually, if I hit a problem, I use my imagination. Here: tough, that's the way it was.' There is almost a penitent tone here, one that in personal terms is entirely understandable, and a response that is entirely consistent with the way that McGovern discusses the meaning of the events elsewhere. However, the notion that the piece is neither creative nor the product of imagination is untenable, and typifies some of the problematic ways in which even the most effective writers are inclined to discuss the qualities of documentary-drama form.

Curiously, even though it achieved a very high profile and many have argued it was a key factor in the Home Secretary, Jack Straw's agreement to initiate a fresh review of evidence in 1997, the reception of *Hillsborough* was not particularly controversial. One simple reason for this was that the conclusions it drew were very close to the first official report on Hillsborough by Lord Justice Taylor first published in interim form in August 1989, only four months after the tragedy occurred. What had so angered and upset the victims' families after the publication of Taylor were subsequent decisions by the coroner and the Director of Public Prosecutions to treat the events as if no one was to blame. This in turn left a lingering idea in the public imagination that this remained a tragedy that was primarily the product of the behaviour of football fans. The Taylor report itself, by contrast, was relatively unambiguous in attributing blame to the actions of the police. This profound contradiction was exacerbated in the eyes of the families by the refusal of the South Yorkshire force to ever offer a full public apology and, in addition, to award high levels of stress-compensation payments to police officers when many of the victims' families were awarded only the most basic funeral expenses.

One further factor behind the almost universal praise for *Hillsborough* as a campaigning documentary drama was its relative fairness in dealing even with those seen as responsible. Whilst the senior police officer who gave the fateful orders, David Duckenfield (Maurice Roeves), is represented as cold and incompetent, even he is not treated with malice. Instead, as the chaos develops in the police control room, a close-up on Duckenfield shows a man out of his depth and desperately trying not to show it. As so often with a McGovern 'villain', the crime is not excused, but seen as all too human. As for the wider representation of the police, McGovern chooses to show us not only some acts of great compassion and even heroism on the part of young policemen, but also the sense of wide-eyed panic that is so reminiscent of the better depictions of ordinary men when faced with the chaos of battle. One young policeman, having been ordered to hurry and deal with a 'pitch invasion at the Liverpool end', draws his truncheon in eager anticipation of beating up 'a few Scousers' only to appear physically wounded when faced with the carnage he saw as he ran onto the football pitch. For a moment all he can do is stand and stare, paralysed with fear and horror, and the viewer is surely invited to empathise with him as well as those suffering all around him.

One exception to the almost universally strong critical reception of *Hillsborough* came, predictably enough, from A. A. Gill's account in *The Sunday Times*, which is loaded with what seems a peculiarly personal loathing not just of the programme, but of anyone such as McGovern who has the temerity to speak directly and powerfully on behalf of a group whose very existence becomes the subject of Gill's bile:

> *Hillsborough* was yet another mawkish hagiography of the cartoon Catholic Ulster-menschen of Liverpool. God's own unemployed, who are spat on and reviled by the mendacious Tory south. McGovern writes

from within a laager of self-imposed oppression and the archaic socialist rants of a dole-fed society, where all misfortune must be the establishment's fault and everyone has a right to be compensated for everything. (Gill, 1996)

Gill is, of course, writing in a newspaper owned by News International who also own the *Sun,* something which the writer fails to acknowledge anywhere in his hyperbole-ridden review. More than anything, though, the tone of the writing serves mainly to confirm one of the things that drove McGovern to write *Hillsborough* in the first place, something which Marcus Free explains in an article that discusses the relationship between Liverpool writers and Irish identity in Britain:

For McGovern the label 'Scouser' signifies birth in Liverpool, but also a cultural sensibility and sense of difference informed by Irish Catholicism. On the anti-Liverpool prejudice following the 1989 Hillsborough football disaster ... he remarked: 'even worse than being a white working-class male football fan was being a white working-class male football fan who happened to be a Scouser because we were not seen as English, we were seen as Irish and Celtic', a perception he confirms: 'it's there in my blood, in my genes, that Scouse thing, that Celtic thing'. (Free, 2011: 57)

If *Hillsborough* was a departure for McGovern in terms of working within the documentary drama form, it is also possible to see from the above that it was a departure entirely consistent with his recurrent preoccupations and moral framework as a writer. The fact that, this time, he was called upon to work with material from such recent history and concerning a cast of characters drawn from the community to which he belonged, inevitably lent the project a particular kind of urgency. As he indicates in the quotation above, it was an urgency informed by a sense that the events, tragic though they were in themselves, were part of a wider political landscape in Britain that had abandoned very large numbers of people of a kind that became easy targets for the likes of the *Sun* when the tragedy of Hillsborough happened, and for the likes of A. A. Gill when he attempted to offer an alternative.

This highly charged discourse around the identity of Liverpool has proved particularly enduring. A number of prominent politicians, including Jack Straw (Norton and Burrell, 1999) and Boris Johnson (Ruddock, 2007), have become entangled in controversy through remarks that have been perceived as trading on negative stereotypes of the city, including, in Johnson's case, reference to Hillsborough. The underlying causes of this are, in all probability, complex, but would certainly include the city's strong associations with, as McGovern puts it, 'that Celtic thing', as well as the city's role as a strong source of left-wing opposition to the Conservative government in the 1980s. In *Hillsborough*

Documentary and historical drama 125

McGovern confronts this discourse in a way that is probably more direct than anywhere else in his work, but, contrary to Gill's reductive implication above, the defence of Liverpool per se never became a recurrent theme, with McGovern often choosing to set his later work away from the city and the pressures he felt when cast as its representative. *Hillsborough* can, then, be seen as the apotheosis of McGovern's engagement with his home city in many ways, an engagement born out of what so many saw as a closing of establishment ranks, but also of an emerging recognition on McGovern's part that his new-found status as a writer enabled him to gain access to audiences, something which he could use in ways that had once been denied to him as part of the *Brookside* team.

Dockers (1999)

Employing a method that would eventually, in other forms, become a staple of his later career, during 1998 McGovern worked with the Scottish novelist and playwright, Irvine Welsh, to allow the story of the 1995–98 Liverpool dockers' dispute to be told for the most part by the striking men and their wives. The mechanism for this collaboration was a series of workshops, run by McGovern and Welsh under the auspices of the Worker's Educational Association, which itself became the subject of a Channel 4 documentary, *Writing the Wrongs* (first broadcast on Channel 4 on 11 July 1999).

Dockers itself (first broadcast on Channel 4 on 11 July 1999) was proposed to McGovern by Channel 4 as a documentary-drama project after he wrote an article in the *Observer* drawing attention to the longrunning industrial dispute. As McGovern himself suggested in *Writing the Wrongs*, he was unashamedly using his power as one of the most successful television writers in the country to draw attention to a dispute that had struggled to gain national attention. At the heart of McGovern's article are some of the reasons why the dispute was relatively invisible. First of all, 1997 was the year of the election of a Labour government for the first time since 1979. Not any Labour government of course, but the so-called 'New Labour' led by Tony Blair and determined to rid itself of its historical associations with industrial unrest. In McGovern's *Observer* article it is this sense of betrayal, both by New Labour and the trade-union leadership, that had aligned itself firmly with its values, that dominates, as indeed it came to dominate the documentary drama itself. Near the end of the piece McGovern adopts the rhetorical device of trying to understand why Bill Morris, then General Secretary of the Transport and General Workers Union, would not throw the Union's full weight behind the striking dockers and declare the dispute official. He imagines, he says, a 'cartoon':

> A rocket is launched into the sky. At the front sits Tony Blair. Behind him sit Bill Morris and the union bigwigs. Behind them, right at the tail-end sits the British working class. Energy is required. The booster rockets are fired and the main rocket climbs higher. An order is given to jettison stage one, now that it's served its purpose, and the working class tumble from the sky. But that doesn't bother Bill and his comrades; they are still hanging on to Tony for dear life. But what's this? More energy is needed. Booster rockets are fired again and stage two is jettisoned, taking Bill and his mates into oblivion. That only leaves Tony but that's OK because he's in orbit now. He doesn't care how he got there. And he's no idea where he's going. But he's up there, and that's what counts. (McGovern, 1997)

By the time of the next general election in 2001, and certainly by the time of the Iraq War in 2003, such attacks on Blair's Labour Party were far more commonplace. What made McGovern's stance in a mainstream broadsheet remarkable was its timing, less than six months after a general election celebrated famously to the tune of D-Ream's *Things Can Only Get Better*, and it was to be a stance that set the tone of the work that eventually led on *Dockers* itself.

Following the publication of the article, Channel 4 approached McGovern about a possible dramatisation of the story behind the dispute. Initially he refused, citing the extent of his other commitments, and suggested Irvine Welsh. By the time it became apparent that Welsh couldn't take on the project either, both men had been in contact with the writer's workshop attended by some of the Liverpool dockers and the idea to use the workshop to create the documentary drama was conceived, and eventually commissioned, by Channel 4.

Although it was born out of an element of expediency, the highly unorthodox (in broadcast television terms at least) method of writing *Dockers* was, in some ways, an extension of the ethical approach that McGovern had already taken when writing *Hillsborough* and which he was to use again on *Sunday*. In slightly different ways it was an approach that would eventually inform much of his later career as he began to work more and more as a writer–producer, often collaborating with new or inexperienced voices. There is no doubt, though, that *Dockers* was a much bolder step, involving as it did a group of people, not only new to writing in any form, but whose lives had been inextricably linked to the events that were to be dramatised. A group who, therefore, possessed an emotional relationship to the key events, something that many would argue made them incapable of taking part in the construction of

Documentary and historical drama 127

a documentary drama that would bear the weight of the scrutiny that it would inevitably come under.

The decision by Channel 4 to commission *Writing the Wrongs* alongside the main dramatisation provides a fascinating set of insights, not only into the writing of *Dockers* itself, but also to McGovern's own thinking about a range of problems that he has wrestled with as a writer throughout his career. In *Writing the Wrongs* we see him working through these, both with a number of the ex-dockers and, memorably, with a number of members of Women of the Waterfront, an organisation formed by some of the wives of the striking men during the dispute.

At one point one of the female members of the group protests quietly that the whole point of the endeavour had been 'to get over our point of view, not to dramatise' and, in a sense, that is an acute way of expressing not only McGovern's dilemma, but the dilemma of all writers of documentary drama. In the first of his two seminal studies of the form Derek Paget sounded a warning about the direction of some varieties of documentary drama, namely that 'while the discourse of factuality is helping to legitimate the fiction, issues are draining away into an exaggerated "human interest" which is ultimately unproductive' (1990: 87). In *Writing the Wrongs* we see numerous instances of McGovern gently negotiating the path between, on the one hand, saying what the fledgling writers understandably want to say to the world in the most straightforward way possible and, on the other, creating watchable, engaging drama.

From the start McGovern is at pains to emphasise structure, the need to find a form that can sustain the often arcane detail of a lengthy industrial dispute for a television audience, albeit at 10pm on Channel 4. Perhaps one of the surprising early decisions is to create fictional, composite families that approximate to some of the real people involved in the dispute, but who do not in any way function as direct representations. It is never articulated in *Writing the Wrongs*, but it seems likely that this was a necessary device to inject at least a little distance between the writing and the very raw events that were obviously still painful for a number of the workshop participants. Prominent in this respect is a key member of Women of the Waterfront, Sue Mitchell, who is seen a number of times passionate and close to tears as she remembers the ways in which key events impacted on her family.

Unlike *Hillsborough* and *Sunday*, then, where McGovern selected key real families as the main characters through which to retell history, here he guides his collaborators towards creating two principal fictional families which possess many of the characteristics of the real people prominent in the strike. The two families were given the fictional names of Walton and Macaulay. The fictional Waltons drew heavily upon the real-life Mitchell family and *Writing the Wrongs* shows Sue Mitchell and, to a lesser extent, her husband as active participants in the writing process itself. The relationship between the fictional Macaulays and any 'real' counterparts is, however, far less clear. This is for the simple reason that John Macaulay (Ricky Tomlinson) is a strike-breaker, a scab. *Writing the Wrongs* does not of course feature anybody from a scab family, as the workshops were set up to assist those who lost their livelihoods through the strike. The creation of the characters and scenes involving the crossing of picket lines and the consequent souring of relations between the main scab characters and his friends are therefore among the most contentious for the writers' group. Agonisingly and fascinatingly, we see the ex-dockers and their wives debate the morality of writing scenes for scabs at all, let alone ones that represented them as sympathetic human beings.

McGovern, on the other hand, in a way that is entirely consistent with all his work, insists that John Macaulay, 'Macca', be utterly credible and even sympathetic. It is one of the strengths of much of his work that he has always insisted not only on the humanity of his 'villains' but also on the fallibility of his 'heroes', and *Dockers* is no exception. In turn, *Writing the Wrongs* is entirely sympathetic in showing us why striking families could barely bring themselves to think sympathetically about a scab, whilst also demonstrating that, dramatically, McGovern is right.

In this context, of course, the casting of Tomlinson was vital. Even if the audience for *Dockers* were not aware of Tomlinson's past as a trade-union activist who had been imprisoned as one of the 'Shrewsbury Two', they would almost certainly have known him as Bobby Grant, fictional trade unionist in *Brookside* (see Chapter 1). In short, Tomlinson the actor had become synonymous with the representation of an old-fashioned trade-union activism which made a great contribution to making John Macaulay a real human being, rather than the pantomime villain that would have undermined the central drama of the strike. In *Writing the Wrongs*, though, we see McGovern the writer push his collaborators even further by creating a scene in which Macaulay confronts Tommy Walton (Ken Stott) with some powerful truths about the reality of their situation. Brought together for the first time since Macaulay's decision to cross the dockers' picket line, Walton confronts his former friend outside a wedding reception. Macaulay's response to the renewed attack is to point to the undeniable lack of support that the dock workers had in Britain at the time. To Walton's counter that they had 'international support' (there had been some remarkable gathering of support amongst dock workers across the world), Macaulay points to the miner's defeat in 1984, even with union support, mocking the way that middle-class 'pop singers and comedians' were the only ones really supporting the dockers, and ending with the devastating line: 'Working-class struggle is always sexy to them who haven't ever known it.' Walton, looking dazed, wanders off inside.

Of course, this is not the whole story. If he allows Macaulay the words to point out the awful truth of the situation, he also supervises a script in which his collaborators are allowed to create characters and scenes that show the ultimate importance of solidarity and staying true to your beliefs. Macaulay may have pragmatically carved out a little economic security, but his home life disintegrates as he loses the respect of his family and friends. Walton, on the other hand, grows as a human being. Through a number of conflicts and doubts about the strike, his relationship with his sons grows into something powerful until, in the final scene of the film, his eldest son Andy (Lee Ross) provides the only vindication that could mean anything for the men who kept faith in the dispute:

> I didn't want to believe in the things that you believed in. I thought you were a bit of a dinosaur, like. I just felt embarrassed by yer ... Dad, I was wrong. You've fought so hard for things, passed them on. I've lost them. But I'm going to get them back one day so I can pass them on. And it doesn't make me feel embarrassed, it makes me feel proud.

Equally importantly, and this is very much reflected through the participants in the writers' workshop as portrayed in *Writing the Wrongs*, is the way that *Dockers* dramatises the journey of those that founded Women of the Waterfront. Perhaps slightly unfortunately, one female character, Jean Walton (Chrissy Rock), is called upon to shoulder nearly all the burden of representing the way that the dispute politicised and changed the lives of a number of women that were married to the striking dockers. Nevertheless, it is a powerful journey that Jean makes, from acting the slightly disapproving mother-in-law when her son's wife, Paula (Christine Tremarco), leaves her child to go out to work, to tireless activism, including making speeches to gatherings of other trade unionists.

It is also a journey for Tommy who, in a scene that one imagines was bravely wrung from bitter experience, initially rails against his wife for becoming so involved and 'neglecting' her own husband. This is a story that became relatively familiar in Britain during the miners' strike of the 1980s, but it is no less powerful for that, and one suspects it is testament to the collaborative nature of the writing that it became a key part of the central narrative of *Dockers*. Given his history with what he has frequently characterised as middle-class feminist activists, this is sensitive territory for McGovern, too. He either writes, or allows one of his collaborators to write, a line for Tommy that is in retrospect a searingly honest self-indictment. Early in the dispute, seeing his wife transform into a valued and important activist, Tommy blurts out to her, 'You're like some hairy-arsed lesbian laying down the law'. To both their credits, though, this is just a transition moment, and by the end there is a sense of comradeship and pride between them at what they have both tried to achieve and the principles to which they have remained faithful.

If such an account is inclined to make *Dockers* seem an impossibly worthy and romantic account of working-class struggle, McGovern the writer never allows this to be the case. Throughout, we are reminded that the only reason the dockers still exist is because 'you can't move a dock'. As Jean Walton says in her speech, far from being the last vestige of old trade unionism, the Liverpool dock workers' dispute 'is the most modern dispute imaginable' because, in essence, it is about the fundamental casualisation of all labour in a Britain with some of the most restrictive anti-trade-union laws in Europe. This is a brutally realistic view of where real power lies in the age of globalisation.

More positively, as is nearly always the case with a McGovern script, it is also a vision of contemporary life shot through with the survival of the human spirit, often expressed through laughter and raucous celebration. As the Waltons watch a televised European football tie between Liverpool and Bergen, the Liverpool and England striker Robbie Fowler celebrates the goal he has just scored by lifting his shirt to reveal the distinctive T-shirt that was the widely recognised symbol of the docks dispute. The T-shirt was itself a piece of witty commentary, as it used the 'CK' symbol of the American fashion house, Calvin Klein, incorporated into the word 'DoCKers', and Fowler's gesture was widely celebrated as one of the few cases of high-profile publicity that the dispute ever attracted. The footballer's act duly attracted a fine from football's governing body, prompting Tommy Walton to observe, 'It's OK to advertise Nike and Reebok, but as soon as Robbie Fowler supports his own community he's in trouble', but the writers cannot resist a little partisan joke as a coda, as Andy Walton quips, 'We gave some T-shirts to the Everton players in case they scored a goal. I'm still waiting!'

From the man dressed as a nun ('I got the wrong fuckin' night!') who interrupts the intense conversation between Tommy Walton and John Macaulay in the Gents at the wedding reception, to the docker who quips to his work-shy friend, 'The last-time I saw any dirt on you was Ash Wednesday', the *Dockers* script is full of a humour and energy that tend to belie its intense focus on the fundamental theme of betrayal. This, too, is the tone of the workshops to which *Writing the Wrongs* allows us access, and which are dominated by the endless banter that goes back and forth between McGovern and his collaborators. In what is perhaps the most directly political of all his works, McGovern and his fellow writers elevate *Dockers* above the merely polemical by achieving what one critic called 'its complexity of tone' (Lawson, 1999). This is achieved not only by becoming what the same review called 'a play of debate', but through presenting us with characters who appeal to us through their sheer wit and exuberance, even when faced with the direst of circumstances.

A curiosity both of the press coverage of *Dockers* and of the insights provided by *Writing the Room* is that there is no mention at all of Ken Loach's documentary about the Liverpool dock workers' dispute, *The Flickering Flame* (BBC2, 1996). Loach's own description of his film perhaps provides some insight both into why this might be and also McGovern's approach to the idea of documentary drama. Comparing *The Flickering Flame* to his previous film, *The Big Flame* (1969), Loach said in an interview:

> The original film was written by Jim Allen at a time when the dock workers were immensely powerful – hence the title. The documentary was about how the last real dock workers were sacked and how their tasks were now being taken by agency workers, without skills, without the tradition and long history of the dockers. The recent film is addressed to what we are reduced to. It was a small film shot in 16mm. It may not be a good film, but the people are so amazing and heroic. (Ryan and Porton, 1998: 24)

Despite the mention of heroism, Loach's sense of his own film is overwhelmingly elegiac. Whilst it shares its central concern of casualisation with *Dockers*, its tone is significantly more detached and, however understandable this may be, full of a sense of defeat. McGovern's approach is, of course, already different by choosing, not only to create documentary drama, but to take this one stage further by creating a leading cast of fictional characters. In a sense this also liberates him and his collaborators to do something that an ostensibly more 'detached' documentary cannot, which is to focus on the humanity at the heart of the dispute. For many this, too, has its dangers, but as we have seen from McGovern's arguments within the workshops he led, this humanity has to be all-encompassing for it to be credible and, if this means some of the best lines reserved for the 'scab', then so be it. If anything, it is Loach's 'amazing and heroic' that suggests something of a gap between him and the people to whom he seeks to give voice.

Ultimately though, *Dockers* will be best remembered for the boldness of the working methods used to create its script. For this reason it is also most productively watched in tandem with *Writing the Wrongs*, something which the producers of the available DVD have recognised by putting them both together. Like much of McGovern's output, *Dockers* has been somewhat neglected, especially considering the high-profile partnership with Irvine Welsh, as well as the work with the members of the writers' group. At a time when arguments around participatory television have been so radically affected by the capacities of social networking and the internet, *Dockers* is likely to remain a rare example, certainly in mainstream British television, of participants being allowed to collaborate in the retelling of their own histories through the construction of narrative. As such it surely deserves greater attention, though it is important to acknowledge that the film was the subject of an unpublished paper by Karen Shepherdson, given at the conference held to mark the twenty-fifth anniversary of Channel 4.[3]

Whilst, to date, McGovern has not attempted (or been permitted to attempt) an exact repetition of such methods, his subsequent work has moved more and more towards collaboration with inexperienced writers in search of the kind of freshness that he has often bemoaned the lack of in British television drama. Aside from the power of what it had to say about the impact of a landmark industrial dispute and its implications for the direction of British politics, *Dockers* can, then, also be seen as an important stage in McGovern's sense of what could be achieved through working alongside other writers in a variety of contexts, something which continues to have a major impact on him right up to the time of writing.

Sunday (2002)

Despite the time gap between the events and the radically different social and political contexts, there are clear similarities and parallels between *Hillsborough* and McGovern's next documentary-drama project written by him alone, *Sunday*, first shown on Channel 4 on 28 January 2002, some six years after the screening of *Hillsborough*. Most obviously, both films belong firmly to the tradition of drama documentaries that take as their starting point a campaign to counteract some kind of injustice. Derek Paget quotes Ian McBride, a senior Granada Television executive who was involved in the commissioning of *Hillsborough*, among other programmes, in justification of the continuation of such a form as a key element of public service broadcasting:

> when conventional means of telling a story are denied – usually when the actual participants are either dead or dutifully dumb. The motivation of the 'heavy-duty' drama-documentary remains primarily journalistic,

and the dramatist brings to that an ability to tell a story which otherwise couldn't be anywhere near as effectively told on television. (Paget, 1998: 208)

Ironically, McGovern's commitment to use his dramatist's skills to make a powerful contribution to the continuing efforts to get to the truth behind the events in the Bogside district of Derry on Sunday 30 January 1972 was paralleled by another film being made on the same subject, but commissioned for ITV and written and directed by Paul Greengrass. Inevitably this has meant that the critical reception of both *Sunday* and Greengrass's *Bloody Sunday* (first broadcast on ITV on Sunday 20 January 2002) has been dominated by comparisons between the two. This has not been an entirely negative phenomenon, of course. The impact of both films being shown close to the thirtieth anniversary of the events resulted in high-profile coverage across the world and succeeded in further raising the profile of the continuing search for truth and justice in which campaigners were engaged. The different approaches of the two films also helped to raise important questions about the documentary-drama form and the choices inherent within its conventions, something that will be explored below. On the other hand, for both films, there was also the unwelcome distraction of a perceived competition, both to be shown first and for a share of the audience. Additionally some inevitably questioned the necessity of two films that dramatised the events, particularly when they were made and shown so close together.

A partial answer to such questions lies in the clear differences in approach that both films take. This is, undoubtedly, at least partly the product of their originators and their respective backgrounds. Whereas McGovern, despite *Hillsborough*, was very firmly a writer of fiction first and foremost, Paul Greengrass's formative experiences came as a journalist on Granada's *World in Action* (ITV, 1963–98) during the 1980s, including work on Ireland. By the time of the making of *Bloody Sunday*, however, Greengrass was developing a strong reputation as a director both of fiction and of high-profile drama documentaries, most notably the *The Murder of Stephen Lawrence* (1999). The end results cannot, of course, be simply attributed to their originators' backgrounds, but it is inescapable that Greengrass's film tends to be far more concerned with the public figures involved in the tragic events, particularly focusing on Ivan Cooper MP (James Nesbitt), a key figure in the civil rights movement in Northern Ireland in the late 1960s and 1970s. On the other hand, McGovern's film dramatised figures from the community, including some of the families whose members were victims of the tragedy.

A certain amount of contemporary critical opinion welcomed both films as complimentary and as important contributions to the ongoing debate about the significance of the events to the recent history of Northern Ireland. This was typified by Gareth McLean's review in the *Guardian* on the day after the screening of *Sunday*:

> Rather than view them as rivals for our attention, we should consider McGovern's and Greengrass's films as companions. Greengrass's communicated the awful panic of the day, its sensory assault dragging into the action with the irresistibility of a whirlwind, while McGovern's effort provided more rounded portraits of characters and a community, and more insight into the repercussions of the events of Bloody Sunday. (McLean, 2002)

However, there were also sharply critical views from elements within the British press, particularly those closest to the establishment. Even an unattributed *Guardian* feature a day after McLean's review above prefers McGovern's work as drama, but casts doubt on elements of its veracity:

> As in *Hillsborough*, McGovern's weakness is his definition of a fact. Scenes presenting the British soldiers in private are high drama but low documentary. But that essentially is the choice. Greengrass is the better journalist. McGovern the greater playwright. I prefer *Sunday* because it never tries to look or sound like what really happened, whereas *Bloody Sunday*, with its pseudo-news style, risks polluting the facts pool on the already blurry story of Northern Ireland. (*Guardian*, 2002: 13)

Such a view raises interesting questions, not just in relation to *Sunday*, but also the debates surrounding documentary drama as a form, particularly in the hands of a writer like McGovern. As the above quotation indicates, the critical disputes about the two films centred not only on the claims of each to veracity, but also their effectiveness as drama. The anonymous writer above suggests that McGovern's approach, though more emotive and less reliant on the re-creation of closely documented events, may be a better film because it never pretends that it is re-creating an external 'reality'. This almost certainly distorts and exaggerates the differences between the two films, but it does accurately reflect the fact that McGovern's film carries a much greater resemblance to what we are used to seeing as 'drama' on British television. For McGovern, this resemblance stems from what he sees as an ethical rather than aesthetic decision, a decision that he has been consistent about in all the contemporary documentary-drama work that he has been involved with, which is one concerning ownership of a story. In a rare, slightly testy, comparison between his own and Paul Greengrass's approach, McGovern makes clear what lay behind the way that he eventually chose to dramatise the events of Bloody Sunday:

Soon after *Dockers* went out, Gaslight Productions, a Derry-based company, asked me to write the story of *Bloody Sunday*. I had been asked before but always refused, arguing that it was a story that should be told by the Irish themselves. But this time I travelled over to Derry to meet a few of the bereaved families. It was then that I realised that Bloody Sunday was our story, too ... It was, I realised, a classic tragedy of colonial power ... I felt that as a son of the colonial power, I had every right to tell that story and so I began work. (McGovern, 2004)

At first glance, this sense of ownership, by dint of membership of an oppressive nation, seems a strange stance for McGovern to take. After all, by the same logic the story of Hillsborough could also have been owned by South Yorkshire Police, but, in the same article, McGovern goes on to make clear the other vital part of his ethical position:

I interviewed in their homes all the families of the dead, all bar three of the wounded, eyewitnesses and former IRA men. In Britain and Belfast, I interviewed British soldiers who were there on the day. More than 60 people in total; Katy Jones went on to interview 100 more ... Now I'm not attacking Paul Greengrass, a fine film-maker, when I say that he did not feel the need to interview the people whose story he was telling; he had adopted a different approach. Little wonder, therefore, that his film, *Bloody Sunday*, and ours, *Sunday*, were very different: his, loosely based on a book, focused on a politician trying to keep two warring factions apart; ours, based on personal testimony, focused on the people on whom a drama-doc should always focus: the victims and their families. (McGovern, 2004)

McGovern goes on to state, perhaps a little disingenuously, that he doesn't wish to criticise Greengrass's approach, despite apparent criticism from him of *Sunday*; nevertheless it is clear from this statement that McGovern's sense of the differences between the two films is rooted in political and ethical positions rather than purely aesthetic choices.

It is perhaps ironic, then, despite his very lengthy period of research, that McGovern would end up writing a script that would inevitably contain more invented dialogue and domestic incident than Greengrass's, by dint of its desire to paint a fuller picture of the Bogside community before and after the events of 30 January 1972. *Sunday* focuses for the most part on the Young family, two of whom, Leo and John, were on the civil rights march on Bloody Sunday only for John to become one of the 13 people shot dead by the British army. Through the Youngs, from the very first film in the scene, McGovern provides the audience with what he saw as the full context for the events of Bloody Sunday. This strategy is typified in many ways by the film's first spoken words, a voice-over by Leo Young (Ciaran McMenamin): 'The coalman gave me the job. I was grateful for it. Because this was Derry in '68. Britain was booming. Europe was booming. But Derry was on the dole.'

From the start, then, McGovern's film is not confined purely to the civil rights movement, but through focusing on ordinary individual members of the Catholic Bogside community he is able to include, to some extent, the social and economic realities of living in the minority community in Northern Ireland. This, in turn, becomes an important element in the balance of dramatic sympathy as the film gets closer to its central events. Immediately following on from Leo's words quoted above, his voice-over slams home the reality of campaigning for any change through a description of the way that Catholics were democratically discriminated against by describing the voting system in local elections. As the camera focuses on a man in a camel coat collecting rent from the street of terraced houses it is explained that he owns a company, something which in Derry in 1968 gave him six votes in local elections, rather than the one vote between the whole household of six Catholic adults occupied by the Duddy family.

Sunday is, therefore, never a film focused solely on the journalistic investigation of the shooting of civilians by the British army. McGovern's use of the voice of Leo Young as historical summariser of the social and political context of Northern Ireland from 1968 does open the film up to charges of didacticism, but equally, because of this opening contextualising scene, the drama that is to unfold looks less like the isolated tragedy that the long-running Saville Inquiry has made it and more like one of the many consequences of systematic social and political discrimination and all the attendant economic hardships that this brought about.

After an account of 1968 and the Northern Irish government's invocation of powers of internment, McGovern's film then turns its attention to the establishment of the lives of the main characters in the film, principally the Young family, but also a number of the other eventual victims. This sequence of scenes is highly reminiscent of *Hillsborough*. In both films the objective at the start seems to have been to counteract the predominant media mythology that has grown up around a group of people that are, essentially, victims of injustice. In *Sunday* the large Young family is seen as very close, teasing, fun-loving and respectful of 'Mammy' (Brid Brennan). Above all, what they are not are members of any paramilitary force, and the decision of John, Leo and Maura (Eva Birthistle) to join the civil rights march on Bloody Sunday is represented partly as a desire for good craic and partly as a response to the everyday injustices they experience as Catholics. In the DVD commentary on the film McGovern comments affectionately on a scene at a local dance where John's romantic aspirations are temporarily held back by his self-consciousness at the state of his old shoes. For McGovern these were his contemporaries, on the verge of adulthood, carefree, despite living with the daily restrictions that were part of life in Derry at the time, something which added great poignancy to the terrible events that were to take place such a short time later.

Whereas in *Hillsborough* McGovern began his film with scenes designed to rebuff the images of violent soccer hooligans, in *Sunday* we see young Catholic men and women enjoying their life rooted in the close Catholic families and communities in which they lived. The justification for such a narrative strategy was perhaps best illustrated in the discussion that Channel 4 screened immediately following the first screening of *Sunday*. The specialist panel included Sir Anthony Farrar-Hockley, who had been the Commander (Land Forces) of the British Army in Northern Ireland until 1971. Some way into the discussion Farrar-Hockley makes routine, casual reference to 'the hooligans' involved in the events of Bloody Sunday, something for which he is taken to task by Eammon McCann, whose books on the tragedy (see for example McCann, Shiels and Hannigan, 1992) are among the key sources of information for historians and journalists. McGovern's opening to *Sunday* and, to some extent his approach to the whole film was, then, powerfully motivated by a desire to rebalance what he saw as a fundamental misreading of the events of Bloody Sunday in the British media as a battle between paramilitaries and the British army. Instead, from the start, the narrative focus is very much upon the ordinary working-class families of Derry on the one hand and, on the other, a smaller number of scenes involving either members of the parachute regiment or senior members of the British establishment, including the then Prime Minister Edward Heath (Corin Redgrave).

McGovern's approach and, in particular, his imagining of the private conversations of soldiers and members of the government, brought a great deal of press criticism. Comparing McGovern's and Greengrass's films, this reviewer accuses the former of a lack of trust in an audience to make up its own mind:

> McGovern ... placed less faith in the viewer's sensibilities: so we sat through slightly clichéd footage of Catholic families going about their daily lives before the shootings, and struggling with their grief afterwards. By contrast with their simple, heartfelt language, the soldiers showed a disturbing tendency to speak in Pinteresque staccato: 'Can't wait for it. The enemy. Face to face. Can't wait for it.' ... *Bloody Sunday* told you what you could think: *Sunday* only told you what you should think. (Hanks, 2002)

Whilst there is little doubt that McGovern's intentions were polemical and that the film had an explicit aim, which was to set the record straight after the gross distortions of the original Widgery Inquiry (now widely discredited, even amongst most members of the British establishment), it seems a distortion to represent the complexity of his narrative in such crude terms. It is hard indeed to accept the idea that the representation of the families consisted of clichés, particularly when, by all accounts, the research process became so intimately involved with the Derry community. McGovern also seeks to remedy such a potential pitfall by focusing so closely on the Young family rather than seek to cover so wide a range of people that any glimpses of characters would almost inevitably result in a very shallow portrayal. The character of Leo Young in particular is particularly complex and intimately related to the struggles and debates amongst the Catholic community at the time. At the film's start we see him entirely concerned with jobs, economic security and a young family, but like so many others he is politicised by the events of Bloody Sunday and, at the end, we are never quite sure whether he has gone through with joining the Provisional IRA along with the others in the queue a few days after the event.

Maura Young, too, is played as a sharp, intelligent young woman, more than capable of bantering with her male siblings and putting them in their place when they need it. Her slightly feisty robust character becomes a powerful dramatic conduit for the grief of the community when she crumbles at the news of her brother John's death. By the end of the film her attitudes to the British, and to the conflict in general, have hardened considerably and she is horrified by her mother's ability to forgive the anonymous soldier who murdered her brother John. This disagreement between mother and daughter exemplifies McGovern's dramatisation of the profound impact on the younger generation of Catholics whose lives became, in many ways, defined by the events of Bloody Sunday.

In terms of McGovern's representation of the paratroopers that were sent into the Bogside on Bloody Sunday there is little doubt that he courts controversy much more directly than Paul Greengrass. Before the events of the day unfold, McGovern presents the men as more unhinged by the prospect of battle than Greengrass does, more at the edge of control with talk of revenge on the 'Fenian bastards' who had caused such difficulties in their lives and the lives of their comrades. Most controversial of all, though, is a scene after the shootings in which the paratroopers are seen back at their barracks, drinking and boasting. Their antics and grotesque banter ('What's up with them?', one asks ironically, 'Can't they take a fucking joke?') are intercut with scenes of families at hospitals discovering their dead and injured. For a moment it is impossible not to feel that the representation of the paratroopers has been ratcheted up to the point of parody, but, even here, McGovern's customary nose for complexity shows us the young soldier whose ammunition count shows that he didn't fire a shot. Nothing is spelt out at this stage, but the body language of his compatriots shows their suspicion and resentment that one of their number is laying claim to any kind of moral superiority in the heat of battle.

McGovern's most unambiguous scorn is, however, reserved for the top of the hierarchy that he has explicitly stated he thinks responsible for the events of Bloody Sunday, an opinion that he says was formed during the exhaustive period of research before he wrote the script for *Sunday*:

> Mr McGovern went into the project believing that individual members of the Parachute Regiment were to blame for Bloody Sunday. 'I no longer think that', he said. 'I think that the blame probably lies in Stormont and at 10 Downing Street. An army that is not controlled by its political masters is no longer an army. It's a rabble. And the Parachute Regiment is no rabble.' (Joseph, 2002)

On the *Sunday* DVD commentary McGovern extends this critique outwards to embrace the idea of Bloody Sunday as a 'colonial tragedy', a story tragically owned by all the British and one that was played out again in the 2000s in Iraq and Afghanistan. In the *Sunday* script one of the results of this shift in McGovern's view is a chilling scene between Edward Heath, Lord Hailsham (Oliver Ford-Davies) and Lord Widgery (Michael Byrne), who was to preside over the ill-fated first Inquiry. Heath and Widgery are seen drawing ominously restrictive boundaries around the parameters of the Inquiry, with the government's intentions made explicit in Heath's final words to Widgery to the effect that the war in Northern Ireland was as much about propaganda as it was about military action.

McGovern's long-term collaborator Christopher Eccleston is also pressed into service to play Major-General Robert Ford, the Commander of Land Forces in Northern Ireland at the time. Eccleston's portrayal is icy and includes an early scene of Ford dictating a memorandum to his superiors back in London, which includes the view that any solution to the ongoing rioting and violence in 'Londonderry' had to include some selective civilian deaths ('after due warning has been given'). Compared to the portrayal by Tim Pigott-Smith in Greengrass's film, Eccleston seems an uneasy loner, always tense with the effort of remaining fully in control. His evidence before Widgery, however, is a masterpiece of deception, a deception that McGovern's script suggests may even have included himself.

Whilst welcoming both the films about Bloody Sunday that were screened on British television in January 2002, Richard Kelly expresses a wish that both Greengrass and McGovern had adopted a somewhat different approach:

> It is possible to admire both the Greengrass and McGovern films while feeling somewhat exhausted by their cumulative effect. You wait thirty years for a Bloody Sunday movie and then two come along at once ... It's (almost) enough to make one wish that Brecht's celebrated device of *Verfremdungseffekt* still enjoyed some currency among our political dramatists: that historical episodes selected for dramatic re-enactment might occasionally be illuminated as pure dialectic, without so much recourse to the conventional carpentry of plot and character to engage our emotions and pique our curiosity. (Kelly, 2002: 75–6)

Whilst few others put it this way, and even fewer expressed similar feelings about Greengrass's film, it is undoubtedly true, as we have seen, that many were highly critical of McGovern's decision to not simply ignore any Brechtian notions, but to come down unreservedly in favour of an approach that placed the emotional impact of Bloody Sunday on families at the heart of his script. Amongst the many criticisms, though, there are also robust defences of such an approach – an approach, given his track record, that was always likely to have been favoured by a dramatist as committed and passionate as McGovern. Richard Kilborn makes one such defence himself and, in so doing, quotes from David Edgar, himself a powerful political dramatist and long-time advocate of documentary drama as a means of accessing different kinds of 'truths':

> The claim being made for Drama Documentaries is that they provide a different kind of access compared to other types of programming. The use of dramatising techniques enables different level of understanding of events, as audiences become emotionally positioned vis-à-vis the characters on whom attention is focused ... As such Drama Documentaries can have an important revealing function in that they point up the role played by personal aspirations or fears in the unfolding of a chain of public events. As David Edgar has commented: ... The dramatic power of drama-documentary lies in its capacity to show us not that certain events occurred (the headlines can do that) or even, perhaps, why they occurred (for such information we can go to the weekly magazines or the history books), but how they occurred: how recognizable human beings rule, fight, judge, meet, negotiate, suppress and overthrow. (Kilborn, 1994: 64)

Edgar's words, in particular, are highly relevant, not just to *Sunday*, but to McGovern's approach to documentary drama in general. His approach, particularly in *Hillsborough* and *Sunday*, is to use his dramatist's instincts and skills to root the drama in characters as real and vivid as he can make them. He does not write saints, far from it, but he writes human beings who are designed to provoke empathy and therefore to have audiences listen to their versions of events. In some ways, then, as I suggested in relation to *Hillsborough*, it is ironic, if understandable, that he should be so insistent on 'facts' and 'accuracy'. As John Corner suggests, *Sunday* (and *Bloody Sunday*) 'ran the risk, in the pre- and post-publicity, of under-recognising the degree of artifice involved in their construction' (2004: 201–2), something which is emphasised again and again on the fascinating commentary on the DVD version of *Sunday*. At a key moment McGovern himself says, 'This allows us to go into the flashback of the killings and every single one we have multi-witnesses for. Do not accuse us of being partisan at this moment, because, you know, we can show you all the statements, play you all the recordings.' Again, given the barrage of accusation rained against him, McGovern's stance is entirely understandable, though, arguably, his view somewhat distorts the reality of working within the documentary-drama form.

In addition, in McGovern's case, the 'artifice' referred to by Corner above was not only about the fleshing-out of character and the partial invention of extended lives, but also the representation of the central dramatic events themselves. Entirely appropriately, he presents the events in fragmented ways, disrupting any idea of neat linear memories whilst at the same time leaving us in no doubt that the total impression that he creates is a verifiable truth. Bravely, he and the director, Charles McDougall, choose to present most of the shootings twice, once in linear narrative time and then again in counterpoint to the witness testimony at the Widgery Inquiry. The lead into this 'flashback' (referred to by McGovern above) is one of the most interesting and contentious elements in the whole film, as it centres on an interview given to McGovern by 'Para 027' (Kenny Doughty). Para 027 was, according to *Sunday*, the dissenting military witness whose written evidence led to him not being called by Widgery. By cutting from a close-up of Para 027's face after being told that he wouldn't give evidence, the film implies that it is his unheard testimony that is the source of the much more brutal and systematic version of the killings that we are then shown. Unlike Greengrass, it is at this point that McGovern is prepared to write a version that shows calculated, systematic slaughter of unarmed civilians of all ages, including one scene where a soldier fires from the hip at a huddled crowd trying to make their escape, something which brought him more criticism than almost anything else.

June 2010 finally saw the publication of the Saville report on the events of Bloody Sunday that had been commissioned by the UK Labour government in 1998. Given McGovern's portrayal of the role of Edward

Heath, it was a supreme irony that it fell to the relatively new Conservative Prime Minister David Cameron to not only announce the findings of Saville, but to offer an unequivocal apology to the families and to the people of Derry some 38 years after Bloody Sunday. Whether this represents total vindication of McGovern's much more hard-hitting dramatic reconstruction of events is, I suppose, still open to some debate. However, Saville did remove much doubt as to the responsibility for Bloody Sunday from the minds of all but the most resistant. In David Cameron's words, the shootings were 'both unjustified and unjustifiable', with his speech in the House of Commons going on to detail the loss of discipline and control on the part of the soldiers as being behind the loss of life. Moreover, any question of any of those who died being armed or a threat of any kind to the soldiers was removed once and for all.

There is no evidence of McGovern's personal reaction to the publication of Saville, suggesting that he felt that he had said all that he had to say in *Sunday* and in subsequent interviews. Certainly he has seemed very reluctant, as we have seen above, to even engage in debate over the relative merits of the versions of the events as presented by his own film and that of Paul Greengrass. He must, though, surely have felt a twinge of vindication when *The Guardian* used the findings of Saville as a way of defending both McGovern's 'Frankie's Story' from the *Accused* series and *Sunday* itself. As was discussed in Chapter 2, 'Frankie's Story' was heavily criticised, particularly by senior military personnel, for its portrayal of young soldiers serving in Afghanistan. In response, the *Guardian* took the relatively unusual step of defending the programme, not in its arts pages, but in a leader column:

> McGovern got the same treatment for his drama about Bloody Sunday, which was also accused of being one-sided, selective with the facts, and over the top in its depiction of violence. Eamonn McCann, one of the organisers of the civil rights protest, wrote at the time of the film's first screening that the hostility to it – and to another television drama on the same events by Paul Greengrass – arose not from concern for the truth, but from an unwillingness to acknowledge it. After the findings of the Saville inquiry few would now say that McGovern's drama *Sunday* was particularly overstated. Those events are long gone, but the war in Afghanistan will drag on for some time. Do we have to wait three decades before it creates drama that is challenging to watch? McGovern should be applauded and defended from the charge that he is being unpatriotic. (*Guardian*, 17 November 2010: 34)

As has been argued above, the placing of undue emphasis on precise veracity is a clear problem for any writer of drama documentaries and,

Documentary and historical drama   143

potentially, one that can undermine the case for the importance of the form itself. However, for a writer of McGovern's powerful ethical and political impulses, someone who has formed a series of close relationships with the subjects of his work in this form, a verdict such as this would undoubtedly be very important. McGovern did not have to wait as long as the victims of Bloody Sunday for public vindication, but it was still some eight years after *Sunday* was broadcast before the publication of anything like such a clear defence of his particular method in an established, nationally read source. It must have felt particularly sweet after the often vitriolic charges of pro-Republican bias and, in particular, criticism of his use of a narrative approach that, it was constantly argued, was so much less 'dispassionate' than that used by Greengrass.

Gunpowder, Treason and Plot

As suggested above, *Gunpowder* could just as easily have ended up as a feature-film project and, in many ways, its production conditions suggest that its final form as a two-part television miniseries belie its creators' original cinematic ambitions. Filmed on location in Romania in order to stretch the budget, the production has all the visual trappings of a cinematic historical epic, complete with castles and sweeping 'Scottish' landscapes (these are an important part of the narrative thread, especially in the first part concerning the 'French' Mary coming to rule over the protestant Scots).

Accounts of the production process also suggest a textbook example of the thinking behind much British feature-film production of the period, whereby shooting would take place in one of a group of former Eastern-bloc countries to take advantage both of cheap labour and facilities as well as landscapes less touched by post-industrial inconveniences. One journalist in full colonial mode describes a visit to Mogosoia Castle: 'we pass higgledy-piggledy haystacks, an old man with a herd of goats, and a number of farmers driving ancient horse-drawn carts with their wives bobbling uncomfortably in the back', before going on to marvel at how far the production's budget would stretch in Romania as opposed to the UK: 'From Mogosoia we move to the nearby Media Pros Studios, built in the Fifties to a Soviet blueprint and recently refurbished. On the 26-acre lot, sets are being hammered together on a scale unimaginable in Britain, where standby carpenters cost £300 a day as opposed to \$6' (Gardner, 2004).

The budget of £4.5 million, an authentic film director attached in the shape of MacKinnon and the use of full-blown sound stages at the Romanian studios all suggest a cinematic ambition that marked yet another departure for McGovern. Whilst not his first venture into feature-film territory, *Gunpowder* represented an altogether different kind of narrative challenge to, say, *Priest* or *Liam* – the irony being that both of these ended up with theatrical releases whilst *Gunpowder* remained a television miniseries – though stories about a 'Mary Queen of Scots film' written by McGovern and starring Scarlett Johansson circulated for several years after the series' television showing.

Amongst the most critically divisive of all of McGovern's work, criticism of the programme tended to focus most of all on questions of authenticity and historical accuracy, making *Gunpowder*'s placing in this chapter all the more useful. Like most of McGovern's work, whether working with documentary evidence or not, *Gunpowder*'s driving force was a powerful narrative created around characters that are nearly always fully fleshed-out human beings with abundant flaws. In his documentary-drama work that relies on recent events, many of the 'characters', their close families or acquaintances were alive and available for interview. When creating a version of Mary Queen of Scots the quality and range of evidence is considerably less, though some argued that *Gunpowder* paid too little attention to the sources that did exist. Gub Neal, one of the film's producers, suggested that McGovern's approach to the Scottish and English royal households was little different from the one he used when working with families in 1990s Derry or Liverpool:

> Jimmy's mission is to create a point of entry where you recognise the world in terms of what's familiar rather than unfamiliar ... And his linchpin is families, whether dysfunctional, mad or indifferent. The *Hillsborough* and *Bloody Sunday* stories were made from the point of view of the family, as was the film he made about the Liverpool dockers. He's very good at looking at these big, overwhelming subject matters from a very ordinary perspective. (Hoggard, 2004: 9)

Whilst Neal's description of McGovern's approach is accurate enough in relation to *Gunpowder*, it tends to gloss over a particular difficulty which lies not so much in representing real characters with little evidence, but rather in representing characters whose mythological status is such that to present them as 'ordinary' risks a particular form of unintentional comic bathos. It is undeniable that the dramatist has to negotiate an altogether different set of difficulties when depicting a 'real' queen and her lover engaged in domestic squabbling or lovemaking, as opposed to a soldier or docker, even when the latter is also a real person.

This said, the larger question of veracity is far more complex than many of the journalistic detractors of *Gunpowder* tend to imply. A 2007 edition of the *European Journal of Cultural Studies* was entirely devoted to the ways that European television has tended to dramatise history, and one of its keynotes is contained in the following sentence from the introductory article, which considers the contemporary tendency 'to think of historiography, whether traditional or televisual', as being 'about arranging and telling stories, not about delivering objective truth' (Bell, 2007: 8). More challengingly, in a piece that focuses largely on documentary drama, the idea of the 'New History' film is posited in a way that suggests at least a relationship to the approach McGovern takes to the Tudors and Stuarts:

> One of the characteristics of the New History film is that it tends to be revisionist: it reveals an alternative history that often challenges received ideas about the historical experience. So, for example, *Culloden* subverts the narrative of romantic Tartanry by characterizing Bonnie Prince Charlie as a drunken coward who flees the field and leaves his supporters to their fate, while *Hiroshima, mon amour* explores the ambivalent feelings of a French woman who had an affair with a German soldier during the Occupation and thus subverts the Gaullist narrative of national resistance. (Chapman, 2007: 25)

It would be wrong, of course, to equate *Gunpowder* too closely with the likes of *Culloden*, which uses formal filmic techniques to foreground its interrogative approach to history in a much more overt way. Nevertheless, Chapman's description of a revisionist approach to more romantic dramatisations of history, particularly those dealing with royal households, has clear relevance to McGovern's work. This is particularly true of the second part of the dramatisation and Robert Carlyle's portrayal of James I. As Gardner's account indicates, apart from the many caricatures of the traditional hate-figure of Henry VIII, McGovern's James became, in the hand of Carlyle, among the least sycophantic portrayals of a ruling monarch in British television history: 'Those for whom James I is synonymous with the Authorised Version of the Bible will be dismayed by the cruel, Machiavellian – not to mention actively bisexual figure cut by Carlyle' (2004).

For many, of course, it was Carlyle's performance that was at the heart of the success of *Gunpowder* as drama, with one review likening the portrayal to a kind of Pol Pot figure (Rampton, 2004: 14), something which, in turn, changes the balances of sympathies around the Gunpowder Plot itself. This latter point places McGovern's version firmly in the revisionist camp, especially considering the remarkably enduring place of Guy Fawkes in British popular consciousness. Someone with the kind of relationship to Catholicism that McGovern has would surely have found such an idea irresistible.

As we have seen above, both McGovern and Gub Neale have resisted the idea of *Gunpowder* having the same responsibility to its central characters as the other documentary-drama work written by McGovern. However, as Bell argues, 'it is important to remember that social narratives, which may include television history programmes, cannot be made at will' (2007: 8), and McGovern's framework included not only existing historical research, but also the powerful contemporary context. Made in the period between the September 2001 attacks in New York and the July 2007 attacks in London, *Gunpowder* was undoubtedly designed to be read in relation to contemporary discourse surrounding terrorism, something that was recognised by most reviews, including this one:

> The other big pull of *Gunpowder, Treason and Plot* is the often startling comparison with today. At one point in the drama, Robert Catesby (Richard Coyle), the Catholic mastermind behind the gunpowder plot, expresses his terrorist aims with a zeal that will have uncomfortable undertones for many viewers. 'In a just and holy war, the Church accepts that innocents may have to die,' he asserts. 'They'll be martyrs.' James, in turn, gives an analysis of the plotters that will strike a chord with audiences. 'We deal with religious fanatics. They welcome death and martyrdom, for it's their gateway to heaven.' (Rampton, 2004: 15)

In an extract from an interview with Carlyle late in the same piece it also becomes clear that such parallels were at the forefront of the minds of those involved in making the films and that they became one of the primary forces behind their approach to history:

> 'What Jimmy has managed to is take a children's nursery rhyme – Remember, remember, the fifth of November – and examine it in today's context. With all the terrorism going on in the world right now, Jimmy's interpretation of the gunpowder plot makes it seem more dramatic and dangerous.' (Rampton, 2004: 15)

Gunpowder's contemporary resonances and the way that this prominent episode in British history could be used to comment upon the politics of the present were undoubtedly part of the attraction of the project for McGovern. As well as giving him a kind of freedom to embellish the historical episode with his own interpretation of the central characters, *Gunpowder* also offered a way of alluding to contemporary debates on terrorism, which had been further polarised by the UK's participation in the invasion of Iraq in 2003, without the problems inherent in dramatising events that were still being played out. The film's depiction of the use of violence in the name of an oppressed religious group is, though, not a simple one. The Protestant King and his court are undoubtedly seen as duplicitous and ruthlessly violent in their suppression of the

England's Catholic minority despite promising tolerance, but equally the gunpowder plotters are portrayed as fanatical and lacking in humanity. If the production values of the two films are heavy on period detail and the traditional iconography of British costume drama, then the avoidance of moral simplicities and overblown heroism prevent it from becoming a Hollywood version of history in the manner of a *Braveheart* (dir. Mel Gibson, 1995).

Perhaps the imagery of one scene in particular is at the heart of the way that McGovern uses contemporary resonance without ever getting close to spurious exact parallels. Some time before the gunpowder plot is hatched McGovern creates a moment where Guy Fawkes, fighting as a Catholic on the side of Spain, comes upon the aftermath of a massacre. The imagery is reminiscent of some of the terrible scenes from Srebrenica during the Bosnian conflict, frequently referred to as the worst atrocity in Europe since the end of the Second World War. Srebrenica saw the systematic slaughter of up to ten thousand Bosnian Muslims by Serb forces in the name of so-called ethnic cleansing, and its scale and ferocity inevitably recalled events in Germany under the Nazis.

The massacre in *Gunpowder* is not of narrative significance and in fact its exact provenance is never fully explained, but the look on Fawkes's face as he surveys the mound of bloody corpses suggests that it is the moment when he is, in contemporary parlance, radicalised. It is the moment when his fighting for Catholicism hardens into an attitude that will countenance the use of a brand of violence that will kill people indiscriminately, including other Catholics. As the gunpowder plotters make their final arrangements, the most vocal is Robert Catesby (Richard Coyle) who, when others plead to be able to warn and spare Catholic friends and relatives, demands silence and suggests that the innocent dead will get their reward because they will go straight to heaven.

Whilst McGovern shows us the ruthless totalitarian power that radicalises the Catholics, he also depicts how the spiral of violence undermines the plotters' moral authority, however much our sympathies might lie with the minority and against the regime of James and his oppressor-in-chief, Lord Cecil (Tim McInnerney). Catesby's determination not to warn the innocent recalls the number of Muslim dead among the 9/11 victims, whilst the constant exhortations to think of the afterlife are all-too familiar to followers of the pattern of radicalisation of young Muslims in the West since 2001. Even the mundane details of buying gunpowder recall similar depictions of the banality of terrorist acts represented in more recent contemporary drama such as Peter

Kosminsky's *Britz* (Channel 4, 2007). In the latter the young men must obtain sufficient quantities of peroxide without attracting suspicion; here it is gunpowder. Finally, as Gub Neale makes clear below, there was at least some intention to draw rather more specific parallels with the USA's conduct of foreign and security policy in the aftermath of the 9/11 attacks:

> the gunpowder plot was for James I what September 11 was for President Bush. Before then, Bush was a dodgy president who had won a dodgy election. He had nothing to unite his people. But after September 11, he went stratospheric in the polls and no one questioned whether he was the rightful president. In the same way, after the gunpowder plot, James I said, 'I have saved you from this heinous plot' and he was given carte blanche by Parliament. He hit the jackpot. (Rampton, 2004: 15)

No doubt to the disappointment of conspiracy theorists, McGovern's allegorical parallels do not suggest that the gunpowder plot was instigated by James or his followers; rather they suggest that once discovered it was allowed to spread and its aftermath was ruthlessly manipulated for propaganda purposes. James is certainly not above slaughtering his own, but the plot itself is conducted by those, it is suggested, who play into the ruthless hands of the King and his followers.

However, not all of McGovern's frame of reference concerns contemporary terrorism and its roots in oppressive state control. James's final line in the film, with its reference to his mother, clearly recalls James Cagney, something again confirmed by Neale, alongside another reference that makes clear the film's cinematic ambitions and broad range of aesthetic inspiration:

> Guy Fawkes is played by a complete unknown. McGovern wanted a genuine enigma, like Kaiser Soze in The Usual Suspects ... 'The Mary, Queen of Scots story is shot outside, so it's very epic, almost western in scale,' explains Neal, 'while the James I story is mostly shot in the studio, so it has a very internalised feel.' The final scene, where a triumphantly nasty James addresses the portrait of his dead mother, is pure Hollywood. 'The inspiration was James Cagney in *White Heat* where he's standing on top of the gasholders saying, "Made it, Ma. Top of the world" and the whole thing explodes!' (Hoggard, 2004)

At one level such observations simply confirm the television miniseries' origins in a feature-film project and the probability that McGovern and Neale were unwilling to abandon that particular vision. The appointment of Gillies Mackinnon is a further indication that the original concept was never fully given up in favour of a more conventionally television-orientated project. On the other hand, the references to key landmarks from very different eras of the gangster film also point both to McGovern's recurrent interest in the moral ambiguities surrounding crime and punishment and a less familiar interest in the way that the best commercial cinema has so often made its anti-heroes the most enduring and engaging characters. Cagney's character in *White Heat* (dir. Raoul Walsh, 1949) is the more obvious of the two connections, principally through its foregrounding of 'Cody' Jarrett's (Cagney) intense relationship with his mother, seen through the prism of film noir's post-war preoccupation with popular psychology. McGovern's screenplay is nowhere near as dependent on such sub-Freudian themes, but at the same time does suggest a strong relationship between James's personality and his being taken away from his mother at an early age. Through both McGovern's writing and Carlyle's searing performance we are once again presented with a character who is not morally absolved from his crimes, but whose complexity makes him the most interesting and attractive character in the series. As well as Cagney one is inevitably reminded of Carlyle's other major collaboration with Neale and McGovern in the role of Albie Kinsella in *Cracker*.

The reference to Kaiser Soze and *The Usual Suspects* (dir. Bryan Singer, 1995) creates a less obvious set of associations which tend to reinforce the idea that the gunpowder plot itself and its perpetrators became mythologised for political reasons in ways that have powerful contemporary parallels. The character of Soze in Singer's film has become best known because of way that the film's ending casts doubt over his existence, despite the fact that his alleged influence has dominated a dark and highly complex plot. McGovern doesn't cast doubt over the existence of Guy Fawkes, but his precise motives and allegiances are kept somewhat shadowy, and the film makes clear that he was nowhere near as central to the political heart of the plot as his enduring status on top of bonfires would suggest. He became something of a convenient bogeyman whose brutal public torture and execution was of great political value to James and his court. At the end of 2011, when one of the year's enduring news images was of the US President and Secretary of State watching a live feed of the killing of Osama Bin Laden by US troops in Afghanistan, one was reminded that the personalising and mythologising of individuals remains an enduring means of exercising power, and that McGovern's identification of contemporary resonance in the gunpowder plot not only holds true, but continues to be strengthened by events some time after the film was made.

Before leaving *Gunpowder, Treason and Plot* it is worth reflecting on one more dimension to the context in which it was produced, namely, the ways in which the historical or 'heritage' film had been evolving in the UK and the likely influence that this had on McGovern and Mackinnon's approach to the project. The following is taken from a description of *Elizabeth* (dir. Shekhar Kapur, 1998), widely thought of as contributing to radical changes to the British 'heritage' film typified by the films made by the partnership of James Ivory and Ismail Merchant:[4]

> The opening sequence shows us forcibly the brutality of the era – there is no chance that we will regard what is to follow as an exercise in nostalgia. A document is sealed and stamped – we track across shackles and chains, to the sound of screaming, and the camera observes from above the violent shaving of a woman's head, with strokes so harsh that her scalp is bloodied. From overhead, we watch as she and her fellow Protestants are dragged out through iron gates to be burnt at the stake ... The black clothes, the gilt, the icons and the burning incense evoke the paintings of Goya. (Church Gibson, 2000: 122–3)

Without in any way wanting to gloss over the important differences between the television miniseries and the cinema, it seems to me that *Gunpowder* positions itself very much in a tradition of anti-nostalgia historical drama, a tradition that this description of *Elizabeth* exemplifies. The cornerstone of such a tradition is perhaps the centrality both of violence and a Machiavellian approach to politics and governance on the part of the British monarch and wider ruling class, something which McGovern's *Gunpowder*, especially the second part, uses very heavily. Equally important is what Church Gibson refers to as an almost operatic visual style and, in the case of *Elizabeth*, camera movements that are designed to reflect the atmosphere of intrigue and plotting that dominated the Elizabethan court. Whilst it would be wrong to claim that McGovern and Mackinnon have created something for television as visually striking as *Elizabeth*, it is also true that there are moments of stylistic innovation that are equally disruptive of any nostalgic heritage tradition. These include direct address to camera and a memorable, very lengthy tracking shot that follows the enraged Boswell in such a way that inevitably recalls *Trainspotting* (dir. Danny Boyle, 1996), not least because Kevin McKidd, who plays Boswell, is also a significant figure in Boyle's evocation of a twentieth-century Scotland in search of an identity.

Later in her analysis of *Elizabeth* Church Gibson suggests that the evolution of the heritage film must now be seen as having embraced postmodernity and possessing an 'element of pastiche' (124). This again is something that can be seen clearly in *Gunpowder*, with its modern sexual innuendo ('There goes a Scotsman in need of his oats', says Darnley of Boswell) and, perhaps above all, the strange figure of 'Hamish', who, like a figure from *Blackadder,* languishes in the prison to which a number of characters are sent at various times during part

Documentary and historical drama 151

one. At times this can seem at odds with the intensity of McGovern's dark portrayal of the court, and there is no escaping that the four-hour piece has some unevenness of tone. Nevertheless, as yet another extension of McGovern's range, his collaboration with a significant director on a genuine epic historical drama must be counted as remarkable from a writer whose natural territory is so often seen as contemporary, working-class and domestic.

McGovern's work for the cinema and single films for television are considered elsewhere in this volume and, to some extent, it can seem incongruous that *Gunpowder*, in many ways the script that has resulted in the most visually expansive of his films, is considered here alongside the likes of *Hillsborough*. *Gunpowder* is, though, primarily an attempt to make sense of a period of British history that is both very well known and widely misunderstood. That McGovern and his collaborators have chosen to use many of the devices of contemporary popular narrative in the pursuit of historical understanding does not make the series any the less serious in intent. Flawed though it is, *Gunpowder* not only provides a reading of history that is illuminating and absorbing, but it does so in such a way as to draw genuine contemporary parallels.

Notes

1 Details of the project 'Acting with facts: performing the real on stage and screen 1990–2010' can be found at www.reading.ac.uk/ftt/research/ftt-actingwithfacts. aspx and a selection of interviews connected with the project at www.youtube.com/watch?v=t_YgT7jvOko (accessed December 2011).
2 For a full account of the setting-up of the Hillsborough Justice Campaign see www.contrast.org/hillsborough/index.shtml (accessed January 2012).
3 An overview of the conference, 'Channel Four – The First 25 Years', together with abstracts, can be found at: www.bfi.org.uk/education/conferences/cFour/abstracts.pdf (accessed January 2012).
4 For a detailed account of the 'English' heritage film, including the work of Merchant–Ivory, see Higson (2003).

Single plays and a conclusion 4

This chapter brings together an account of McGovern's single plays for television and ends with a brief Conclusion to the book. In certain respects it would also have been useful to cover McGovern's work for cinema in *Priest, Heart* and *Liam*, which offer interesting points of comparison to the single plays for television, particularly through the intensity of their scrutiny of the Catholic Church. However, strictly speaking, cinema is beyond the scope of this series, and space restrictions dictate that such a boundary needs to be drawn.

There is an inevitable risk of distorting the shape of McGovern's career in bringing these films together, for a number of reasons. To begin with, they do not represent a sustained trajectory towards the writing of either single television drama or feature films on his part. Many of them are fitted around the writing of his two major series of the 1990s, *Cracker* and *The Lakes*, whilst the earlier plays for television represent a period in which McGovern was establishing his credentials as an independent writer, away from the confines of *Brookside*.

In addition, the production contexts for the films represent a very large range – from the very small budget for *Traitors* in the BBC2 'Screenplay' slot to work of a kind that gets close to being a feature film for theatrical release with someone who would soon become an internationally established director, Michael Winterbottom. The parameters for such contexts were not defined only by budgets, but also the level of freedom and agency afforded to a writer as well as the overall principles of any given television slot as defined by commissioning editors and executive producer.

As always with McGovern, one is left marvelling at both his versatility and, despite powerful political and ethical principles, his ability to work with such a variety of people and within radically different commissioning environments. As a result, this chapter tends to confirm the idea of McGovern as part pragmatic writer who understands the privilege and value of being able to work, but also someone who, whilst undoubtedly finding his voice, is set upon exploring distinctive territory.

If his ambivalent relationship to his Catholic faith is present throughout all of his work it looms even larger in a number of his single films (particularly if one includes those that were written for theatrical release). It is possible to speculate therefore that the relative freedom of the single play or feature tended to be the place where more explicit and direct inclusion of matters of faith were allowed to surface, with *Traitors* (as well as *Priest* and *Liam*) containing explicit discussion on matters of doctrine as well as the Church's wider social and cultural role. However, it would be wrong to suggest that Catholicism dominates this dimension to McGovern's work at the expense of all other recurrent concerns. All the single films have, to a certain extent, something to say about the operation of class and power, though both the means that are employed and the role of such questions in the respective narratives are very different.

Inevitably, though, we see McGovern experimenting with what he always characterises as the craft skills of the writer. Narrative structure, storytelling, ways of revealing character are all seen in a much greater variety of forms in this chapter than any other. This is mainly to do with a writer experimenting and gaining confidence in his own voice, but also to do with the range of collaborators that McGovern worked with on these projects, some of whom, such as Charles McDougall, would become frequent collaborators. Others, such as Stephen Frears and Antonia Bird, themselves cinema-orientated auteurs, only ever worked once with McGovern.

This chapter, then, unlike the others, will be less about patterns of consistent development within a form, often establishing McGovern's considerable contribution to its evolution, and more about watching the emergence both of a voice and of someone working out how to engage with the industries within which he chooses to operate. Some of the work here is not even available outside the confines of research collections. It is hoped, therefore, that by trying to set such work, for the first time, within the context of the whole of McGovern's output it will provide opportunities to see the plays themselves in new light and also to suggest patterns that would emerge more strongly as McGovern became an established force in the wider industry.

Traitors (1990)

First broadcast on the long-defunct 'Screenplay' slot on BBC2 on 5 November 1990, *Traitors* was McGovern's first fully realised attempt to engage with one of the key moments of British history in respect of the relationship between the state and the Catholic Church, namely the so-called 'Gunpowder Plot'. As was discussed in Chapter 3, McGovern's interest in these events eventually formed a key part of a much longer work, *Gunpowder, Treason and Plot*, broadcast in 2004.

Of all the work discussed in this volume it is perhaps *Traitors* that is the least typical, in formal terms, of the entirety of McGovern's output. Made on what seems to have been a very small budget and set entirely in a studio, *Traitors* can reasonably be seen as the most austere and visually restrained of McGovern's single films.

McGovern's script for *Traitors*, rather like *Gunpowder* over a decade later, treats Guido Fawkes (David Chittenden) himself as a peripheral figure and instead chooses to focus attention on Father Garnet (Geoffrey Hutchings), a Catholic priest who, within the sanctity of the confessional, hears of the plot to blow up Parliament. Much of the screen time is taken up with a lengthy interrogation of Garnett by Robert Cecil (Anton Lesser) who, in McGovern's version, becomes a calculating Machiavellian villain hell-bent on ridding England of the scourge of Catholicism.

Structurally, *Traitors* revolves around the brutal torture of Garnet on the rack, but what is particularly remarkable is that Garnet's silence is seen not as approval of the plot that he has knowledge of, but of a belief that the function of confession must survive at all costs. At one point he says that 'a million mortal souls depend upon it', and one of the leaders of the Gunpowder Plot itself, Robert Catesby (Tim Woodward), uses the strength of Garnet's belief to enable him to 'confess' his sins in the sure knowledge that he will not be betrayed. In turn, for Cecil, the objective of getting Garnet, a leading Jesuit, to break the confessional seal comes to override any need to obtain information (Cecil's spies have long secured enough of this for him).

Whilst the sheer austerity of the dimly lit and studio-bound production seems a product both of the end of the era of the majority of single dramas on television and of McGovern's comparatively novice status as a writer (despite nearly a decade's experience on *Brookside*), some of the ways in which the script approaches the historical events anticipate McGovern's later work. The most obvious of these is the way that contemporary political parallels are drawn and signalled. Early on in the piece we see the plotters themselves agonising over whether what they are going to attempt is justified, and they raise the explicit question of

Single plays and a conclusion 155

whether or not they could be seen to be 'at war'. This has been a key debate for those throughout history who have sought to reconcile their actions with their moral dilemmas about the taking of human life. In Britain in the late twentieth century this was a question of particular significance for Irish republican groups who sought to justify military actions in the North of Ireland through a rhetoric of being 'at war' with Britain. In *Traitors* such a position is made clear by Catesby, who asserts that 'in a just and holy war, the Church accepts that innocents may have to die', to which Garnet retorts, 'We are not at war.'

This anticipates the much more extended parallels that McGovern was later to suggest between the authorities' approach to dealing with the Gunpowder Plot and the behaviour of governments in the immediate aftermath of the events of 11 September 2001 (in *Gunpowder, Treason and Plot*). In addition, it also points to his eventual interest in Bloody Sunday and all that it implied about the idea of a 'war' being waged in Northern Ireland. Furthermore, as the agonised dialogue between Cecil and Garnet progresses, it becomes clear that McGovern's interpretation of the historical evidence has led him to imply a much greater degree of manipulation of events, on Cecil's part at least, than is popularly thought. Not only does McGovern show Cecil allowing the plotters to proceed with their actions for a long time after there is plenty of evidence to arrest them, but he suggests that he actively facilitated some of those actions in order to maximise the propaganda effect of high-profile Catholics being discovered in a plot that would have caused so much bloodshed.

Traitors is, then, in many ways, a play about a powerful state and all the means that it has at its disposal to suppress opposition and dissent. Despite the low budget (or perhaps because of it), we see endless scenes of the slow torture on the rack, of Cecil in clandestine meetings with a variety of apparatchiks and of rudimentary surveillance by undercover agents. It is little wonder that McGovern returned to the subject for *Gunpowder*, in a post 9/11 world in which such matters became more the subject of public conjecture. In 1990, however, there were already plenty of contemporary parallels with which to interest an audience, as this review suggests:

> the theological dilemma that first traps Garnet now looks entirely relevant: the concept of the Just War. This may have started out, like much else in the script, as a reference to Northern Ireland. But only a few days ago there were clerics on *Newsnight* debating the issue in the context of the Gulf. (Herbert, 1990)

It is clear, then, that in *Traitors*, McGovern was continuing with the emerging career trajectory of engaging with uncomfortable truths about the behaviour of the state, especially when it feels endangered or threatened, the trajectory on which he had embarked on a *Brookside* still interested in stories about trade unionism and bogus schemes to keep people out of the unemployment statistics. That he chose to do so in such a comparatively confined way is slightly surprising, given what the rest of the decade would bring from him, though as McGovern would be the first to admit, it was almost certainly partly the product of pragmatism and the availability for a particular kind of slot that dictated that he would choose to write in this way about a historical event with which he was evidently very preoccupied.

As Herbert later puts it, *Traitors* is 'a challenging hour of television' consisting principally of a series of moral and theological debates between characters, interspersed with the screams of torture victims echoing down the dimly lit stone corridors built in a BBC studio. The brief flurry of action when the plotters are apprehended forces home the clearest contemporary reference of them all as the soldiers are ordered to 'shoot to kill'[1] by Cecil. Nevertheless, the overall conception and challenge to accepted versions of history are characteristically bold, and there are also flickers of a more playful McGovern beneath the restraint: one element of Cecil's machinations involves moving the date of the sitting of Parliament to November. When asked why it could not be October Cecil replies, 'because it wouldn't rhyme'. Part knowing joke and part comment on the propagandist intentions of Cecil (Remember, remember ...), the exchange is not so much typical of *Traitors* as a glimpse of one strain of a writer's talent beginning to emerge.

In terms of television history *Traitors* feels like part of the end of something on British television. The *Screenplay* slot in which it was screened finished altogether in 1993 and even that was seen as what Lez Cooke describes as 'a showcase for feature-length filmed dramas' (in fact, *Traitors* was only one hour in length). Cooke goes on to quote Alan Plater on why any discussion of the single television play was 'close to archaeology': 'The reasons are obvious enough. Plays are unpredictable and dangerous: tricky qualities for a conformist society, and an industry increasingly market-driven, to use the American jargon' (Plater, 1987, cited in Cooke, 2003: 141).

Plater goes on to describe his own instincts in response to this, namely, to subvert the system to 'cheat' or 'write a play but pretend it's a genre series'. Perhaps McGovern read Plater at some point, because this is a good description of the strategy that the younger writer not only adopted, but refined in a number of different directions, so that by the end of the 2000s he was practically back at the single play. During the early 1990s, however, with *Traitors* and the other single dramas discussed below, McGovern took advantage of being one of the last to be able to enjoy the opportunities to learn and develop that the single drama offers, as well as trying to avoid being, in Plater's words again, a writer 'who can sing any tune except their own'.

Needle (1990)

Broadcast just a few weeks before *Traitors*, *Needle* (BBC1, 1990) was commissioned for the *Play on One* season, another attempt by the BBC both to breathe new life into the single-play format and to bring on new writers. It brought McGovern together for the first time with director Gilles Mackinnon, with whom he was to collaborate on the much higher-budget *Gunpowder, Treason and Plot* (see Chapter 3).

In comparison to *Traitors*, *Needle* is much more familiar McGovern territory. As an opening title tells us, it focuses on 'a city in the North of England in the near future', though generally any futuristic element is quite muted (but this may be something to do with the benefit of hindsight). The title reveals more, in a way, about the intention of the piece to present a particular kind of urban landscape as the central 'character' in the play as the opening scenes provide a montage of drug-related crime and vigilantism, suggesting an environment that is out of control.

In some senses McGovern's narrative strategy in *Needle* foreshadows those that came to the fore in his work in documentary drama. In seeking to draw a kaleidoscopic picture of a city in the grip of a heroin epidemic, McGovern chooses to do it through the morality tale of a young couple and the impact that drug use and addiction have on their lives. Whilst the difficulties of individualising a widespread social issue are clear and discussed further in Chapter 3, McGovern attempts to counter these through a parallel strand to the drama that involves high-ranking police officers, politicians and the media whose various approaches to the 'problem' form a background to the disintegrating lives of the young couple.

The quasi-documentary style strand to the drama can be seen partly as a response to the barrage of official approaches to the twin problems of drug use and the spread of HIV/Aids in inner cities in Britain during the 1980s. For some reviewers this element to *Needle* was the least successful and too dominated by the constraints of the form, with one calling it an 'almost mind-numbing drift of social realist clichés' (White, 1990: 14). It is, however, possible to argue that MacKinnon and McGovern set out to create a wider world lacking in the detailed reality experienced by the central characters Danny (Sean McKee) and Paula

(Emma Bird). Politicians and the police appear to operate in response to the moral panics set in train by the media, resulting precisely in what White called 'social realist clichés' – politicians trading shamelessly on the fears of vulnerable people whose accounts of heroin users and HIV sufferers have come from the pages of tabloid newspapers.

The representation of Danny and Emma, a young couple with a child, is much closer to the later McGovern, with even their names anticipating a pair of characters in *The Lakes* later in the decade. Whereas, in *The Lakes*, it is addictive gambling that undermines Danny's determination to make a stable life for his partner and child, here it is heroin use. Early on in *Needle* we see Danny working on the Mersey ferry (surely a powerful emblem of a Liverpool that still had jobs for the majority), displaying a flair for cheeky Scouse banter, but generally well liked and reliable. As he moves from smoking to intravenous heroin use, so his ability to maintain any kind of façade of normality declines and he loses his job. Eventually the inevitable happens and theft to feed his drug habit leads to a prison sentence and, ultimately, to the unsafe needle-sharing that is the play's central political issue.

If this sounds something like a slightly conventional morality tale, then there is an element of truth in that. The images of dealers' houses in the direst ex-council flats have, since 1990 when the film was made, become commonplace via high-profile films such as *Trainspotting* (dir. Danny Boyle, 1996), and the portrayal of the intimate relationship between drugs and HIV/Aids is in danger of simplifying the issues involved. However, it is important to remember that McGovern was writing from a very different historical vantage point, one in which the spread of drug use and sexually transmitted diseases was the final straw after a long decade of rising unemployment and economic decline. Moreover, McGovern's script frequently works hard against any reductive portrayal of conventional urban misery. This is usually through humour, for example in the following exchange between Paula's disapproving Dad (Pete Postlethwaite) and Danny:

Danny: I cut myself shaving.
Paula's father: What did you use, a fuckin' machete?

Or later, after Danny collides full pelt with a lamp-post, nearly knocking himself out, when arguing with Paula he speculates that it is her 'Dad in disguise'.

There is also a strange poetry about some of the babblings of the heroin smokers, tiny glimpses of the lucidity and escape for which they are prepared to suffer the indignities of their chaotic lives. One unnamed man babbles about films in a way that echoes McGovern's own remarks about polite costume drama, 'A Room with a View, you can stick it up you arse, Mean Streets, Taxi Drive ...' (the sentence just tails off), whilst Danny himself muses about the function of bees, calling them 'idle, crafty bastards'. Tellingly, there is little of this once the supply of heroin becomes restricted, and Danny's group turns to intravenous use in order to eke out what they can obtain. The more powerful and dangerous effects of heroin consumed in this way turn the men (it is mostly men in McGovern's account) into useless zombies, and the whole tone of the script becomes altogether darker.

A further strength of Needle is its resistance of simple political solutions. In fact it is deeply critical of those who impose them and who, in turn, unleash forces that they cannot control. An advice-centre worker begs the politicians not to bow to media pressure to stop a free needle-exchange scheme. When the advice is ignored the inevitable spread of infections and other horrors becomes the subject of Mackinnon's unflinching camera. More controversially, though, in prison we see Danny sharing a needle with a fellow inmate who is homosexual and promiscuous. Though we never learn whether or not Danny has become HIV-positive the dangers of his behaviour are made clear. Such a portrayal of intravenous drug use, homosexuality and HIV/Aids as being intimately connected can be seen as, unwittingly perhaps, pandering to a moral majority that the film's serious intent is designed to challenge.

As Jim White's review points out, the film ends on a moment of bitter nobility from both of the main characters. Finding herself pregnant again, whilst Danny is in prison, Paula determines to give him another chance, despite a litany of broken promises and repossessions. As Paula stands outside the prison gates Danny emerges, only to walk straight past her, determined not to taint her with the HIV that he thinks he may have contracted whilst inside. Paula is left very alone in the desolate landscape that surrounds the prison. It is a terrible moment, but one that is typical of McGovern's general determination to resist easy judgements or solutions. If Needle is somewhat didactic compared to his later work, it still resists judgements that condemn completely and offers us a sense of the survival of the spirit in the worst of circumstances.

Gas and Candles (1991)

If Needle can be seen as McGovern operating in similar territory to his later, more mature, work then Gas and Candles (first broadcast on BBC1 on 1 August 1991) contains a number of detours from that territory and up what one can only assume McGovern found to be blind alleys.

Adapted from a stage play by David Henry Wilson, much of the action takes place on a studio set with the appearance of something from an earlier phase of television drama's history. The piece as a whole possesses a degree of reflexivity and it may well be that this very stagy, confined piece of design is part of the narrative of confinement that McGovern offers us. On the other hand, there is also a sense that McGovern's adaptation from a three-handed stage play has not quite made the leap across to television.

The two principal characters, Bill (Bert Parnaby) and Betty (Edna Doré), are first presented as bickering pensioners from central casting. The play opens with them returning from yet another funeral, with Bert, in particular, bemoaning his descent into old age and all the indignities that this brings. Betty is more resilient and frequently resorts to black humour in order to shake Bill out of his torpor. Her running line of attack centres on Bill's affliction with piles and the embarrassment he feels about it.

The plight of those who feel the impact of contemporary Western society's dismissal of the elderly is, to some extent, a recurring McGovern theme from his storylines for the widower Harry Cross (Bill Dean) in *Brookside* to the creation of Stan (Jim Broadbent) in *The Street*. For McGovern, old age is another variant on his concern for the marginalised and powerless, and *Gas and Candles* is perhaps his most extended treatise on the idea, albeit by means that are less than typical of his work as a whole.

The most obviously 'experimental' dimension to *Gas and Candles* is the sudden and rather isolated use of song bursting out from a naturalistic frame in a way that is far more Dennis Potter than Jimmy McGovern. The song in question revolves around the twin refrains, 'If you're over 65 join a queue' and 'If you're over 65 just be grateful you're alive'. These are sung by elderly people in a montage of settings that are commonly seen as marking the territory of the old and infirm: the post office, doctors, day-care centres and offices of government welfare departments. In one of the few moments of unbridled exuberance that *Gas and Candles* allows, a chorus of extras sings along, dances and generally performs in ironic counterpoint to the content of the lyrics themselves. This, fleetingly, is the Potter of *Pennies from Heaven* (BBC1, 1978), in which the dark truths of the central character's life are slowly revealed against the backdrop of the cheery songs from the sheet music that he makes his life selling.

Curiously though, the sequence above is not repeated anywhere else in the play which, via a series of farce-like events, descends into black comedy. As Bill returns from the shops, having inadvertently stolen a tin of salmon, an Irish terrorist attempts to assassinate the Home Secretary in another part of the city where they live. Unaware of the latter incident, Bill and Betty hear the sounds of sirens and police helicopters and assume they are coming for Bill. In fact the gunman has been seen entering the tower block in which the couple live, and so the police have it surrounded.

As Bill and Betty ultimately turn the situation around to their advantage the black-farce elements come to the fore. However, in originally having the couple assume that so much police attention is over a stolen tin of salmon, the narrative runs the risk of turning them into precisely the rather stereotyped, naive and paranoid old people that it eventually encourages us to see differently. This is somewhat true of much of the first half of the play as the obsession with minor ailments is joined by tales of the war, and complaints about a whole litany of 1990s social bogeys, including the spread of drug-taking and the advance of supermarkets. The cumulative effect of this and the stifling studio set are never quite overcome by the way that Betty and Bill manage to turn things to their advantage later on.

This said, the way that the second half tries to combine a kind of fantasy with the grim ruthlessness of the authorities trying to end what they think is a terrorist siege is bold television, even if not always successful. Through a series of misunderstandings straight out of old-fashioned situation comedy, the police come to think that Bill and Edna have become hostages in their own flat, imprisoned by 'Mr Shah', a 'Persian'. In fact Mr Shah is a cat, who Bill truthfully describes as being in the flat with them in response to a police door-to-door search.

As the siege progresses Bill and Betty are able to extract a number of small 'luxuries' from the police in the guise of them being demanded by 'Mr Shah', until eventually the authorities turn ruthless. This latter phase sees the couple leading a grotesque parody of a pensioner's existence, with light and heat turned off and only cat food to eat. In one of the genuinely poignant moments of the play they dance in the semi-darkness to a dance tune of their youth, clinging desperately to the comfort of the past.

Close to the end we see plans being prepared outside for the flat to be stormed, and there is a chilling slot of three coffins being delivered, one each for Bill and Betty and one for 'Mr Shah'. The doctrine of no surrender to terrorists is being upheld at all costs. In the end this glimpse into the darkness and ruthlessness of British officialdom beneath the surface of smiling bobbies is undercut, and the ending sees the couple flying to Australia to see their daughter at the taxpayer's expense, in return for their silence on how they outwitted the Home Secretary and hordes of armed policemen.

Gas and Candles has a lot to say about the exclusion of the impoverished elderly from a Britain obsessed with youth and 'progress', and it attempts to be innovative in the way that the narrative unfolds. It is also unafraid of the real horror beneath the grumbles about minor ailments and queues. In a strangely structured, but very affecting, subplot Bill's brother, Tom (Lesley Sands), is shown to have starved his crippled wife to death because he could no longer care for her. This is the dark reverse side of the farce-like main plot in which Bill and Betty eventually triumph.

Ultimately, though, Gas *and Candles* seems very much a test bed for the various strands to McGovern's emerging voice and one that is hampered by its origins as a stage play. For most of his career McGovern showed himself to be anything but a writer who thought in stage terms. He became an absolute master of the pace and economy required of modern television drama, and *Gas and Candles* is quite possibly one of the vehicles by which he learnt the difficulties and restraints of dialogue-heavy studio-based drama. Whilst it is tempting to dismiss *Gas and Candles* as another part of the death throes of regular single-play slots (it was part of the very last series of 'Play on One'), it is also possible to see in it a willingness to be inventive on McGovern's part, whatever the constraints. A number of times in this book McGovern's pragmatism as a writer has surfaced, a quality born from someone desperate to gain a foothold in television whilst being able to retain a distinctive voice. In the case of *Gas and Candles,* an established theatre piece and some gentle black comedy also allowed him to open up the plight of pensioners as well as comment obliquely on the question of dealing with terrorism. To do this whilst also trying out different voices and styles reveals an early talent in McGovern for being able to work with established forms and schedule slots and turn their constraints to his advantage.

Go Now (1995)

McGovern's final single drama for television came four years after the transmission of *Gas and Candles* and is a much more confident, contemporary piece, reflective perhaps of a writer who had already received serious acclaim for *Cracker* as well as his first single-authored series, *Hearts and Minds.*

Like *Needle, Go Now* (first broadcast on BBC2 on 16 October 1995) paired McGovern with another director who would later go on to stake a claim to be recognised as a genuine British cinema auteur, this time Michael Winterbottom (with whom McGovern had already worked on

Single plays and a conclusion   163

Cracker). Such early-career pairings are a reminder of another dimension that has been lost in the demise of the single play, in this case the nurturing of writers and directors by creating opportunities for emerging talents to work on projects together.

Go Now was part of a short-lived approach to commissioning single drama through creating broad thematic frameworks for a short season. In this case the season consisted of a series of three plays by different writers which was shown under the collective title of *Love Bites* on BBC2. There was also some flirting with the idea of a theatrical release for *Go Now*, with the film being shown at a number of international film festivals during the course of 1995, including Edinburgh. However, the film never secured proper cinema distribution and can be seen as reflective of a new caution on the part of broadcasters' confidence in feature-film production after the boom years of the 1980s. In this respect, then, *Go Now* can be seen as a bridge between McGovern's early single dramas for television discussed above and his later work on fully-fledged features that secured full theatrical release.

In one other respect, also, *Go Now* anticipates later McGovern in that a co-writer credit is given to Paul Powell, who McGovern met at a disabled workshop in Liverpool. Powell, who suffers from multiple sclerosis (MS) himself, initially penned a short stand-alone film about the disease which McGovern reworked into a feature-length script (Roberts, 1995). Though there is no evidence at this stage that McGovern was actively seeking to develop new voices, *Go Now* suggests that such an instinct was present in McGovern from a relatively early stage in his career, something that was to grow and take a number of different forms right up to his most recent work.

The desire to work with new voices is of course another dimension to McGovern's constant attraction both to providing a platform to those without a proper 'voice' and to the constant search for 'stories' that are fresh and capable of sustaining interest. Powell's take on multiple sclerosis tends to focus less on the traditional, generalised pathos of most medical drama and more on the physical detail of the disease itself. In McGovern's own words, what attracted him further to Powell's story was the approach that he took to the telling of what could have become a very maudlin tale: 'You can find humour in the direst of circumstances and Paul was writing about the things you or I would be wondering – like how does MS affect your job, your relationships, your sex life?' (Roberts, 1995).

Perhaps unsurprisingly, it was the last of these that became the focus of tabloid press attention prior to transmission, with the *Evening Standard* typifying a tone that was, at best, distasteful, when previewing a play that is ultimately about the savage attack of a disease on person's neurological system: 'The BBC today unveiled a trio of new Saturday night dramas littered with raunchy sex scenes, foul language and drugs' (O'Carroll, 1995). The *Evening Standard* piece goes on further to dwell particularly on the 'bad' language of *Go Now*, which it describes quaintly as 'locker-room', a reference to the depiction of the amateur football career of the central character, Nick Cameron (Robert Carlyle).

What the *Evening Standard*'s mildly prurient preview fails to acknowledge is that the use of strong language, the graphic depiction of different dimensions of Nick's sex life and the detailed portrayal of his ongoing symptoms are all part of a script that seeks to distance itself from the sentimentality that tends to be inherent in drama concerned with serious illness. Not only does the script use humour, mainly of the dark variety as delivered by Nick's best friend, Tony (James Nesbitt), it also doesn't shy away from the sexual impotence that is offered in powerful contrast to the scenes from the early physical relationship between Nick and his partner, Karen (Juliet Aubrey).

However, it is not solely through his sex life that Nick is seen, pre-illness, as an active, highly masculine character. Much of the film revolves around the comically not very good football team for whom Nick turns out every weekend. Almost as important as the football is the endless stream of banter that surrounds the game, along with the enraged ranting of their despairing coach (Berwick Kaler), and McGovern cleverly uses this as a barometer which charts Nick's decline. After one episode in the bar when Nick struggles to play pool and Tony deliberately lets him win, Nick berates his old comrades about patronising him. Later, when Tony tries to respond to this in an extended diatribe concerning Nick's impotence and how he should let him stand in for him with Karen, it becomes clear that a balance has not yet been struck. Moreover, in reality, there is no balance to be struck and it is not only Nick that must live with MS, but all those who are fond of him and who will always be anxiously searching for the right ways to respond to his difficulties.

One of the key things about *Go Now* is that it is not a film defined by disease alone. In a rare venture outside the north of England McGovern delivers a script that is as sensitive to the nuances of class and taste as his other work. Set in a recognisable, though never named, Bristol, *Go Now* depicts a world that is as close to middle-class bohemian as McGovern has ever got in his writing. In a way this is curious, as Karen works as a hotel manager whilst Nick is a builder, albeit working on stone casts which we assume are intended for a church. Nevertheless, their life, after a brief whirlwind romance and moving in together, revolves around an attractively untidy flat, drinking in contemporary-looking bars and walks along the river. It is as if McGovern and Winterbottom are at pains to distance the drama from what are so often the conventional tropes of misery and decline, so that when the disease does actually strike the impact feels all the greater.

The setting and the early euphoria of Nick and Karen's romance sets up one of the film's most painful sequences when, on hearing of Nick's diagnosis, his working-class Glaswegian family come and visit. Whereas Karen is as determined to be as open and frank as possible about Nick's condition, his mother and father are kind and loving, but find Nick's illness very difficult to discuss. Nick's mother immediately assumes that she will take him back to Glasgow and care for him as an invalid, whilst his father drinks enough to unleash his feelings, finally bursting into Nick's room at night and repeatedly imploring him to 'Walk to me, son.' However, McGovern's detour into the impact of class on such a situation is not reductive. Karen and Nick's parents get along and eventually are able to share thoughts on ways to support Nick; they are seen as a different dimension of a loving, supportive network rather than as any kind of simplistic set of oppositions, something which receives its full confirmation in the final scene of the film as Nick and Karen are married.

In the trajectory of McGovern's career *Go Now* seems an important marker. Made almost simultaneously with *Priest*, it confirmed McGovern's status as someone who worked with bright young directorial talent that spanned both television and feature film. Also, in the shape of Carlyle, Aubrey, Nesbitt and Sophie Okonedo, who played Karen's friend, Paula, it saw his work able to attract some of the best of a generation of young actors who would become central to different parts of the industry for the next decade. In short, *Go Now* was part of the process in which McGovern, on the back of *Cracker*, was moving from a post-*Brookside* period of finding a voice to one where he was becoming one of the reasons people signed up to a project. As one reviewer put it at the time: 'In the wake of *Cracker* and after some years of relative anonymity on *Brookside*, he is one of the very few television writers whose name attached to a project is enough to get it green-lighted' (Rampton, 1995).

Conclusion

Part of the reason for embarking on this book was a sense of McGovern's neglect at the hands of television scholarship that, for all its problematising of notions of quality, has tended to be wary of what it seems to see as his resort to populist, mainly social-realist narratives. Having now spent an extended period looking at all of McGovern's work for both television and cinema, I find it even more surprising that McGovern has been ignored in such a comprehensive way at a time when the study of television drama has expanded so rapidly.

Of course it would not be enough to merely point to the extraordinary range of McGovern's work, however remarkable that might be, but what I have tried to argue is that, in so many of the key areas of the development of British television drama since the early 1980s, McGovern has made a significant contribution to the future direction of the form. In some cases it is possible to argue that he and his collaborators have, through the directions they have chosen to take, been responsible for instigating some key changes themselves; in others that they have built upon new directions, perhaps set in train by others, but developed by McGovern in ways that have been important for the direction of the genre or television format.

Something that runs across a number of McGovern's most significant contributions and which has helped to define the overall trajectory of his working life is his ever-increasing tendency to employ collaboration with teams of writers as a working method. The precise details of such collaborations have, of course varied. They range from the very radical (in broadcast television terms) *Dockers* and its involvement of dock workers and their families in the writing of the final script, to the more familiar idea of becoming an executive producer to a less experienced group of professional writers in the case of *Moving On*.

Even this is too simple a summation, though, when *Moving On* is seen part of a radical attempt to reintroduce original drama into the moribund daytime schedules and its ambition to attract actors and directors who are already established international stars. *Moving On* was not an exercise in breaking in new writers in ghettoised work to be hidden away in the schedules, but an attempt to shift the television landscape, an attempt that has, as we have seen already, attracted the likes of John Simm, Corin Redgrave, Dominic West and Sheila Hancock to work on daytime television.

In the case of *The Street*, the idea of collaboration was extended to the potential audience, with the production team taking out newspaper advertisements asking for stories. As we have seen, McGovern freely admits that the vast majority of these tended to be derivative and heavily influenced by existing television. However, those that did not fall into this category justified the exercise and McGovern's desire to break free of formulaic narrative. The additional factor of introducing several new writers to television, with McGovern overseeing the process, helped turn *The Street* into a series with a distinct identity.

Building upon the work of the likes of Paul Abbott, then, McGovern has taken the idea of flexi-narrative in different directions and, in *The Street* and *Accused*, has succeeded in re-establishing prime-time space that is equivalent to the single play. Of course, the idea of what has often been termed an 'anthology' series is not in itself new, but its reappearance in the prime-time schedules on BBC1 represents a major breakthrough for writers. From *The Street* to *Accused*, the idea arguably became more radical, and the latter consisted entirely of single dramas linked only by the overall concept of an individual accused of a crime in circumstances that presented the audience with, often, profoundly challenging questions of morality.

As we have seen, though, McGovern's contribution to the evolution of television has not been a relentless pursuit of the apparent Holy Grail, and, for some, ultimate mark of the writer's freedom, the single play. His contribution to genuinely significant shifts in the operation of a number of television genres have, arguably, been just as important. First, on *Brookside*, whilst by no means being the dominant authorial voice in the early days of the series, McGovern clearly became one of the most powerful writers on a team that effected a clear change of direction for British soap opera. This was a change that most critics saw as leading to the BBC's introduction of *EastEnders* which, for good or ill, remains one of the enduring cornerstones of British television. It is possible to argue that the direction that *Brookside* took most closely identified with McGovern was already being reversed, even before he left the show. However, whilst it is true that the left-orientated radicalism typified by the character of the trade-union activist, Bobby Grant, was less and less part of *Brookside*'s storylines, it is also the case that a whole range of robust narratives, social and political dilemmas and powerful characters not only sustained *Brookside* through a very turbulent era in British television, but were an enormous influence on producers' sense of what could be achieved within the framework of the genre.

Secondly, the influence of *Cracker* on the direction both of the crime genre overall and the representational boundaries of its heroes was, at the very least, considerable. As Chapter 1 makes clear, there is no sense that McGovern was the sole authorial voice. Not only was the series partly the idea of producer Gub Neale, but *Cracker* also used a number of writers as well as directors that have since established themselves as powerful creative forces in their own right. However, as Neale is the first to acknowledge, his idea of 'a town marshal with a pocket full of Jung' (Duguid, 2009: 8) really only took flight when he managed to persuade McGovern at his most angry (over the BBC's stalling on the script of *Priest*) to embrace the concept. However, if anger is definitely a powerful driving force within *Cracker* it is to the series' subtler qualities that we should look for its lasting influence on the crime genre. Writing at a time when we have seen innumerable series of *Waking the Dead* and *Silent Witness*, to name but two examples of series in which investigating police officers are of less significance than those who pore over the minds and bodies of criminals and victims, it easy to forget what a rarity such a perspective was before *Cracker*. Even now the psychologist is much rarer than the pathologist, and McGovern's full use of a profession that seeks to open up the emotional dimension of crime has not been surpassed. This privileging of emotional revelation has had an impact on the crime genre that goes much wider than the mere introduction of a wider range of investigative professions. Along with another close contemporary, *Prime Suspect* (ITV, 1993–2006), *Cracker* can fairly be credited with a major influence on the genre in the direction of much subtler motivations, a greater complexity in the characters on both sides of the investigation of crime and 'heroes' who are not only flawed (we had already had those in the 'tough-guy' heroes of the 1970s), but emotionally self-reflexive.

I have also suggested throughout this book that McGovern's writing offers a relationship to ideas of realism that is far less straightforward than superficial critical opinion generally suggests. Inevitably, such a relationship varies considerably, particularly because of the range of genres and television formats in which McGovern has chosen to operate. It is in some of the later work, notably *The Street*, that the relationship between McGovern's work and notions of working-class realism become most interestingly fractured. There are moments where, in the most subtle way, the narrative takes a turn into a mode that approaches magic realism: the pair of twins swapped, not at birth but in death; the little girl dressed as a fairy who persuades the old man not to take his life; and the mother of the murdered baby who returns to persuade the murderer to have a child of his own to redeem his terrible act. All of these plot lines and a number of others in a similar vein happen within the aesthetic framework of *The Street* with its undeniably strong relationship, signalled in the title, to a particular kind of northern, working-class realism. Whilst it is unwise to build too substantial an analysis on the basis of McGovern's passing references to himself as 'the poor man's Thomas Hardy' (see Chapter 2), it is also true that somewhere in the mix of Hardy's use of fate and a more contemporary sense of 'magic' in narrative lies a strain in McGovern's writing that inescapably distances his later work, especially from reductive ideas of social realism.

McGovern's impact on documentary drama, whilst not groundbreaking in the sense of formal innovation, also showed a strong tendency to extend the boundaries of the working methods that tended to be the norm in the making of broadcast television. *Dockers*, already mentioned above in relation to the overall arc of McGovern's collaborative method, was by far the most extreme example, as McGovern and Irvine Welsh set about writing a mainstream drama through a creative writing class for ex-dockers and their families. Equally, both the length of the research period for *Sunday* and the extent to which McGovern worked with the Hillsborough Family Support Group on *Hillsborough* were also examples of his powerful commitment to a particularly rigorous ethical code. Writing at a time when mutations of the documentary-drama form include *My Big Fat Gypsy Wedding* and 'scripted reality' shows such as *The Only Way is Essex*, the ethical underpinning of all of McGovern's engagements with documentary drama looks a particularly important benchmark for work that engages at any level with ideas of the 'real'.

Stella Bruzzi (2000: 123) describes *Priest* as one of the few contemporary films that takes religion seriously and this could, of course, apply more generally to McGovern the writer. Despite his numerous attacks on a whole range of contemporary Catholic practices, particularly in relation to education, McGovern has barely attempted to write anything that is not suffused with, at the very least, some manifestation of Catholic doctrine. Guilt, sin and confession are the cornerstones of his narrative approach, even when there is not an actual Catholic in sight, though there is usually at least one of those as well. Priests, with whom McGovern admits to having a lifelong fascination, are everywhere and of all varieties. What saves McGovern's work from drowning, in what can become a somewhat relentless stream of Catholic tropes, is that what seems to attract him to them is not faith, but the power of the Catholic 'apparatus' as dramatic device. The idea of the confessional, almost above all others, full of secrets that are bound to emerge at some point, full of intimacy, often of the wholly inappropriate variety, typifies what McGovern appears to relish in Catholicism.

On the other hand, his profound ambivalence over the status of his own faith, expressed so many times in interviews, leads him to present a similarly ambivalent vision of the Church and its devotees. McGovern's Catholics are at their most appealing when most fallible and least doctrinaire. For a man who so often expresses such strong opinions McGovern is very attracted to weakness, particularly when the character acknowledges such weakness in themselves. One suspects that Father Matthew Thomas in *Priest* is McGovern's ultimate good priest: unable to keep his vow of chastity, fond of a drink and a sing-song, highly sceptical about the Church's ability to reach new souls in such a poor parish but, ultimately, committed to the Church having a role in lives that so many, including politicians on the left, have abandoned.

The one dimension to the Catholic Church that is universally reviled in McGovern's work is its hierarchy. For McGovern, Catholicism in the widest sense is part of a complex pattern of exclusion from power in Britain, something exemplified by his long-term fascination with the Tudor–Stuart succession and the Gunpowder Plot. It is, though, working-class, usually Irish, Catholicism that is at the heart of his contemporary world-view in a way that fits into a wider dramatisation of what could be termed 'internal colonialism'. In *Hillsborough*, *Dockers* and *Sunday* (as well as *Liam* and *Priest*) in particular, but also in more subtle ways throughout his work, we see the Irish (in interviews, as we have seen, he broadens this to 'Celts', emphasising the colonial framework), the Catholics, the northern working class as the collectively marginalised. It would be a crude, bleak world-view if McGovern's dramatic intelligence did not also drive him to make the majority of the oppressors seem both human and fallible. One of his absolute golden rules, one which we saw him passing on in *Writing the Wrongs*, is that the devil must have good tunes, if not necessarily the best, and it is a rule that almost always keeps him from the trap of formulaic predictability.

It would be wrong to leave this section without a brief return to one more major question that has continued to follow McGovern around, one that I suspect is another contributory factor in his neglect by television academics, namely his endless struggles with the contemporary representation of gender. As we saw, particularly in the discussions of *Brookside* and *Cracker* cited in Chapter 1, the received wisdom on McGovern is that he tries to have it both ways, typically creating a fascinating and complex character in Edward Fitzgerald, the psychologist at the heart of *Cracker*, only for the role to become an apologia for the exercise of good, old-fashioned masculinity. As will be apparent, my sense of McGovern's approach is that it is altogether more complex than that and has certainly become more and more so as his career has gone on. The interviews that make reference to his 1980s conflicts with 'middle-class feminists' who, as he saw it, were part of a wider marginalisation of the working class by the British left are, of course, part of the case for the prosecution. However, with the benefit of hindsight and, after ten years of New Labour governments, there may be more people with sympathy for the general tenor of McGovern's complaints, if not the precise detail. Against this, though, must surely be set the endless stream of rich, complex roles for women that he has written, often played by some of the best actors of the period and in ways that suggest that his sense of the complexity of gender politics is altogether subtler than most have given him credit for.

At the time of writing McGovern is in Australia working on a series with the working title *Redfern Now*, for ABC, the Australian network. The series is to be produced by Blackfella Films for ABC's 'Indigenous Department'. These bare facts alone give a clear indication that, once again, McGovern's instincts are leading him into new and interesting territory with rich narrative possibilities. However, when these possibilities were expanded upon on one of the leading Australian television blogs the connections to the choices that McGovern has made in his later career become even clearer: 'the explosive and dramatic stories of six households in Redfern. Nestled in the heart of Sydney, Redfern is one of Australia's most famous suburbs – an area full of contradictions; Aboriginal icon, centre of black struggle, and a real estate goldmine' (Knox, 2011). In the same piece it is confirmed that McGovern's role in the series is to oversee the work of 'indigenous Australians' and also that the production of *Redfern Now* will create 250 jobs in the Australian television industry, most of them for indigenous people.

It is clear, then, that right up until the time of writing, McGovern is continuing with a trajectory that has seen him work more and more on projects that provide opportunities for emerging writers, often from marginalised communities. In the case of *Redfern Now* the opportunities are very specific and, to an extent, take McGovern's work much more firmly in the direction of what in the USA would be called 'affirmative action', a direction that would not be available in the same form within the institutional arrangements of British television. According to another Australian online source the funding arrangements for *Redfern Now* include an element of public subsidy: 'The ACT TV Indigenous Department has partnered with the Indigenous Department of Screen Australia and Screen NSW to lead the way with this groundbreaking series, which tells the stories of six households in Redfern, one of Australia's most infamous suburbs' (Artshub, 2011). We might deduce from this that, at the heart of his latest initiative, is the combination of pragmatist and visionary radical that runs throughout McGovern's career. Whilst part of the story behind why he has chosen to go and work on a project in Australia might be the availability of funding, the other half is the excitement of nurturing what is Australia's first significant, prime-time indigenous television series. In *Redfern Now* we can see the McGovern who chose to work with the forgotten dockers of Liverpool to tell their story when not even the majority of the mainstream trade-union movement wanted to remember it, but we also see the hungry writer, so thrilled to have his big break on *Brookside* that he devised elaborate strategies in order to make sure that his response to the new storylines would be the first to hit the producer's desk.

McGovern remains, then, a writer who always wants to work and who understands the realities of contemporary television institutions, but also one who has continued to find ways to make radical interventions within the spaces of popular television forms. He has never given the kind of interviews or made the kind of speeches about the problems of radicalism within television of a Dennis Potter or, in a different vein, a Trevor Griffiths, with his advocacy of 'strategic penetration' (see Tulloch, 2006). However, I would want to argue that McGovern's impact on the British television landscape has been at least as significant. Even those who remain sceptical about what they would regard as the inherent limits of McGovern's engagement with form surely have to acknowledge the boldness of what he has been able to achieve in terms of collaborative working. Whilst *Dockers* remains the most overtly radical of all his work in terms of the nature of the collaboration involved, in more subtle ways the engagements with communities on *Hillsborough* and *Sunday*, the airing of new voices in prime time on *The Street* and the assault on the dead zone of daytime in *Moving On* all stand as remarkable examples of a writer using their reputation to open up new television spaces in an era where such ventures have become so difficult. McGovern has never attempted to hide his own pragmatic streak and he also acknowledges the realities of those such as Phil Redmond, who carry the burden of people's jobs alongside being faced with the limits of what they can do within popular television (see Chapter 1). On the other hand this has rarely meant, for McGovern, any sustained attempt to avoid controversy or confrontation both with the conventional establishment and those on the left who, he feels, have ignored the people that he knows best.

McGovern's is a career of real substance and one that has made a great contribution to the survival of serious popular drama made in Britain, something that is of particular value in an era so dominated by the critical adulation of drama from the USA. Such a comparison is not intended to denigrate the latter, but rather to end this book with a reminder of the critical neglect of the breadth and sustained engagement with television forms, as well as with life in modern Britain, of one of our very finest television writers. I hope this book will not only help to address this neglect but also stimulate others to return to McGovern's work in a renewed spirit of critical enquiry.

Note

1 One of the best sources of information on the British army's alleged policy of shoot to kill when dealing with particular categories of paramilitary suspects in Northern Ireland is the drama documentary *Shoot to Kill* (ITV, 1990), written by Michael Eaton and directed by Peter Kosminsky. Ken Loach's feature film *Hidden Agenda* (1990) also dealt with fictional events with close parallels to the allegations around a 'shoot-to-kill' policy.

References

(Note that all references to British newspaper articles give the page number where reference is to the paper edition. In cases where no page number is given the reference is to an online version.)

Books and articles

Adetunji, Joe (2010) 'BBC defends Jimmy McGovern army bullying drama', guardian.co.uk, 21 November, www.guardian.co.uk/uk/2010/nov/21/bbc-defends-jimmy-mcgovern-army-drama (accessed October 2011).

Armstrong, Richard (2003) 'Social Realism' BFI *Screenonline*, www.screenonline.org.uk/film/id/1037898/index.html (accessed November 2011).

Artshub (2011) (unattributed) 'Redfern Now to create 250 Indigenous jobs', November 2011, www.artshub.com.au/au/news-article/news/arts/redfern-now-to-create-250–indigenous-jobs-186353 (accessed March 2012).

Banks-Smith, Nancy (2007) 'Last Night's TV: The Street', *Guardian*, 14 December.

Barnett, Steven and Emily Seymour (1999) *'A Shrinking Iceberg Travelling South ...' Changing Trends in British Television: A Case Study of Drama and Current Affairs*, London: Campaign for Quality Television.

BBC (2004) 'Gunpowder, Treason and Plot – the creation of an epic', www.bbc.co.uk/pressoffice/pressreleases/stories/2004/02_february/27/gunpowder_creation.shtml (accessed August 2012).

BBC (2006a) 'Gunpowder, Treason and Plot – background', www.bbc.co.uk/northernireland/drama/gunpowder/background.shtml (accessed September 2011).

BBC (2006b) 'The Street', www.bbc.co.uk/liverpool/content/articles/2006/02/20/200206_inside_out_street_mcgovern_feature.shtml (accessed September 2011).

BBC (2007) 'The Street by Jimmy McGovern is back for a second series on BBC One starting Thursday 8 November 2007 at 9pm', www.bbc.co.uk/pressoffice/pressreleases/stories/2007/10_october/19/street.shtml (accessed November 2011).

References

BBC (2010a) 'Accused – Introduction' (Press Pack), www.bbc.co.uk/pressoffice/pressreleases/stories/2010/10_october/26/accused.shtm (accessed November 2011).

BBC (2010b) 'Jimmy McGovern army drama "fails soldiers" says veteran', 16 November, www.bbc.co.uk/news/entertainment-arts-11764240 (accessed November 2011).

Bell, Erin (2007) 'Televising History: The Past(s) on the Small Screen', *European Journal of Cultural Studies*, 10:5, pp 5–12.

Bennett, Tony, Susan Boyd-Bowman, Colin Mercer and Janet Woollacott (eds) (1981) *Popular Television and Film*, London: British Film Institute and the Open University.

Bignell, Jonathan (2010) 'Docudramatizing the Real: Developments in British TV Docudrama since 1990', *Studies in Documentary Film*, 4:3 (Winter), pp 195–208.

Billen, Andrew (2010) 'Another cock and bull story', *The Times*, 2 November.

Brunsdon, Charlotte (1993) 'Identity in Feminist Television Criticism', *Media, Culture & Society*, 15:2 (April), pp 309–20.

Brunsdon, Charlotte (1998) 'Structure of Anxiety: Recent British Television Crime Fiction', *Screen*, 39:3 (Autumn), pp 223–43.

Brunsdon, Charlotte, Julie D'Acci and Lynn Spigel (eds) (1997) *Feminist Television Criticism: A Reader*, Oxford: Oxford University Press.

Bruzzi, Stella (2000) 'Two Sisters, the Fogey, the Priest and his Lover: Sexual Plurality in 1990s British Cinema', in Robert Murphy (ed.), *British Cinema of the 90s*, London: BFI, pp 123–34.

Butler, Robert (1995) 'The man who raped Sheila Grant', *Independent*, 5 February, www.independent.co.uk/arts-entertainment/the-man-who-raped-sheila-grant-1571642.html?service=Print (accessed October 2012).

Byrom, Howard (2006) 'Streets ahead', http://ideasfactory.com/writing/features/writ_feature75.htm (accessed July 2011).

Cathode Ray (1997) 'The Box', *Sight and Sound*, 7:10, p 10.

Caughie, John (2000) *Television Drama: Realism, Modernism and British Culture*, Oxford: Oxford University Press.

Cavendish, Dominic (2007) 'Jimmy McGovern's crusade against boredom', *Daily Telegraph*, 8 September, www.telegraph.co.uk/culture/theatre/3667792/Jimmy-McGoverns-crusade-against-boredom.html (accessed August 2012).

Chapman, James (2007) 'Re-presenting War: British Television Drama-documentary and the Second World War', *European Journal of Cultural Studies*, 10: 5, pp 13–34.

Chater, David (2010) 'Rewind the 60s/The Indian Doctor', *The Times*, 15 November.

Church Gibson, Pamela (2000) 'Fewer Weddings and More Funerals: Changes in the Heritage Film', in Robert Murphy (ed.), *British Cinema of the 90s*, London: British Film Institute, pp 115–24.

Cohen, Stanley (2002) *Folk Devils and Moral Panics* (3rd edn), London: Macmillan.

References

Conlan, Tara (2010) 'Christopher Eccleston to star in Jimmy McGovern crime drama', *Guardian*, 11 May, www.guardian.co.uk/media/2010/may/11/accused-christopher-eccleston-jimmy-mcgovern (accessed September 2011).

Cooke, Lez (2003) *British Television Drama: A History*, London: British Film Institute.

Cooke, Lez (2005) 'The New Social Realism of *Clocking Off*', in J. Bignell and S. Lacey (eds), *Popular Television Drama: Critical Perspectives*, Manchester: Manchester University Press, pp 183–97.

Cooke, Rachel (2010) 'Accused', *New Statesman*, 18 November.

Coppock, Vicki, Deena Haydon and Ingrid Richter (1995) *The Illusions of 'Post-Feminism': New Women, Old Myths*, London: Taylor & Francis.

Corner, John (2004) '*Bloody Sunday* and *Sunday*', in Glen Creeber, *Fifty Key Television Programmes*, London: Edward Arnold, pp 198–202.

Crampton, Robert (1995) 'Scouse Grit', *The Times*, 11 March.

Crampton, Robert (1996) 'Nothing but the truth', *The Times*, 16 November.

Creeber, Glen (2002) 'Old Sleuth or New Man? Investigations into Rape, Murder and Masculinity in *Cracker* (1993–1996)', *Journal of Media and Cultural Studies*, 16:2, pp 169–83.

Creeber, Glen (2004) *Serial Television: Big Drama on the Small Screen*, London: British Film Institute.

Cumming, Ed (2010) 'Jimmy McGovern returns with a courtroom drama to remember', *Daily Telegraph*, 12 November.

Dugan, Emily (2007) 'The only black faces at the BBC are in the canteen says McGovern', *Independent*, 1 September.

Dugdale, John (2011) 'What *The Tudors* has taught us', www.guardian.co.uk/tv-and-radio/tvandradioblog/2011/apr/01/the-tudors-history-revelations (accessed September 2011).

Duguid, Mark (2009) *Cracker*, London, British Film Institute.

Duguid, Mark (2010a) 'McGovern, Jimmy', BFI *Screenonline*, www.screenonline.org.uk/people/id/510555/ (accessed October 2011).

Duguid, Mark (2010b) 'That Was Then, This is Now', *Sight and Sound*, 20:6 (June), pp 50–4.

Du Noyer, Paul (2008) 'Jimmy McGovern: Trouble Is His Business', www.pauldunoyer.com/pages/journalism/journalism_item.asp?journalismID=194 (accessed November 2011).

Ellis, John (2008) 'What Did Channel 4 Do for Us? Reassessing the Early Years', *Screen*, 49:3 (Autumn), pp 331–42a.

Ferguson, Euan (2003) 'Ten years on', *Observer*, 9 February.

Free, Marcus (2011) 'On the Edge: The Irish in Britain as a Troubled and Troubling Presence in the Work of Jimmy McGovern and Alan Bleasdale', *Irish Studies Review*, 19:1 (February), pp 55–64.

French, Philip (2001) 'Love and death on the dole', *Observer*, 25 February, www.guardian.co.uk/film/2001/feb/25/philipfrench (accessed September 2011).

Gardner, Anthony (2004) 'Gunpowder, treason and plot', *Daily Telegraph*

Magazine, www.anthonygardner.co.uk/features/gunpowder_plot.html (accessed October 2011).
Geraghty, Christine (1984), 'Brookside', *Marxism Today*, February, pp 37–8.
Geraghty, Christine (1991) *Women and Soap: A Study in Prime Time Soaps*, London: Polity.
Geraghty, Christine (1992) 'British Soaps in the 1980's', in Dominic Strinati and Stephen Wragg (eds), *Come on Down? Popular Culture in Post-War Britain*, London: Routledge, pp 131–49.
Geraghty, Christine (1995) 'Social Issues and Realist Soaps: A Study of British Soaps in the 1980/1990s', in Robert Allen (ed.), *To be continued ... Soap Operas Around the World*, London: Routledge, pp 66–80.
Gill, A. A. (1996) 'Making a drama out of a crisis', *Sunday Times*, 8 December.
Glover, Stephen (2010) 'I'm no supporter of this war, but I despair at the BBC's denigration of our troops', *Daily Mail*, 24 November.
Hanks, Robert (2002) 'Television review', *Independent*, 29 January.
Hari, Johann (2002) 'The *New Statesman* Interview: Jimmy McGovern', *New Statesman*, 28 January.
Hattenstone, Simon and Tom O'Sullivan (1999) 'Those who were left behind', *Guardian*, 8 May.
Healey, Tim and Karen Ross (2002) 'Growing old invisibly: older viewers talk television', *Media, Culture & Society*, 24:1 (January), pp 105–20.
Henderson, Lesley (2007) *Social Issues in Television Fiction*, Edinburgh: Edinburgh University Press.
Herbert, Hugh (1990) 'By the light of a Roman candle', *Guardian*, 6 November.
Higson, Andrew (2003) *English Heritage, English Cinema*, Oxford: Oxford University Press.
Hoggard, Liz (2004) 'More grit to their mill. Using Hollywood techniques to tackle complex subjects, edgy writer-led drama is back and booming on TV', *Observer*, 14 March.
Holmwood, Leigh (2008) 'Jimmy McGovern to make BBC daytime drama set in Liverpool', *Guardian*, 4 July, www.guardian.co.uk/media/2008/jul/04/bbc.television4 (accessed August 2012).
Jeffries, Stuart (1996) 'A walk through the storm', *Guardian*, 6 December.
Jones, Catherine (2010) 'Liverpool writer Jimmy McGovern's new drama series Accused starts on BBC1 tonight', *Liverpool Echo*, 15 November.
Joseph, Claudia (2002) 'Bloody Sunday: "The Irish suffered, but it was a great tragedy for Britain too"', *Independent on Sunday*, 20 January.
Keelan, Liam (2010) 'The changing face of BBC Daytime: Moving On, The Indian Doctor, Land Girls and more', www.bbc.co.uk/blogs/tv/2010/07/bbc-daytime-moving-on.shtml (accessed August 2012).
Kelly, Richard (2002) 'It Won't Go Away, You Know – *Bloody Sunday* and *Sunday*', *Critical Quarterly*, 44:2, pp 73–83.
Kibble-White, Graham (2002) *Twenty Years of Brookside*, London: Carlton.
Kilborn, Richard (1994) 'Drama over Lockerbie: A New Look at Television Drama-documentaries', *Historical Journal of Film, Radio and Television*, 14:1, pp 59–76.

References

Knowledge Bulletin (2011) 'Sky+; Drama Audiences Flock To Time-Shifting', www.theknowledgeonline.com/the-knowledge-bulletin/post/Sky-Drama-Audiences-Flock-To-Time-Shifting (accessed August 2012).

Knox, David (2011) 'Indigenous jobs on *Redfern Now*', *TV Tonight* ('Australia's leading TV blog'), 7 November, www.tvtonight.com.au/2011/11/indigenous-jobs-on-redfern-now.html (accessed March 2012).

Lacey, Stephen (2007) *Tony Garnett*, Manchester: Manchester University Press.

Lawson, Mark (1999) 'Work experience', *Guardian*, 5 July.

Lawson, Mark (2011) 'The BBC's biggest change since digital expansion', *Guardian*, 6 October, www.guardian.co.uk/commentisfree/2011/oct/06/bbc-biggest-change-american-schedules (accessed November 2011).

MacCabe, Colin (1981) 'Realism and the Cinema: Notes on some Brechtian Theses', in Tony Bennett, Susan Boyd-Bowman, Colin Mercer and Janet Woollacott (eds), *Popular Television and Film*, London: British Film Institute and the Open University, pp 216–35.

Male, Howard (2010) 'Accused, BBC One', *The Arts Desk*, http://theartsdesk.com/tv/accused-bbc-one (accessed November 2011).

McArthur (1981) '*Days of Hope*', in Tony Bennett, Susan Boyd-Bowman, Colin Mercer and Janet Woollacott (eds), *Popular Television and Film*, London: British Film Institute and the Open University, pp 302–9. (First published in *Screen*, 16:4 (Winter 1975/6).

McCann, Eamonn, Maureen Shiels and Bridie Hannigan (1992) *Bloody Sunday in Derry: What Really Happened*, Belfast: Brandon.

McGilliard, Graeme (2010) 'Why I owe my career to this great writer', *Manchester Evening News*, 9 November, p 23.

McGovern, Jimmy (1997) 'This article is written by the man who wrote *Cracker*, *Hillsborough*, and *The Lakes*. If you're expecting the usual story of passion, grit and broken hearts, you're not trying hard enough', *Observer*, 5 October.

McGovern, Jimmy (2001) 'Whose story is it anyway?', *Observer*, 18 February, www.guardian.co.uk/film/2001/feb/18/features (accessed September 2011).

McGovern, Jimmy (2004) 'The power of truth', *Guardian*, 10 June.

McGovern, Jimmy (2009) Interview at the Manchester Literary Festival, reproduced in the BBC Writer's Room at www.bbc.co.uk/writersroom/insight/jimmy_mcgovern_4.shtml (accessed October 2011).

McLean, Gareth (2002) 'Troubles in mind', *Guardian*, 29 January.

Modleski, Tania (1979) 'The search for tomorrow in today's soap operas: notes on a feminine narrative form', *Film Quarterly*, 33:1, pp 12–21.

Moran, Caitlin (2006) 'A Cracker vs. a load of Horrocks', *The Times*, 30 September.

Naughton, John (2006) 'Street fighting man', *Radio Times*, 8 April, pp 26–9.

Nelson, Robin (1997) *TV Drama in Transition: Forms, Values and Cultural Change*, Basingstoke: Palgrave Macmillan.

Nelson, Robin (2007) *State of Play: Contemporary "High-End" TV Drama*, Manchester: Manchester University Press.

Norton, Cherry and Ian Burrell (1999) 'Straw says sorry for insult to Liverpool', *Independent*, 21 April.

O'Carroll, Lisa (1995) 'BBC dramas set to turn the airwaves blue', *Evening Standard* (London), 5 September, p 21.

Orwell, George (1941) 'The meaning of a poem', broadcast talk in the BBC's Overseas Service, 14 May; printed in *The Listener*, 12 June.

Paget, Derek (1990) *True Stories? Documentary Drama on Radio, Stage and Screen*, Manchester: Manchester University Press.

Paget, Derek (1998) *No Other Way To tell It: Dramadoc/Docudrama on Television*, Manchester: Manchester University Press.

Pawling, C. and T. Perkins (1992) 'Popular Drama and Realism: The Case of Television', in A. Page (ed.), *The Death of the Playwright?*, Basingstoke: Macmillan, pp 34–43.

Potter, Dennis (1994) *Seeing the Blossom: Two Interviews and a Lecture*, London: Faber & Faber.

Preston, Peter (2011) www.guardian.co.uk/commentisfree/2011/oct/16/lets-do-timeshift-tv-habits, 16 October (accessed August 2012).

Rampton, James (1995) 'Pain, with no jokes taken out', *Independent*, 16 September.

Rampton, James (2004) 'Method and Madness', *Independent*, 10 March, pp 14–15.

Rampton, James (2006) 'Street Life', *Independent*, 11 April.

Rees, Jasper (1997) 'Jimmy's as deep as they come; the Monday interview: Jimmy McGovern', *Independent*, 25 August.

Roberts, Tyler (1995) 'Prejudice against disability exposed', *Scotsman*, 13 September, p 14.

Robinson, James (2010) 'BBC: *Accused* is "a piece of fiction"', *Guardian*, 23 November.

Ruddock, Andy (2007) '"Get a Real Job": Authenticity on the Performance, Reception and Study of Celebrity', Particip@tions, 4:1 (May), www.participations.org/Volume%204/Issue%201/4_01_ruddock.htm (accessed January 2012).

Ryan, Susan and Richard Porton (1998) 'The Politics of Everyday Life: An Interview with Ken Loach', *Cineaste*, 24:1 (Winter), pp 22–8.

Salmon, Peter (2011) Drama from the North – Jimmy McGovern in Manchester, www.bbc.co.uk/blogs/aboutthebbc/2011/06/jimmy-mcgovern-drama-from-the-north.shtml (accessed September 2011).

Smith, Philip (2007) '"I've Got a Theory about Scousers": Jimmy McGovern and Linda La Plante', in Michael Murphy and Deryn Rees-Jones, *Writing Liverpool*, Liverpool: Liverpool University Press, pp 210–27.

Stubbs, David (2011) 'Box Set Club: *The Street*', www.guardian.co.uk/tv-and-radio/tvandradioblog/2011/sep/13/box-set-club-the-street (accessed November 2011).

Sutcliffe, Tom (1996) 'TV: Review: Hillsborough', *Independent*, 16 December.

Thornham, Sue and Tony Purvis (2005) *Television Drama: Theories and Identities*, Basingstoke: Palgrave Macmillan.

References

Thorpe, Vanessa (2010) 'TV drama must stop relying on irony and costumes, says Jimmy McGovern', *Observer*, 7 November, www.guardian.co.uk/tv-and-radio/2010/nov/07/jimmy-mcgovern-tv-drama-irony (accessed October 2011).

Tulloch, John (2006) *Trevor Griffiths*, Manchester: Manchester University Press.

Walker, Ed (1996) 'Medicine and the Media: A day Sheffield Will Never Forget', *British Medical Journal*, 313 (December), p 1491.

Ward, David (2007) 'Cottoning on to a soulful story', *Guardian*, 14 November, www.guardian.co.uk/culture/2007/sep/14/europeancapitalofculture2008.theatre (accessed September 2011).

White, Jim (1990) 'All the gear', *Independent*, 13 September.

Williams, Elaine (1995) 'Cynic's guide to the inner-city burn-out cases', *Times Education Supplement*, 10 February.

Woodhead, Lesley (1999) '*The Guardian* Lecture: Dramatised Documentary', in Alan Rosenthal, *Why Docudrama? Fact–Fiction on Film and TV*, Carbondale: Southern Illinois University Press, pp 101–10.

Woodin, Tom (2005) 'Muddying the Waters: Changes in Class and Identity in a Working-Class Cultural Organization', *Sociology*, 39, pp 1001–11.

Websites

http://dontbuythesun.co.uk/site/
http://film.guardian.co.uk/features/featurepages/0,4120,1235247,00.html
http://news.bbc.co.uk/1/hi/programmes/newsnight/review/3543601.stm
www.bafta.org/access-all-areas/videos/bafta-writers-in-conversation-with-jimmy-mcgovern-and-writers-from-the-street,382,BA.html
www.bbc.co.uk/drama/thestreet/jimmy_mcgovern.shtml
www.bbc.co.uk/northernireland/drama/gunpowder/background.shtml
www.crackertv.co.uk/youmagazineinterview.htm
www.edgehill.ac.uk/EdgeHill/Publications/Edgeways/issue13/inconversation.htm
www.newstatesman.com/200201280022
www.screenwritersfestival.com/news.php?id=2
www.sundayfilm.net/Interview.htm
www.timesonline.co.uk/article/0,,22871-2375861.html

Index

Note: 'n' indicates that the reference is in a numbered note on a page. Page numbers in bold refer to main entries.

Abbott, Paul 1, 10, 17, 52, 61-2, 64, 67-8, 75, 107, 109, 167
Accused 3, 20–1, 23, 64, 66–7, **93–110**, 142, 167
   'Alison's Story' 100–2, 105
   'Frankie's Story' 21, 95, 100–6, 142
   'Helen's Story' 102, 107
   'Kenny's Story' 94
   'Willy's Story' 94, 96–100, 102
Allen, Jim 34, 69, 131
American television drama 28, 66, 68, 107, 109, 110n.2, 156
auteur 6, 7, 111, 153, 162
authorship (and television drama) 10, 19, 26, 82, 107
autobiography 10, 25, 57

Bennett, Jana 104–5
Between the Lines 51
Big Flame, The 131
Bird, Antonia 6, 7, 53
Blackfella Films 171
Blair, David 60, 69–70, 77–85 passim, 94–100 passim, 107
Blair, Tony 80, 96, 125–6
Bleasdale, Alan 2, 22, 26
Bloody Sunday 14, 133–43 passim, 155
Brecht, Berthold 36, 140

British Broadcasting Corporation (BBC)
   and the army 21, 104–6, 110n.6, 110n.7
   commissioning 7, 58, 52–3
   and daytime television 18, 67, 86–93
   and film 22
   and history 16
   radio drama 22
   Radio 6 controversy 110n.4
   and single drama 5–6, 118
   and social realism 67–8
   and writers 109, 167
Broadbent, Jim 74, 76, 160
Brocklehurst, Danny 71, 94
Brookside 1, 3–6, 8–9, 12, 23, 24, **25–41**, 42–7 passim, 62, 68, 75, 81, 87, 92–3, 96, 116–18, 125, 128, 152, 154, 156, 160, 165, 167, 170–1
Bulger, James 79–81, 110n.3

Can't Pay, Won't Pay! 19, 26
Carlyle, Robert 147–9, 153, 164–5
Catesby, Robert 146–7, 154–5
Catholic/Catholicism 22, 152–3
   in *Accused* 96, 98–100
   in *Brookside* 31
   in *Cracker* 45

Index

and guilt 10, 12
in *Gunpowder Treason and Plot* 145–6
in *Hearts and Minds* 54
in *Hillsborough* 123–4
in *The Lakes* 10, 57–60
and McGovern's life 25, 60, 169–70
and the priesthood 23
in *The Street* 76
in *Sunday* 13, 136–8
and working-class life 3, 10, 12
Cathy Come Home 9, 35, 65, 113
Cecil, Lord Robert 147, 151, 154–6 *passim*
Channel 4 (Four) 1, 4–7, 13, 22, 25, 34, 40, 53, 61, 66, 72, 125–7, 132, 137, 148, 151n. 3
class 1–3, 8, 11–12, 17, 19, 22–6 *passim*, 27–8, 30–2, 36–9, 42–52, 56, 59, 61, 67, 74–81, 87, 95–101, 105–6, 115–20, 124–30 *passim*, 137, 150–3, 164–5, 168–70
classic realist text 35
Clocking Off 17–18, 66–85 *passim*
Coltrane, Robbie 42, 44–53, 81, 83, 96
Coronation Street 9, 23, 27, 29, 36, 39, 74
Cracker 1, 3, 6–9, 10, 15–16, 17, 20–1, 24–5, **41–53**, 57–8, 60–2, 71, 83, 93–4, 114, 116, 118, 149, 152, 162–3, 165, 167–8, 170
'The Mad Woman in the Attic' 45
'Men Should Weep' 43, 46
'To Be a Somebody' 8, 48–52, 116
Crossroads 36, 39

Dannatt, General Sir Richard 104
Davies, Russell T. 1, 66, 107–8
Davies, Terence 11
Days of Hope (and *Days of Hope* debate) 35, 73

Distant Voices, Still Lives 11
Dockers 11–15 *passim*, 83, 93, 111, 113, **125–32**, 135, 166, 169–70, 172
documentary drama 1, 14–15, 112–15, 122–7, 131–46 *passim*, 157, 168–9
Duckenfield, Chief Inspector David 123

Eastenders 9, 29, 30, 31, 68, 167
Eccleston, Christopher 8, 21, 46, 55, 68, 94, 96, 118–20, 139
Edinburgh Film Festival, The 34, 65
elderly people and television 18, 74, 84, 87, 89, 160
Elizabeth 150

Farrar-Hockley, Sir Anthony 137
Fawkes Guy (Guido) 145, 147–9, 151
Felix Randal 22–3
feminism/feminist 3, 25–6, 28, 37–8, 43, 45, 101, 120, 129, 170
flexi-narrative 66–9, 72, 86, 109, 110n.2, 167
Flickering Flame, The 131
Fo, Dario 19, 26
Fowler, Robbie 130
Frears, Stephen 2, 12, 153

Garnett, Tony 2, 34–5, 69, 93, 108,
Gas and Candles 5, **159–62**
Gaslight Productions 13, 135
gender 27–8, 31, 37, 42–7 *passim*, 51, 56, 81, 101, 170–1
Glover, John (and family) 117–19
Go Now 6, 7, 162, 165
Greengrass, Paul 14–15, 133–43 *passim*
Gunpowder, Treason and Plot 14–16, 22, 111, **143–51**, 154–5, 157

Hancock, Sheila 18, 88, 89, 166
Hardy, Thomas 75–6, 97, 100, 168
Hatton, Derek 33
Heart 11, 22, 152

Index   183

Heartbeat 59, 65
Hearts and Minds 3, 6–8, 24–5, 53–7, 96, 162
Heath, Edward 137, 139, 142
Heffer, Eric 33
Hicks, Trevor (and family) 117–20
Hillsborough 1, 13–16, 21, 40, 43, 48, 58, 79–80, 93, 111–12, **113–25**, 126–7, 144, 151, 151n.2, 169, 170, 172
  in relation to *Brookside* 40, 43, 47,
  in relation to *Cracker* 8–9, 47, 50–1
  in relation to *Sunday* 132–41 *passim*
Hillsborough Family Support Group 21, 169
historical drama (television) 16, 111–13, 143–151 *passim*
Hopkins, Gerard Manley 22–3, 59–60

ITV (Independent Television) 6, 9, 14, 17, 23, 27, 42, 57–8, 113–18 *passim*, 121, 133, 168, 173n.1

Johnston, Sue 31, 37–9

King Cotton 19
Kinnock, Neil 33

Lakes, The 9–10, 22–5 *passim*, **57–62**, 66, 71, 75, 83, 152, 158
La Plante, Lynda 2, 58
LA Productions 64, 92
Liam 7, 11–12, 22, 60, 144, 152–3, 170
Loach, Ken 9, 11, 12, 34, 35, 69, 131, 173n.1
Long Day Closes 11
Love Bites 6, 16

McDonough, Terry 76, 84
McDougall, Charles 131, 141, 153
Mackinnon, Gillies 15, 111, 143, 148–159 *passim*

magic realism 3, 110, 168
Marchant, Tony 2, 66, 107
Massey, Anna 18, 89
Merseyside Film Production Fund 11
Mersey Television 9, 26
Militant Tendency 32–3
miniseries 111, 143, 144, 148, 150
modernism (and television drama) 34
Moving On 17–19, 64–7, **86–93**, 109, 166, 172
  'Malaise' 91
  'The Rain Has Stopped' 88–9
  'Sauce for the Goose' 89
  'The Test' 89

Neale, Gub 6, 15–16, 41, 144–9 *passim*, 167
Needle 5, 41, **157–9**, 162
New Labour 13, 79, 125, 170
Nutter, Alice 92, 94, 107

Plater, Alan 2, 156–7
Play for Today 17, 69, 72, 83, 93, 107
Play on One 157, 162
Poliakoff, Stephen 1
Potter, Dennis 2, 19, 34–5, 65, 110n.1, 160, 172
Powell, Paul Henry 6, 163
Priest 6, 7, 15, 22, 41, 53, 60, 114, 144, 152–3, 165, 167, 169–70
Prime Suspect 51, 168

'quality' television drama 1, 6, 11, 18–19, 45, 64, 107–8

race/racism 48–9, 56
realism 3, 17, 22, 30, 34–6, 39–40, 61, 68–9, 73–8 *passim*, 84–5, 95, 97–8, 102, 110, 168
  see also social realist
Redfern Now 110n.5, 171
Redmond, Phil 26–30 *passim*, 38, 40, 172

RSJ Films 64, 93, 107
Russell, Willy 22, 26

Salmon, Peter 9, 58
Saville Enquiry 15, 136, 141–2
Screen 4, 35–6
Screenplay 152, 154
sexual politics 37, 42–4, 47, 51
  see also feminism, white working-class male
Sharpe, Leslie 18, 70
Simm, John 9, 18, 59, 91, 166
soap opera 5, 9, 18, 25–39 *passim*, 68–70, 76, 116, 167
social realist 2, 3, 17, 62, 67, 75–6, 84–5, 165
Spearitt, Eddie (and family) 117–22 *passim*
Spencer, Roxy 64, 107
Street, The 3–4, 10, 17–18, 20, 62, 64, **67–86**, 87–98 *passim*, 107, 110, 160, 166–8, 172
  'The Accident' 69, 73
  'The Promise' 77–82
  'Stan' 69, 72–5, 87
  'Twin' 76, 84
Sun, The 43, 50, 80, 116–19, 122, 124
Sunday 13–16 *passim*, 103, 111, 113, 116, 126–7, **132–43**, 169–70, 172

television history 1, 12–16 *passim*, 25, 52, 58, 145–6, 156

Thatcher, Margaret 33, 59, 65, 96
Thompson, Mark 21, 103
Tomlinson, Ricky 31–2, 96, 118, 119, 120, 128
trade unions (and television drama) 6, 24, 32, 37, 48, 54, 125, 128, 130, 167, 171
Trainspotting 13, 150, 158
Traitors 5, 152–3, **154–7**
'trojan horse' (and broadcast television drama) 33

Wall, General Sir Peter 21, 103
Wednesday Play, The 17, 69
Welsh, Irvine 13, 125–6
West, Dominic 18, 91, 166
white working class male 3, 26, 37–8, 116, 124
  see also class
Widgery Inquiry 138–9, 141
Williams, Sita 64, 83, 107
Wilson, David Henry 160
Wilson, Esther 92, 94–5
Windhover, The 23, 60
Winterbottom, Michael 7, 53, 152, 162, 165
Women of the Waterfront 127–9
Workers' Educational Association (WEA) 13
Writing the Wrongs 125–31 *passim*, 170

Young, Leo (and family) 135–8